"A highly entertaining, rapid-fire, hard-to-put-down...
The record producer/label founder/hotelier/film pro...
us on a rip-roaring ride through the '60s, '70s, and '80...
exciting years in popular music ... *The Islander*...
320 pages long. I could have read 320 more."
—*Air Mail*

"A superior story from start to finish, *The Islander* permits access to a
remarkable world, but without any self-aggrandizing razzmatazz ...
To the credit of Blackwell's collaborator, the veteran journalist
Paul Morley, [this] story is told with a disciplined coherence
that plunges deep beneath the surface."
—*The Telegraph*

"A rip-roaring yarn, the ultimate behind-the-scenes insider look
at the coolest label ever on the planet."
—*The Quietus*

"[Blackwell] candidly details both his hits and his misses
in a highly readable new memoir."
—*The Guardian*

"A memoir of a singular music mogul, his record label, and an era before
rock became so corporate ... Highly recommended."
—*Kirkus Reviews*, **starred review**

"Rock & Roll Hall of Fame inductee Blackwell, founder of Island
Records, delivers a fascinating behind-the-scenes account of his
consequential career as a record producer ... but most impressive is his
refreshing self-awareness ... Music lovers shouldn't miss this."
—*Publishers Weekly*

"*The Islander*, among its many pleasures, doubles as a firsthand
history of the development of Jamaican music ... Best of all,
one is always sent scurrying back to the music."
—*The Wall Street Journal*

"Fascinating."
—*8/10, Uncut*

WELL ... IS AN ADVENTURER, AN ENTREPRENEUR, A BUCCANEER, A VISIONARY, AND A GENTLEMAN." —**BONO**

"I read Chris Blackwell's autobiography in one sitting, unable to tear myself away. From 'My Boy Lollipop' and Bob Marley, via Swinging London and punk, and all the way to Talking Heads and U2, I felt like I was reading the inside story of the music of my life."

—**Salman Rushdie**, author of *New York Times* bestseller *Quichotte*

"C.B. had this way of throwing me in the deep end knowing that I would thrive on being challenged. As you'll read in *The Islander* he knows how to get the very best out of people—he's a mover and a shaker and a mischief maker."

—**Grace Jones**, author of *New York Times* bestseller *I'll Never Write My Memoirs*

"As you're about to find out through the pages in this book, Chris Blackwell—who looms large in U2's life, and was our lifeline into the music world—is an adventurer, an entrepreneur, a buccaneer, a visionary, and a gentleman. I'm proud to know him."

—**Bono**

"[Blackwell] is indisputably one of the greatest record executives in history. If you're even a minor fan of music books, stop reading this article and buy his autobiography, *The Islander,* which was written (beautifully) with Paul Morley—seriously, it's on the level of Elton John's *Me* and Patti Smith's *Just Kids* for all-time great music memoirs."

—*Variety*

"A highly entertaining, rapid-fire, hard-to-put-down memoir. The record producer/label founder/hotelier/film producer takes us on a rip-roaring ride through the '60s, '70s, and '80s, the most exciting years in popular music . . . *The Islander* is 320 pages long. I could have read 320 more."

—*Air Mail*

"*The Islander,* among its many pleasure, doubles as a firsthand history of the development of Jamaican music . . . [and] offers a vivid series of John Aubrey–esque 'Brief Lives' of Mr. Blackwell's most notable artists . . . Mr. Blackwell's sympathy for his subjects reveals unspoken truths we feel we might easily have intuited if only we'd listened to the music hard enough . . . I have never read anything better on Tom Waits, let alone in so few words . . . Best of all, one is always sent scurrying back to the music."

—*The Wall Street Journal*

"A superior story from start to finish, *The Islander* permits access to a remarkable world, but without any self-aggrandizing razzmatazz . . . to the credit of Blackwell's collaborator, the veteran journalist Paul Morley, [this] story is told with a disciplined coherence that plunges deep beneath the surface."

—*The Telegraph*

"A thoroughly quotable autobiography . . . a book that's hard to put down."

—*Mojo*

"This compelling autobiography charts the rise of the Island Records founder who became as much of a legend as the acts he championed . . . Blackwell helped revolutionize popular music, his label becoming a byword for uncompromised artistry and era-shaping acts . . . His story, warmly told with an unobtrusive ghostwriter, is unique in popular music, its hero being not Blackwell but Jamaica itself."

—*The Guardian*

"Fascinating."

—8/10, *Uncut*

"A rip-roaring yarn, the ultimate behind-the-scenes insider look at the coolest label ever on the planet."

—*The Quietus*

"[Blackwell] candidly details both his hits and his misses in a highly readable new memoir. The dizzying list of stars it covers spans oceans, genres, and eras, including Bob Marley, U2, Cat Stevens, Robert Palmer, and Steve Winwood, who was, for years, the label's MVP. A deeper look at his catalogue shows an uncanny knack for promoting some of Britain's boldest acts, like King Crimson, Free, Mott the Hoople, Fairport Convention, and Roxy Music, as well some of its most sensitive, like Sandy Denny, Nick Drake, and John Martyn. Then there are those Island artists who cannot be classified in any way, like Grace Jones, John Cale, Marianne Faithfull, and Eno."

—*The Guardian*

"Fascinating autobiography of the Island Records founder. *The Islander* is a treasure."

—*Prog*

"A memoir of a singular music mogul, his record label, and an era before rock became so corporate . . . Before music even enters the story, he recalls being punched by Errol Flynn and hanging out with Ian Fleming . . . Blackwell chronicles how he straddled the cultures of London and Jamaica and how an indifferent student with few career prospects learned the music business from the ground up . . . Highly recommended."

—*Kirkus*, **starred review**

"Rock & Roll Hall of Fame inductee Blackwell, founder of Island Records, delivers a fascinating behind-the-scenes account of his consequential career as a record producer . . . Throughout, Blackwell provides engrossing details of his road to success—including discovering such famed musicians as Bono and Cat Stevens—but most impressive is his refreshing self-awareness; as he writes, 'There's no two ways about it: I am a member of the Lucky Sperm Club. I was born into wealth and position.' Music lovers shouldn't miss this."

—*Publishers Weekly*

THE
ISLANDER

MY LIFE IN MUSIC AND BEYOND

CHRIS BLACKWELL
WITH PAUL MORLEY

G

GALLERY BOOKS

NEW YORK   LONDON   TORONTO   SYDNEY   NEW DELHI

Gallery Books
An Imprint of Simon & Schuster, Inc.
1230 Avenue of the Americas
New York, NY 10020

First Gallery Books trade paperback edition February 2023

GALLERY BOOKS and colophon are registered trademarks of Simon & Schuster, Inc.

For information about special discounts for bulk purchases, please contact Simon & Schuster Special Sales at 1-866-506-1949 or business@simonandschuster.com.

The Simon & Schuster Speakers Bureau can bring authors to your live event. For more information or to book an event, contact the Simon & Schuster Speakers Bureau at 1-866-248-3049 or visit our website at www.simonspeakers.com.

Interior design by Jaime Putorti

Manufactured in the United States of America

10 9 8 7 6 5 4 3 2 1

Library of Congress Cataloging-in-Publication Data for the hardcover is available.

ISBN 978-1-9821-7269-5
ISBN 978-1-9821-7270-1 (pbk)
ISBN 978-1-9821-7271-8 (ebook)

For all those who traveled with me in my life:

those who are still here

and those who are no longer here

CONTENTS

NEARLY THE END . . .

I was eighteen years old when a Rastaman saved my life.

I have sometimes embroidered the first part of this story to make me look a little less stupid and give the narrative a dramatic boost. I've said that I was out to sea in a tiny sailboat, all by myself. That I got caught in a violent storm. That I thought I wasn't going to make it. That the mast was struck by lightning and the boat had split, and I was holding on to a charred piece of the splintered hull and eventually was thrown up against some rocks along a barren stretch of isolated coast, whereupon I was knocked unconscious.

The truth is a little more prosaic. I wasn't on my own. It wasn't a sailboat. I was out in a motorboat with a male friend from England who was in the Jamaican Regiment whose name I cannot recall, and a female companion who I do remember, Lorraine. It was 1955. I was a directionless Anglo-Irish-Jamaican boarding-school flameout who, for kicks, decided to take a boat ride on the Caribbean with his mates. We set off from Kingston Harbor, passing the sleepy fishing village of Port Royal, a remnant of the colonial city of the same name that provided the setting for *Captain Blood*, the lavish, jolly 1935 swashbuckler that made a film star of Errol Flynn.

Three hundred years before our little voyage, the English navy had invaded Jamaica and claimed it from the island's previous colonizer, Spain. Under British rule, Port Royal became the largest English-speaking city in the New World outside of Boston: a privateer's paradise, home to pirates, beggars, prostitutes, and sundry other gold-chasing chancers of loose morals. But its infamy was brief: in 1692, as if by divine retribution, Port Royal was finished off by a tsunami, exacerbating a demise already begun by fires, earthquakes, and hurricanes.

I am ashamed to say I hadn't filled up my boat's tank with enough petrol, and we soon ran out of fuel. We pulled up on an unfamiliar stretch of shore then, a long way past Hellshire Beach, just southwest of Port Royal. This didn't initially strike me as a problem. It was about five in the afternoon, not yet dark, and civilization was surely only a matter of minutes away. After all, this very area had once been the commercial center of the world, even if we were now a fair way from Kingston or Montego Bay.

I directed my English friend to head inland on foot, assuming he would soon come across a road. I stayed behind with Lorraine. For an hour or two, we bided our time blithely, thinking it wouldn't be long before he found help. But then events took a turn that requires no exaggeration to make dramatic.

My friend suddenly reappeared, his face pained, his body covered in scratches and streaks of blood. He hadn't found anything but dense jungle. "There's no way out," he said. The tide was coming in and we were huddled upon a small, shrinking sliver of beach. It was now past seven. I made an executive decision: we would lie down on the driest area of sand, and in the morning I would walk along the coast to find help.

We slept under the stars as best we could. We didn't have much fresh water to drink, and we were hemmed in between the sea and what turned out to be not a proper coastline but a treacherous mangrove swamp. In the right light and conditions, the mangroves are beautiful, a dense tangle of flora providing shelter for hundreds of animal species. But to us, they were more menacing than anything else. The bird and insect sounds that normally seemed a gentle, dreamy part of the coastal ambience now seemed to be warnings of impending doom.

In the morning, I set out. At low tide, when the ground was cracked and dry, it was easy to walk amongst the roots. But soon the crusty surface gave way to thick mud. The mangroves became a combination of labyrinth and quicksand, exceedingly difficult for me to navigate.

I somehow managed to walk for hours, looking for any kind of clearing, shouting for help. I had foolishly set off without taking any of the water we had—a cocksure white boy who, to this point, had never thought of Jamaica as anything but a delightful Eden. The sea was always a liberation, never a trap. Even during this walk, the water was a lovely teal color under the green canopy of the mangroves. But there was no safe harbor to swim to.

A deep thirst started to kick in. At one point I reached a small section of beach that seemed to be moving. I thought I was delirious, hallucinating under the hot midday sun. Eventually I realized the moving beach was actually thousands of crabs, a writhing mass of them crammed together between the sea and the mangrove forest. As I moved closer, they got excited, darting around my feet as swiftly as lizards. I had no defenses; if they chose to come after me as hungry predators, I was a definite goner. What an exit: death by crab.

By late in the afternoon I was still walking, still searching, losing hope. My thirst had advanced from serious to desperate, and I was scarily weak. But then: in a small clearing, I spied a tiny, lopsided wooden hut held together with bits of string. It was the first sign of life I had seen for hours. We might be saved after all! Adrenalized, I walked towards the hut and looked through a little window, really just a crude cut-out hole.

To my terror, I laid eyes on the first Rastafari I had ever seen in my life.

He was a bearded and inscrutable man. His hair was long, stiff, and matted, as if made of bark. He looked as though he was somewhere between being as old as time and as young as me. He was wearing the kind of basic shirt and trousers that didn't seem to have ever been bought in a shop. Maybe he'd made them himself, or found them at the side of the road. Badly dehydrated, utterly lost, and near collapse, I now stood face-to-face with one of the "black heart men" that white Anglo-Jamaican parents warned their kids about.

I had heard a little about the so-called cult of Rastafari. The Rastas were eccentrics who swore allegiance to the emperor of Ethiopia, Haile Selassie, whom they believed to be the messiah incarnate. They traced their origins to the 1930s, when a Black Jamaican preacher named Leonard Howell became the first person to call himself a Rastafari. Howell grew out his beard after seeing a photograph of Haile Selassie on the cover of *Time*, bearded and handsome in a brocaded uniform and sash. Haile Selassie's civilian name was Tafari Makonnen. *Ras* was a noble honorific. Ras + Tafari = Rastafari.

If you grew up in white Jamaican society in the 1940s and '50s, as I did, you were conditioned to regard these men more as a violent gang than as a new religious order or social movement. The colonial government viewed the Rastas as a threat, and there were folkloric horror stories of them capturing, burning, and sacrificing children. They spoke in a mangled, cryptic dialect that signaled a headstrong disregard for English rule. They wore their hair in matted plaits called dreadlocks, which made them look intimidating.

I never quite bought into this propaganda, as no Rastafari had ever caused harm to me or anyone I knew. The Rastas deliberately kept their distance, absenting themselves from a white society that held them in ill regard. They populated the working-class areas of Montego Bay known as Railway Lane and Barnett Lane, roamed the black-sand beaches of Jamaica's south coast, and set up communities in the bush up in the hills, far from my stomping grounds in upperclass Kingston.

But because I had never so much as laid eyes upon a Rasta, they still existed in my head as bogeymen. In my confused, parched state, on the verge of passing out, I looked at the man before me and thought, *This might be the end.*

Instead, he beckoned me towards him, motioning me into his rickety beach hut. Defaulting to my ingrained English-style politeness, I absurdly asked the man, "Do you, by any chance, have some water?" Immediately I noted an ethereal gentleness about him. Moving with a dancer's grace, he brought me a little gourd filled with water. Whatever fear I had felt moments earlier instantly dissipated. Still wobbly and faint, I asked the man if I could lie down. He carefully cleared a spot for me in the corner of the hut. Within seconds, I was asleep.

Two or three hours later, I awoke to find five more Rastas in the hut along with my host; the six of them sat around softly reading to each other from the Bible. For a split second, my fear returned—*Oh God, there's more of them!*—but the first thing they did upon seeing that I was awake was offer me some ital food: *ital* being the Rasta term, derived from *vital*, for their plant-based diet, which, per their philosophy, imbued people with energy and good health while not bringing death to God's creatures.

Once again, I was overcome by the incredible, almost mystic gentleness that surrounded me. These were good men of faith. They were not burning children or plotting a violent revolution. Without hesitation, they had taken in and looked after a frail, helpless white boy who had stumbled across them and collapsed in their midst.

As I ate, they carried on reading to each other from the Bible, discussing amongst themselves what they were reading. Thoughtful debate and exchange seemed an important part of their lives. Once I had regained my strength, they took me by boat back to Port Royal. While I was sleeping, they had found my boat and my friends. When I got to the port, my friends were there, having also been rescued by these kind, enigmatic outsiders who exuded mysterious, uplifting warmth, and generosity.

It had been an incredible, life-changing experience. It would be another seventeen years before I began working with Rastafari's most celebrated advocate and ambassador, Bob Marley. Reggae didn't yet exist. Nor, for that matter, did its precursor, ska. But a seed was planted that day. I had begun to understand the important contribution that Rastafarians were making to the culture and future of Jamaica as the nation moved towards independence from British rule. But never would I have imagined at that point that, in a matter of decades, these peaceful men with dreads would form a central part of Jamaica's international identity.

THE
ISLANDER

— CHAPTER ONE —

SCHOOL VERSUS ERROL FLYNN

There's no two ways about it: I am a member of the Lucky Sperm Club. I was born into wealth and position, albeit of a particularly mixed sort endemic to Jamaica. I am Jamaican, but I am also English, Irish, Portuguese, Spanish, Jewish, and Catholic. The island was and remains a nexus for trade, pleasure-seeking, and cultural collisions. There is no such thing as a "pure" Jamaican unless you are describing the island's original inhabitants, the Taínos, the descendants of the indigenous Arawak peoples of South America who migrated northward and named their new home Xamayca, land of wood and water.

The Taínos were largely wiped out by the Spanish in the decades that followed Christopher Columbus's "discovery" of Jamaica in 1494. "The land seems to touch the sky," Columbus marveled as he took in the paradisiacal view, conveniently paying no heed to the people who had lived there peacefully for hundreds of years until the arrival of the Spanish. The Taínos loved games, music, and dancing for the sheer joy of it, and an island chief greeting Columbus was accompanied by a ceremonial band of musicians playing trumpets made from leaves, flutes carved out of wild cane, and manatee-skin drums fashioned out of the trunks of trumpet trees. They used drums for worship and wars; and for entertainment the flutes, trumpets, and a form of harp; and their music was a natural way for them to communicate with people landing amongst them out of nowhere speaking a different language.

My mother was born Blanche Adelaide Lindo. The Lindos were Sephardic Jews who rose to prominence as merchants in medieval Spain. When the Spanish Inquisition began, the Lindos fled, making and losing fortunes in Portugal, the Canary Islands, Venice, Amsterdam, London, Barbados, Costa Rica, and, finally and most prominently, Jamaica. By the time my mother was born, her father and his seven brothers were the banana kings of Costa Rica, where Blanche was born on December 9, 1912. They owned 25,000 acres of land and exported five million stems per year of their "green gold."

When my mother was two, her father relocated the family to Jamaica, where the Lindo brothers developed 8,000 acres of land into sugarcane fields. This inspired them to buy the rum manufacturers Appleton Estate and J. Wray & Nephew, making the Lindos the world's first family of rum. Wray & Nephew was run by my maternal grandfather, Percy Lindo, the youngest of the eight brothers. Percy is my middle name.

My father was born Joseph Middleton Blackwell in Windsor, England, on August 13, 1913. His father, born in County Mayo, Ireland, was a descendant of the founders of the Crosse & Blackwell food company, though too distant from them to reap the benefits of great wealth. Like the Lindos, the Blackwells reproduced in biblical abundance. My father was one of ten children, which goes some way towards explaining why the family fortune eluded him.

There's no doubt, Dad had a formidable education. He attended Beaumont College, a Jesuit public school, and from there continued at the Royal Military Academy Sandhurst, the latter-day alma mater of princes William and Harry. After his training, he served as a major in the Irish Guards, the British Army regiment perhaps best known for the red tunics and tall bearskin hats they wear to the annual Trooping the Colour ceremony, in which various household regiments escort the king or queen in a procession down the Mall from Buckingham Palace.

Though he was addressed for the remainder of his life as "Major Blackwell," my father was perhaps less-than-ideal officer material. In 1935, the year of King George V's seventieth birthday, he slept in and missed the entire Trooping the Colour. Another time, after a heavy drinking session, he drove his car into the gates of Buckingham Palace, which, needless to say, did not go down well.

I think the reason I have never been much of a drinker is that, when I was eleven, my father grandly announced that I was now old enough to drink. He airily waved his hand at the bottles of spirits before us and asked me what I wanted. Since my father drank whiskey and soda, I asked for one of those. It was vile; drinking it actually caused me physical pain. He had successfully warned me off the temptation of drink, whether that was his intention or not.

My parents met at a fashionable members-only club in the West End of London in the early 1930s. Dad, known as Blackie, was a cunning rascal. Mum was stunning and athletic, at ease both flitting through high society and snorkeling amongst Jamaica's coral reefs. She was a friend of Ian Fleming's and an inspiration for two of his most memorable female foils to James Bond: the independent, provocative nature girl Honeychile Rider, who, as played by Ursula Andress in *Dr. No*, emerges from the sea clad only in a bikini and knife scabbard; and the acrobat-turned-burglar Pussy Galore, who, as played by Honor Blackman in *Goldfinger*, literally took a roll in the hay with Sean Connery.

By marrying outside the Jewish faith, my mother scandalously deviated from centuries of family tradition. The Irish on my father's side were equally alarmed at him breaking away from Catholicism to marry a "Jamaican Jew." Both were displaying their independence, their willful determination to do things their own way. Their union doubled up a considerable free-spiritedness that they passed on to me, their only child.

My parents moved from London to Jamaica in 1938, not much more than six months after my birth on June 22, 1937. That was a thing that was done in the colonial era—women from prominent families delivered their babies in the mother country and then returned to Jamaica. We set up house in a Lindo family estate in Kingston known as Terra Nova, a European-style mansion set imposingly on Waterloo Road, between the Blue Mountains and the harbor. It has since been converted into a hotel.

This was where I spent the first several years of my life, a sickly child suffering from bronchial asthma so extreme I spent days on end in bed and barely attended school. At eight I was still struggling to learn how to read and write. I seldom mixed with other children, more often conversing with elderly relatives. I don't remember having birthday parties or attending them.

My father joined the Jamaican regiment of the Irish Guards, and my mother worked in the family firm. Theirs was a genteel colonial existence. Dad stood six foot four and seemed to stretch all the way to the sky. I walked alongside him to the barracks where he was stationed. He commuted home by horse and buggy. Dad loved horses and, with Mum, owned several. The English had introduced polo to the island, and I took pride in leading one of my father's horses, Brown Bomber, into the paddock after a win.

The people I tended to spend the most time with were the Black staff who looked after Terra Nova. There were about fifteen members of staff attending to the estate's house, stables, and gardens. There are no photos of me from that time with other children, but there are lots of pictures I took of the staff, arranged in rows, like in a school photo.

I was obviously in a vastly different position to them, the only child of the house, a right Little Lord Fauntleroy, really. I didn't understand that they looked upon me as the young gentleman of the house and that it was their job to be nice to me. But I do believe I got to know them and even become friends with them. Our conversations were friendly and free of awkwardness. I learned a lot from them about life, and Jamaica.

Most of Jamaica's Black people are the descendants of people from Africa who were enslaved by Spanish and English colonizers. After the English vanquished the island's Spanish occupiers in the seventeenth century, the Spanish released whatever enslaved people of theirs hadn't already run away. These Black freedmen found safe harbor in Jamaica's mountainous interior, some of them partnering with the island's last remaining Taínos. This population of ex-slaves and their progeny became known as Maroons, a name derived from the Spanish word *cimarrón*, meaning wild and undomesticated. When English rule brought with it a new wave of enslaved Africans, the Maroons took in their runaways too. On unforgivingly hilly land, they established their own farming systems, religious customs, and language. One of the more notable Maroon settlements, which still exists as a village in St. Elizabeth Parish, is called Me-no-Sen-You-no-Come, a sort of patois version of the phrase "out of sight, out of mind."

The Maroons established one of Jamaica's earliest indigenous genres, a heavy rhythmic drumming—a composite of West African influences—that reverberated through the hills at night, audible even to the white folks in the posher precincts of Kingston.

In 1838, all Black people in Jamaica had been emancipated from slavery. This, however, did not do much to improve their lot under British rule, where they lived as politically disenfranchised second-class citizens. One day, I witnessed something that shattered the illusion of the English as kind, genteel employers. My mother had been asked by her brothers Roy and Cecil to help manage the Lindo family's banana plantation. I was sometimes taken out by horse and buggy to visit them. On this particular occasion, I saw a dead Black field worker casually slung over the shoulder of a foreman. The worker had been caught trying to steal some bananas for himself and then tried to make a getaway. He was shot as he ran—killed for the sake of a few bananas.

It was a terrible sight, an abrupt whip-crack of reality. To the Lindos, this seemed a normal form of punishment, a routine way of maintaining order. But I knew, even in my youthfulness, that this simply wasn't right. The memory of that dead man never left me. My constant revisiting and processing of the image of his slumped body made me realize that I was not spiritually aligned with the people who controlled the island. There was a big chasm between the nineteenth-century world of the Lindos and the modern world that I was racing towards. My mind was changed by this awful incident, glimpsed through a crack in the otherwise carefully maintained façade of the colonial world.

MEANWHILE, LIFE CARRIED on as though nothing had happened. My mother threw glittery parties for the cream of Anglo-Jamaican society. I grew accustomed to mixing amongst the guests, and Ian Fleming, Noël Coward, and Errol Flynn became unofficial mentors to me.

The Tasmanian-born Flynn was a criminally good-looking man and a flamboyant hedonist with a roving eye for both women and men. One of his favorite targets was my mother, and he was even more turned on when she resisted his considerable wooing charms and infamous, merry swagger. She had her ways of deflecting Flynn's attention, including telling him that she had boils on her backside. That put him off for a short while, but inevitably he would try again. His avid pursuit of my mother may have explained why Fleming, with his own tender feelings for my mother, so disliked Flynn. (Coward was surprised to discover that he *liked* Flynn, having read his "bloodcurdling autobiography, with its unnecessary vulgarity." Upon meeting Flynn, Coward wrote, "I found him to be most gracious and pleasant, one of the most charming individuals I've ever met. So it worked out fine.")

Because Errol fancied my mother, he treated me generously and allowed me aboard his two-masted schooner, *Zaca*, a prized invitation for Jamaica's elite. He even allowed me on the net at the front of the boat.

Errol happened upon Jamaica by accident after the war. His beloved *Zaca* was blown off course during a hurricane after a trip through the Panama Canal, forcing him to dock in Kingston. He loved what he saw, and, being Errol Flynn, immediately wanted more. He bought a local hotel, a 2,000-acre ranch, and a 64-acre island in Port Antonio's harbor.

Flynn's cinematic heyday was in the 1930s and '40s. By the time I knew him, he was a diminished man, afflicted by addictions to alcohol, opium, and gambling, the last of which cost him much of his fortune. He was living on the *Zaca*, which he kept moored at Navy Island off Port Antonio. Still, Errol knew how to live large. He was the first person I ever saw water-ski, with a nonchalance that made it seem like he was just going for a stroll. When I was fifteen, I watched as he glided onto the Port Antonio beach dressed for cocktails, with a cigarette holder in his fist and a dachshund under his arm. It was the coolest thing I have ever seen. Some say the phrase "in like Flynn," which was popular at the time, derived from the roguish way he approached seducing a woman. He ended up calling his memoirs *My Wicked Wicked Ways* but he toyed with calling them *In Like Me*.

Errol was cross with me just once, when I was around eighteen and tried to steal one of his girlfriends. He was notoriously unfaithful to his own wives, but this didn't stop him from punching me in the face with all the force of a living legend who had played Robin Hood on the big screen. He loved a punch-up and had been known to get into bare-knuckled fistfights with the director John Huston, one of his drinking pals, just for the fun of it. It was the only time I have ever been hit in my life.

Errol was once beaten up by a posse of lesbians in Paris after some altercation, drove a Cadillac into a swimming pool while nonchalantly smoking a cigar, released a large alligator into Port Antonio's main high street, and planned on building a New Orleans–style brothel in Kingston. By the time I got to hanging out with Grace Jones or Marianne Faithfull, who had their own extreme ways of living a daring life, I'd pretty much seen everything.

Flynn legitimately deserves credit for helping establish Jamaica's tourism industry. His magnetism drew other movie stars to the island, amongst them Ginger Rogers, Katharine Hepburn, and Bette Davis, and he helped popularize river-rafting down Jamaica's Rio Grande. He had noticed that the banana farmers ferried their cargo down to the steamships in Port Antonio Harbor on bamboo rafts. This gave him the idea to host moonlight floating parties that sometimes turned into races pitting him against such guests as Noël Coward and Coward's longtime partner, Graham Payn.

More significantly, as far as I am concerned, Errol helped popularize indigenous Jamaican music. For his parties, he frequently hired a local band of Black musicians who called themselves the Navy Island Swamp Boys. It's believed that it was Errol's idea to change their name to the Jolly Boys, because they clearly were having irreverent fun, overlaying their music with salty, entendre-laden lyrics about Jamaican life. The Jolly Boys exist to this day, though their original members are long gone.

The Jolly Boys played a genre of music known as mento: a distinctively Jamaican hybrid of West African, European, and American folk influences. Mento was Jamaica's original country music, played on acoustic instruments, with a lilting, mellow beat that anticipated reggae and Brazilian bossa nova. Its most recognizable song is Harry Belafonte's "Day-O (The Banana Boat Song)," which is frequently mischaracterized as calypso, a similar-but-not-the-same Trinidadian idiom—not least because "Day-O" originally appeared on a 1956 album by Belafonte entitled *Calypso*. Ten years my senior, Belafonte was born in Harlem to Jamaican parents. Like me, he is a character-istically Jamaican mix of ancestries: part African, part Scottish, part Dutch, part Jewish, part Catholic. He too spent his early years on the island—we overlapped from 1938 to 1940—and had his worldview shaped by the social inequities he witnessed between Jamaica's English rulers and its largely Black citizenry. The cheery call-and-response vocals of "Day-O" mask the fact that the song is about struggling workers pulling grueling shifts on the plantations.

Mento, as old-fashioned as it sounds now, pointed the way for-ward for Black Jamaican music. It was also where the tradition arose, in an echo of how freed slaves assumed the noble names of their for-mer masters, of musicians taking up such European titles as Lord, Duke, Count, Prince, and King. The heyday of mento saw perfor-mance bills bearing the names of such artists as Count Lasher, Lord Flea, Lord Power, Lord Beginner, Lord Creator, and Lord Lebby.

Errol died in 1959 at the age of fifty, a victim of his appetites. The story is that he was buried with half a dozen bottles of his favorite whiskey. One way or another he taught me an awful lot, about how to be, and how not to be. And when it comes to wildness, I learned to let others be wild, and just watch from a safe distance.

IAN FLEMING FIRST visited Jamaica during World War II, when he was an intelligence officer. Afterwards, desperate to escape the bleak, run-down austerity of postwar Britain, he purchased a strip of land on the lush north coast near the banana port of Oracabessa and built a modest three-room house. He named it Goldeneye, after a sabotage mission he had planned during the war.

Like Flynn, Fleming was a social animal, albeit far more restrained. He and Noël Coward presided over a circle of wealthy English who chose to spend their winters on the island. Goldeneye, and Jamaica itself, offered the illusion that Britain remained an imperial power rather than a fast-contracting empire. This was put into especially stark relief when Anthony Eden, the UK prime minister, spent three weeks at Goldeneye in 1956 as he recovered from the Suez Crisis, in which Britain was humiliated by Egypt. Eden's wife, Clarissa Spencer-Churchill, a niece of Winston Churchill, found Jamaica beautiful, but she also characterized it as sinister: there were strange tom-toms beating throughout the night, she told friends back home, as if the island itself were alive.

Fleming wrote his first James Bond novel, *Casino Royale*, at Goldeneye in 1952, drawing upon his own wartime experiences in British intelligence. The book's success prompted him to write thirteen more Bond novels, three of which—*Dr. No*, *Live and Let Die*, and *The Man with the Golden Gun*—featured Jamaican locations. The novels were written in six-week bursts every winter, every year until Fleming's death in 1964. In that period, Jamaica underwent a tectonic shift, transitioning from a British colony to an independently ruled nation (albeit still a member of the Commonwealth) in 1962. As this was happening, Fleming's carefully curated vision of Jamaica as a gentlemen's playground exerted a powerful pull on the public imagination: a last flare of confident British imperialism before the white bureaucrats beat a hasty retreat back to London. Bond, too, would play a role in Jamaica's tourism boom and rising international profile, all the more so after the surprise success of the very first Bond film, *Dr. No*, which I worked on as a production assistant and location scout.

Fleming and my mother met in 1956. My parents' marriage did not survive the 1940s—they split in 1949—and Mum and Ian formed a close relationship. They shared an interest in the outdoors, swimming, water-skiing, and snorkeling, and from them I learned to love the water, where I felt as much at home as I did on land.

MY PARENTS AND I had moved back to England, my birthplace, near the end of World War II. It was thought that the northern European air might be better for my asthma than the sticky, close Jamaican air. I also needed the education that had been seriously lacking as I aimlessly wandered the gardens of our house, either on my own or pestering the staff, who had become part of my little world. I needed a dose of reality, or at least something that lifted me out of myself and gave me the energy to fight my condition.

The journey by boat back to Southampton took us into dangerous waters. There were plenty of threats in the ocean between Jamaica and Europe, the ship felt very exposed, and it was a scary few days. It did not get much safer when we arrived in London, checking into the Grosvenor Hotel by Hyde Park in Mayfair. Bombs were still falling upon London into the last year of the war, V-2 rockets that you couldn't hear coming. One landed near enough to the hotel to send our plates jumping off the table when we were having breakfast.

The move to London left me even more on my own, because there was no working staff to engage with me in our high-class Mayfair apartment. My parents went out most evenings, leaving me at home without a babysitter. Cold as their approach was, I grew to appreciate the sense of freedom my solitary life gave me, the feeling of being responsible for myself and finding things to do.

School, however, was hell. I was sent away to my father's alma mater, St. John's Beaumont School in Windsor. My father marrying a Jew made it imperative to his mother and my grandmother, a religious maniac, that I be sent to a Catholic school. I hated the place. I was too ill most of the time to do much of anything. Sometimes I required oxygen care in a tent. When I did manage to make it to classes, I really loathed them, and my teachers loathed me, not least because I picked verbal fights with them during lessons. I had an argument with a teacher when he was talking about heaven. The school's motto was "Heavenly Matters over Earthly Matters." I asked if my dog would go to heaven. He said no because it was not a human being, and heaven was strictly for human beings. I was furious. I loved my dog more than most people at the time, and it definitely put me off Catholicism.

My next stop was another preparatory school, St. Peter's Court, in Broadstairs, Kent, overlooking the English Channel on the Kent coast. My parents decided that the location of St. John's Beaumont, in the damp Thames Valley, was causing me breathing problems. That, rather than the fact that I had been told my dog would not go to heaven, was the reason for my transfer. In any event, the sea air coming in from the coast in Broadstairs truly did help clear my airways, and I certainly preferred St. Peter's Court to my old school.

I wasn't a great student. I was absolutely hopeless at English and slightly better at math, but for some reason I excelled at Latin, which was enough to help me pass by the slimmest of margins into one of England's most ancient and respectable schools, Harrow, founded in 1572 under a royal charter of Queen Elizabeth I. Harrow and its main rival, Eton, are elite, exclusive institutions for the rich, privileged, queue-jumping establishment. Confusingly, especially to Americans, they are known to the British as public schools, though they are anything but public, and they continue to have a mesmerizing hold over the British people, whose leaders are drawn disproportionately from a small group of Harrovians and Etonians.

It will not surprise you that I failed to fit in at Harrow. I was very much an outsider, at the bottom of the social food chain. Mercifully, I was not subjected to the very worst customs of "fagging," the inelegant public-school term for institutionalized bullying. Fagging was intrinsic to school life, meant to instill character. It was based on the notion that those who are destined to rule must first learn to obey. In many instances, it was, as its slur of a name suggests, a cover for nonconsensual sexual acts between boys, what the Victorians called "irregularities." My fagging tasks, as far as I can remember, never went much further than warming toilet seats for the senior boys and polishing their leather belts. I was more like a tea boy than a submissive sex slave.

Alongside the fagging, I was caned a lot by the teachers, usually for breaking arcane rules dating back to the eighteenth and nineteenth centuries. My most common offense was my failure to wear the famous shallow straw hat with a black band that all Harrovians were meant to when outside. I would claim that my hat was lost, stolen, or damaged, but the truth was, I just didn't want to wear such a stupid old-fashioned thing. I never took to the other clothing requirements either: the stiff blue blazers we were supposed to wear during the week and the formal Sunday uniform of tailcoat and striped trousers. My Harrow experience led to my lifelong affinity for extremely casual wear: flip-flops and shorts whenever possible.

In one instance, I was caned publicly, in front of the entire student body, which evidently had not happened in 130 years. My offense? Dropping some candy wrappers on school grounds. I think the schoolmasters were making an example of me because I had a reputation as a rebel. I would break out at night and head into town to buy alcohol and cigarettes, which I would then sell to other pupils. One day the masters discovered a stash of bottles that I had foolishly left lying around, probably thinking I was too clever for them. I wasn't. Maybe deep down, or not so deep down, I was looking for a way out.

My mother was summoned, and a careful diplomatic solution was reached. I was not formally expelled, but the headmaster said to Mum with typical English understatement, "Christopher might be happier elsewhere." That was the end of my formal education, at age sixteen. I became one of Harrow's unmentionable dropouts, which suited me.

The main legacy of my "public" schooling is my accent, which combines easygoing traces of Jamaican speech with a posh—some have even said arrogant-sounding—Harrow tone. This accent has served its purpose, impressing or intimidating people, depending on their own social insecurities, and exciting certain Americans seeking a glimpse into some sort of illusory English fantasy. I also learned that forceful but fetching English manners are useful in matters of persuasion, especially when gently mixed with something more Jamaican and elusively headstrong.

My Harrow non-expulsion expulsion sent me back to Jamaica, where the start of my adult life awaited me.

CHAPTER TWO

THE FIFTIES, JAMAICA: FINDING A PURPOSE

My parents' divorce proved fortuitous in a way, in that their separate paths exposed me to a very particular set of circumstances that pointed me towards my future in the music business. My mother stayed in Jamaica, where I could sense change afoot as the country prepared for independence and the newly invigorated Black population was asserting itself culturally. My father remarried, to an American woman, and made his new home in Lake Forest, Illinois. My summer visits there put me within minutes of Chicago at the very beginning of that city's blues boom. I educated myself in Chicago's manifold independent record labels: Vee-Jay, home of John Lee Hooker and Jimmy Reed; J.O.B., home of Snooky Pryor and Johnny Shines; Chance, home of Homesick James; and the great Chess, home of Muddy Waters and Willie Dixon.

Not that I foresaw a life in music at that time. For all of my academic failure, I had a ready-made future in the Lindo family business. There would always be a well-paid position for me at Wray & Nephew, the island's leading rum manufacturer. That is, until there wasn't. In the mid-1950s, much to my surprise, my uncles sold their rum businesses. So much for my secure future.

At this point, my adventurous Blackwell genes kicked in, along with some life lessons picked up from Errol Flynn. I simply went with the flow, taking life as it came, my luck coming in fits and starts, and sometimes disappearing altogether.

Not long after my rescue by the Rastamen at Hellshire Beach, I found myself back in London, at a party at the Dorchester Hotel thrown by the showman Mike Todd, at the time the husband of Elizabeth Taylor and one of the biggest producers in Hollywood. The party celebrated the launch of Todd's bloated, star-packed comedy *Around the World in 80 Days*, which seemed more an excuse to throw glamorous launch parties than a proper film.

My mother attended the party, as did the man who was at that time the governor of Jamaica, Sir Hugh Foot, a friend of hers. Sir Hugh politely asked, "How's Christopher doing?" My mother rolled her eyes, more or less labeling me a lost cause. I was in England for one last try at finding my place in straight society, trying to learn the ropes of accountancy at the esteemed firm Price Waterhouse. It wasn't going well—this plan was as ill-considered for me as Harrow had been.

Sir Hugh threw my mother a lifeline by saying he had a job for me. I would serve as one of his gofers, running errands and assisting him at public functions—basically the kind of role that being a Harrow fag was meant to prepare you for. Mother was skeptical, telling Sir Hugh that she didn't think I even knew how to get out of bed in the morning. Sir Hugh told her to leave things to him.

For two years, I worked at his side in Kingston, in the process getting to know such local politicians as Norman Manley and Alexander Bustamante, who would become Jamaica's first premier and first prime minister under independent rule. Sir Hugh, the product of an enlightened and liberal family, was a class act who got on well with Bustamante and Manley, developing a great relationship with the people he recognized to be the future of the island. He was one of the most popular governors of Jamaica, a steadying influence as the prospect of independence came closer.

Nearly twenty years later, I hired one of Sir Hugh's sons, Benjamin Foot, to work for me as the minder to a strong-willed group I had just signed to my record label, Island Records. They were called the Wailers, and their members were Bob Marley, Peter Tosh, and Bunny Wailer. Benjamin was basically serving in the same sort of gofer capacity for them as I had for his father, albeit with different briefs. I hadn't planned it, but the group was being looked after by the son of a former governor of Jamaica—he was having to follow their demanding, unforgiving orders based on a particularly alien set of rituals. A key part of his duties was ensuring that the group received its full daily quota of marijuana every morning, the smoking of which began before breakfast.

I later learned from Benjamin that his father had faced political pressure in the 1950s to crack down on the Rastafari as a disruptive force. But Sir Hugh resisted, admiring the Rastas for their independence and ingenuity in building a society for themselves. I hadn't planned for this bit of historical symmetry, but it wasn't lost on the Wailers that they were giving orders to the son of a former governor of colonial-era Jamaica. Bob told me the group appreciated the irony.

My distinguished service to Jamaica as an aide to Sir Hugh Foot ended when his governorship did, in 1957. I drifted a bit more, briefly trying my hand at showing real estate, selling air conditioners, and teaching water-skiing. My best customer at the last job was a skinny, easygoing Rasta who, unlike my white customers, always paid me on time. I grew healthier in this period too, my asthma abating and my physical confidence growing, which made my mum happy enough, even though I had still failed to launch as a responsible and respectable adult.

Finally I happened upon a freelance job that lined up with my personal interests. One of my friends had the concession in Jamaica for Wurlitzer, a major manufacturer of jukeboxes. I persuaded him to let me lease some of his jukeboxes, which were growing in popularity in the 1950s amongst Jamaicans who couldn't afford to keep a radio in their own homes. Before long, I was responsible for sixty-three jukeboxes on the island, from the cities on the coast to places up in the hills in the middle of nowhere. In one of those places miles from anywhere, I would deal with a seven-year-old, because the Chinese owner of the bar didn't speak English. It was one of those jobs for which there were no real qualifications, and I was pretty good at it.

MOST OF THE jukebox demand was for American product: blues, R&B, boogie-woogie, gospel, doo-wop, Fats Domino, Rosco Gordon, Lloyd Price, and Little Richard. Before long, though, some mento and calypso records came into the mix, by the likes of Count Lasher, George Moxley, and Lord Flea. The foremost mento label—the only game in town, really—was MRS, which stood for Motta's Recording Studio.

Motta was Stanley Motta, who ran an electronics and camera store on Hanover Street in Kingston. Shrewdly recognizing that tourists might want to take some recorded Jamaican music home with them, he set up a no-frills studio where artists recorded their songs in one take, on one track. Motta also stocked amplifiers and speakers, which became another plank of Jamaica's postwar music boom.

The best sound system was built by Hedley Jones, a Black inventor who had served in the Royal Air Force as an engineer during the war. A high-fidelity obsessive, he was keen to build amplifiers that would better showcase the jazz records he sourced from America than even those of the top-range US and British manufacturers. A Kingston hardware store owner named Tom Wong was so impressed by the sound quality of Jones's rig that he ordered an amplifier and speaker set from him.

Wong, a Jamaican of Chinese and African heritage, initially used his PA setup to play music for the open-air dance parties of a well-to-do clientele—taking the place of the big bands that the swells had hired before the advance of recorded music. But Wong found that he had an equally willing market for his wares in Black neighborhoods, where he experimented further.

He hung speakers from trees and pushed the volume into the red. The result was a vital sonic power that made entire neighborhoods shake. The horns echoed through the hills and the bass was enough to wake the dead, as it should be. Wong called his rig—a combination of a turntable, a tube amplifier, and some bulky speaker boxes, bound together in a classically Jamaican rewiring of technologies and traditions—a sound system.

Wong's system inspired imitators and competitors, all of which were essentially throbbing mobile discos, replete with DJs and hype men. When I started going to sound systems, the thing that hooked me the most was the sheer bone-shaking volume, a loudness that live music had yet to achieve. There was nothing like it outside of Jamaica until the Who and Led Zeppelin pushed the limits of amplification in the late 1960s.

As rival sound systems joined the competition, Jamaica became the loudest island on earth, with ever-larger crowds gathering for showdowns between the systems. Who had the best tunes? Who had the loudest, toughest sound?

Wong assumed the performing name Tom the Great Sebastian, after a Barnum & Bailey trapeze artist. For a while, Tom reigned supreme in the sound-system world, fighting off the likes of Sir Nick the Champ and Count Smith the Blues Blaster. But he was eclipsed in the mid-1950s by three brilliant innovators who understood and shaped what Jamaican ears preferred: Duke Reid, Sir Coxsone Dodd, and "King" Edwards the Giant, the cultural conquistadors whose influence ultimately extended well beyond Jamaica and the 1950s.

The King Edwards sound system was run by brothers Vincent and George; in a way there were two Kings, inspired early on by Tom the Great Sebastian, and amongst the first to go for bigger amplifiers and bigger sound—bigger than the rest, who were forced to keep up—to champion their favorite American records by the likes of Smiley Lewis and Shirley and Lee.

Arthur Stanley Reid was an ex-policeman who began hosting parties to promote Treasure Isle, the liquor and haberdashery store he owned with his wife, Lucille. Selling liquor was originally the priority, with the music just a way of drawing a crowd of customers. One song wasn't enough. There had to be a sequence of really good songs, and Reid had to work out a flow of them. As Duke Reid, he started to connect his record player to purpose-built larger speakers, which became ever larger and more powerful over the years, making the music much more of a local event, a performance.

Reid developed an act. He carted his equipment from place to place in a Bedford Trojan van with DUKE REID—THE TROJAN KING OF SOUNDS painted on its side. He played the part of extreme party host, a show-business gangster carried on his throne to his turntables wearing a gold crown and flamboyant costumes complete with pistols and a belt of bullets.

Clement Dodd, a cricket fan, took his handle from an English cricketer named Alec Coxon. Sixteen years Reid's junior, Dodd started out working for Reid, hunting down exclusive new records. Coxsone had logged time in the American South as a migrant worker, picking fruit for more money than he could make working at home. While his mates spent their cash on clothes, he bought records. He had direct exposure to new American postwar music, bringing back new beats and rare discs for Reid to play. Before long, Coxsone broke off from Reid, eager to be a frontman himself, setting up his own sound system and a rivalry with his former boss.

Jukeboxes weren't as cool as sound systems, but they were equally important in terms of disseminating new music in Kingston and across the island. (The ska pioneer Prince Buster started out as a jukebox operator.) I traveled Jamaica's uneven roads, constantly changing the records in my machines in Kingston and in the bars up on the mountains and down in the coastal villages. In most of these places, radio sets, record players, and live concerts were rare, which encouraged the kind of communal listening that also fueled the sound-system rivalries.

Running my jukeboxes was the very best way of discovering on the ground what kind of music people liked—which, at the time, was predominantly American R&B and country. You'd get instant market research about which new sounds were working and which weren't. I found myself in crowded, tiny rooms where everyone was packed in tight, desperate to hear something new that made their bodies move. If I put on a record they didn't like, they jeered and I hung my head: the record was a flop. But if I played something they liked, they were beside themselves, shouting, "TUNE!"

I became a version of what was becoming known, in sound-system parlance, as a selector: a person responsible for picking out the best songs and the best sequence in which to play them to keep the party going. I loved the real-time market-research aspect of it. It was an exhilarating, physical job.

Coxsone Dodd, Duke Reid, and King Edwards as the Big Three with their private stashes of hot 45s would soon be joined at the end of the 1950s by Cecil Bustamente Campbell, aka Prince Buster, the voice of the people straight from the dark, intimidating Kingston side streets, determined to dethrone the established leaders, breaking free of the Coxsone stable to set out on his own. Eventually, he would be one of the rare operators to have their own crew of artists, DJs, and singers, and also release records under his own name.

When he found his access to buying American records blocked by some suspicious shenanigans regarding his immigrant status, he was quick to turn to producing and recording his own music to play, exclusives fronted by himself, Owen Gray, and Eric "Monty" Morris.

It was mayhem, and the to-and-fro, the competitive battles between systems with their fierce electronics set up in dusty yards, in open fields, sound fiends setting the pace, ignited a new form of Jamaican music. The sound systems launched the Jamaican music business.

Your record-hunting rivals would be going to Louisiana, Nashville, New York, North and South Carolina, all over the place, traveling by bus to find that one record, that absolute scoop that would make their name, or keep their reputation intact. We were all in competition, which forced us to make discoveries and transform ourselves as we chased sounds and listeners.

When you found a record nobody else had, you'd scrape off the label, so no one knew who the singer was. Obviously, today, it's impossible to think that you wouldn't know what a record was, because everything is so readily available. But in those days, that was not the case. You'd scratch the labels off to guard your treasure and retain exclusivity, which was your advantage over others. If a rival had a tune you didn't have, that would really hurt you. If you had a record no one else had, you could hurt them. To survive, you needed a tune that no one else had. And then another tune that no one else had to follow that. You had to make sure you had the best records and that you strung them together in the best way. It was ruthless. And, as I discovered, the helter-skelter, cutthroat nature of doing business with the sound systems was the best training for working in the record business.

I would supply some of the sound systems with records I had found in New York for sixty cents. Scraping off the label so that it was anonymous could make a good record very desireable, and you could get ten, twenty dollars for it. The sound system guys were cool with that as long as I sold only one copy to them exclusively. Beware selling a great and expensive new record to two systems at the same time. That was an absolute no-go. That's when things could take a vicious twist. It was best to stick to the code, which wasn't written down, but you got the idea.

Sometimes, getting the record no one else had, or the one someone else had but had made anonymous by removing the label, involved an immense search. Having blasted Tom Wong out of the way, Reid had been used to getting it all his own way until his old employee Dodd found some records he didn't have, including one that more or less became Dodd's theme tune. Reid went on the search when he was next in America to get hold of the track but at the time he didn't know what it was called or who it was by, and to this day it remains a mystery. Some records would remain a mystery, their titles and artists taken to the grave by the sound man.

He listened to thousands of songs until he managed to find it in a record shop in Philadelphia. Apparently, he jumped for joy and laughed like a maniac. At a showdown set up on his return at a regular venue, Forrester's Hall, Dodd thought it was a scam that Reid could play all his exclusives. At midnight, Reid defiantly played the track, and Dodd fainted on the spot. Reid ruled once more. Or something like that.

MY MEMORIES OF record-hunting in America have taken on the quality of dreams. It's hard to believe that it was all real, but it all led to a new kind of knowledge. I seemed to have the knack for meeting the right people, who would take me to the right places. On one trip to New York in 1958, I went out on a hot, steamy night with a songwriter with whom I had become friends, Syd Shaw, who had written some great romantic songs covered by Nina Simone, Eartha Kitt, Sarah Vaughan, Vic Damone, Duke Ellington, Johnny Mathis, and Lena Horne.

After midnight, we ended up at Café Bohemia on Barrow Street in Greenwich Village, where the first great Miles Davis Quintet was playing, getting up to speed. We were just ten feet away from Miles, the music right in our faces. It was intense, and I found it hard to contain myself, but the vibe was that you quietly paid attention, gently applauded, and acted as if it was all just routine stuff: Miles blowing music apart, paying no mind to the audience, sometimes turning his back to us, his thoughts miles away.

Syd managed to get us backstage to meet Miles. I suddenly found myself in a small smoky room with the great trumpeter and a few others. I think John Coltrane and Philly Joe Jones were also present, but I only had eyes for Miles. He was delicate-looking, even a little vulnerable, with those hooded eyes and that famous raspy whisper. All of this made him even more magnetic.

Syd and I were the only white guys there. At that time in America, it was uncommon for a white kid to be hanging around with Blacks, but coming from where I did, working with Dodd and Reid, I was used to it. Miles took a liking to me. I think he noticed that I wasn't as nervous as most white people were in his company—often they broke out in flop sweat, which tickled him. I had learned from dealing with sound-system royalty how to pick up the rhythm and fall in with the mood. We started hanging out.

Miles was the best teacher, always amused when I asked him questions. I was pretty cocky at the time, and I once asked him why he played so many bad notes, unlike Bix Beiderbecke and Louis Armstrong, who always played clean. He didn't blink. He didn't bite my head off. "Because I try and play what I hear in my head," he said, "not what I know I can already play." That, to me, was the essence of jazz, trying to get somewhere new and not worrying if you made mistakes as long as you got there in the end. On a tightrope, and wobbling a little, but eventually gliding across that tightrope.

Only once did Miles tell me off. We were listening to some music, something fast, and my leg was unconsciously jiggling to the beat, which irritated him. "Slow down, man!" he scolded me. "Enjoy it in your head. Keep it to yourself." In other words, keep cool.

The other thing Miles taught me about, besides music, was cars. He had an affinity for flashy motors, especially fast European ones. When he jumped from the Prestige label to Columbia in the mid-fifties, he blew his first advance on a beautiful Mercedes 190SL soft-top convertible, as sleek and bewitching as one of his solos. It was such an exotic-looking piece of machinery at the time—still is. He had been paid $300 an album by Prestige, so this was his Columbia-fueled, $4,000 way of expressing defiance at the music industry's shabby treatment of Black artists.

I was in the car with Miles a couple of times and I remember how quiet it was as we shot across 110th Street late at night, at what seemed like a hundred miles an hour. It was dangerous driving with Miles, but it imbued in me a passion for cars, and for buying a good one when I had the funds. Later on, if ever I had some unexpected extra cash, I would buy a car I fancied. When Free's "All Right Now" became a big hit in 1970, I spent my windfall on a sporty black Mercedes two-seater coupe I had imported directly from Germany.

Here's another thing I picked up from Miles: drive fast to test the mettle of the person sitting next to you in the passenger seat. One day in the Bahamas in 1980, my passenger was Nick Stewart, the head of A&R at Island Records (a label's "Artists and Repertoire" department was traditionally responsible for talent scouting and artist development). As we drove to Island's Compass Point Studios in Nassau, he was trying to sell me on signing a four-piece rock group that he, and many others at Island Records, really wanted to sign.

I had misgivings. The group was from Ireland and didn't strike me at the time as a good fit for us. I picked up some speed, just to see how committed Nick was to this band he wanted me to go and see. He stuck with his pitch well, steadily telling me that they had a great guitarist and a very forceful singer. I asked a few more questions about the group, testing his resolve. Nick stuck to his guns. Then I put my foot on the gas some more. I didn't say anything, but he knew the acceleration was me saying, *I'll think about it.* So I thought about it. And I did indeed sign U2.

*   *   *

MY ABILITY TO get over to America regularly meant I was a good source for rare records. Sometimes a title alone would point you in the right direction—Lionel Hampton's "Hey! Ba-Ba-Re-Bop," Joe Liggins and His Honeydrippers' "Groovy Groove," Willis Jackson's "Howling at Midnight," and Paul Gayten's "Tickle Toe" were all winners. Sometimes you'd click with an artist who never let you down, like my beloved Professor Longhair—the Fess!—who was as influential on Jamaican music as he was on Fats Domino, Elvis Presley, Dr. John, Huey "Piano" Smith, and Allen Toussaint.

I picked up tangy, tangled Afro-Caribbean influences on Longhair's playing, what Jelly Roll Morton described as "the Spanish tinge," a slow Latin element in the blues. Longhair, otherwise known as Roy Byrd of New Orleans, had a way of slipping and sliding around the beat as he played piano, essentially deconstructing the rhythm with a natural but idiosyncratic grace that connected with Jamaican ears in the 1950s.

Sounds were continually cross-pollinating as they traveled between the North American continent and the islands. In the era of the slave trade, a large number of enslaved people came through the Caribbean en route to America, spending some time working on the islands before reaching their real destination—a practice the slavers called "seasoning." Some of these enslaved people performed music rooted in their African homelands, picking up island influences as they did, whether Latin rhythms or the Afro-Caribbean drumming of the Maroons.

Then this music traveled to the American South, where it sneaked into the jump blues of Professor Longhair, and from there it would flow back to the Caribbean, where a lot of it had begun in the first place. Jamaicans responded so positively to the American records played by the sound systems and jukeboxes because these imports sounded more like Jamaican music *should* than mento, which, as the fifties became the sixties, seemed increasingly like tame tourist music.

Fats Domino was revered in Jamaica. He played strident chiming chords with his right hand and a cocky walking bass with his left, which, when interpreted by Jamaican musicians, resulted in a very distinctive Jamaican lope and swagger. Just as the swing and back-beat of his 1949 song "The Fat Man" helped set up rock and roll, the bouncing beat of his 1959 hit "Be My Guest" helped create ska. Fats's Jamaican listeners were taken with the song's skeletal, unfussy arrangement and, with their Jamaican genius for taking something they loved and making it their own, played their instruments to the off beat rather than the on beat.

Bob Marley and Jimmy Cliff both credited Fats Domino as a major influence on their early sound. Fats's Jamaican acolytes didn't necessarily think of what they were doing as playing on the off beat; they were just after something that sounded rougher and harder than mento. They were hitting the beat where it sounded better, where it took the listener by surprise and made feet move.

The Big Three of the sound systems, Duke, Coxsone, and King, were my contemporaries, a new breed of businessman with an ear for talent and picking hits. But whereas they ran companies, complete with employees and signature battle cries, I was a sole proprietor. I operated in the shadows, behind the scenes. I knew that I was no showman. How could I be, considering my background and the color of my skin, as well as my natural proclivity for keeping to myself?

Still, we all shared the same hunger for new records and new sounds. The competitive element of it, the chase to be the first to discover something new, stayed with me throughout my life in the record business. I liked it when it was a fight, when it wasn't comfort-able, when you weren't bound by rules or an orderly system, when you were in a battle with others on the hunt for talent.

As time went on, though, there weren't enough records to go round. The product, the repertoire, started to dry up. Dodd, Reid, and Edwards knew what they had to do next: make records, not just play them. I needed to follow suit.

*   *   *

I STARTED TO think deeply about records themselves. How were they made, and who made them? Where did they come from? Well, they came from the recording studio, something of a mystery at the time. So that was the next place I needed to be in order to get to the essence of the music I loved. I became obsessed with the idea of making one of these records that was so powerful that, when you played it in a bar, you changed the energy of the crowd in an instant.

I felt I had learned enough about records to start making them myself—not only the music but the actual object, the record itself, pressed onto a label that you grew to trust because its releases were consistently good. Something entrepreneurial stirred inside me, although I didn't initially think of the record business as a great one to get into. It didn't even seem like a business, period. It certainly wasn't organized like one in Jamaica.

I did feel that I was spending far too much money buying records for my jukeboxes and that it would be worth seeing if I could make my own. I didn't necessarily think there was a future in it, but it seemed one way of sourcing records. Filling all my jukeboxes with a steady stream of new, in-demand records was getting expensive.

The next step was to have my own label, which in hindsight seems logical, though not so much at the time. And the name for the label I wanted to have fell into my lap. In 1957, crowned as the Calypso King, a sex symbol and pioneering Black icon, Harry Belafonte had starred alongside James Mason, Joan Fontaine, and Joan Collins in *Island in the Sun,* Robert Rossen's film adaptation of Alec Waugh's 1955 interracial romance set on an imaginary West Indian isle. The novel glanced against the complicated political realities of the time, the tensions between the old order and a new nationalist movement, between tourist paradise and tough economic reality; but it ended more as a colonial romance supplying a little cheer to Brits anxious about losing their place in the world. The book allowed them to be already nostalgic for the empire even as it was melting away, offering glimpses of how the British would cling to often delusional feelings of superiority and authority as their power shrank.

Along with the song called "Island in the Sun" that Belafonte sang for the movie, a subtle challenging of white misconceptions of the Caribbean, the title gave me an idea for the name of the record label I formed at the end of the 1950s. Island Records would emerge out of the same postwar Jamaican winds of change that whispered through the book and film.

The very first album I recorded and released on Island Records was *Lance Hayward at the Half Moon Hotel*, which came out in 1959. It was made very much in the spirit of the great jazz labels, Blue Note, Prestige, and Verve. I was twenty-two—hence the album's catalogue number, CB22. The cover was a striking red flame graphic inspired by staring at the stylish albums released by those design-conscious jazz companies, and the very first label logo Island had was an orange sun—I was clearly after some heat. The address on the back said Island Records, Box 258, Jamaica W.I. Island was in business.

I discovered my debut recording artists while I was working at the Half Moon Hotel in Montego Bay. I was holding down the resort's water-skiing concession—a way of getting by until something else came along. My cousin Barbara's dad owned the hotel, and she and I both loved jazz.

Barbara persuaded her father to put on a jazz act at the hotel, and they brought in a young, blind jazz pianist from Bermuda named Lance Hayward, whose music was very much in the mood of Oscar Peterson and early Nat King Cole. Nothing too troubling or distracting for the well-heeled, cocktail-sipping hotel clientele, but jazz nonetheless, swinging nice and easy. I made friends with Lance and started to make rash promises about making a record with him, probably having drunk a couple of rums too many.

I must have sounded like I knew what I was doing, because Lance believed me and kept asking, "When are we going to make that record?" I started to investigate how to do it. This was a time when recording studios in Jamaica were technically very basic, if they existed at all, and most music was recorded in local radio stations, usually surreptitiously, after hours.

This was the earliest era of Jamaican recording, and I was trying to do it at the same time as the artful sound-system royalty were getting hold of a one-track, a two-track machine, grabbing talent from outside their shops, players and singers with nothing much to do, ready for action, making records that weren't available in the shops, often just an acetate, a sneaky instrumental version of some American hit, anything to keep supplying the sound systems with some fresh-feeling rhythm, some hard bass and tricky movement for the DJs to use behind their messages and call-outs.

Initially I was a little more orthodox with my talent spotting, finding professional musicians in the swanky hotels and the cricket club dances. Lance was my first experience recording an album, designing a sleeve, getting it printed. To get it made I went over to New York, where I could buy more records to sell to the sound systems and fill my jukeboxes but now more excited by the idea that I could make my own records to sell. Sound systems were still rounding up crowds and turning up the volume, but I could sense, after all that record handling I'd done, that making records was where the action was heading.

I took Lance and the band in a Volkswagen van down to what became known as Federal Records on Marcus Garvey Drive in Kingston, where the Lebanese/Cuban businessman and furniture salesman Ken Khouri recorded in a couple of converted rooms—amongst the first generation of Jamaican recording entrepreneurs, he was one of the main reasons there was such a thing as a Jamaican recording industry. He was known as Papa Khouri, a real godfather of Jamaican music.

Ken had gotten into the music business by accident. A gadget freak, he had traveled to Miami to buy a car and met a man in dire financial straits who was desperately trying to unload a disc-recording machine. Khouri paid $350 for it, unsure if he'd been ripped off or had scored a bargain.

He started recording mento and calypso acts in local nightclubs, sending his recordings to England to be pressed into 78 rpm records. Bitten by the record-making bug, Khouri invested in more equipment and built a tiny pressing plant next to the studio, which became known as Federal Records.

Before I brought Lance and his band to Marcus Garvey Drive, I had never before been inside a recording studio, didn't know what they consisted of, and had no idea what to do. One thing I could do very well at the time, however, given my background and training at Harrow, was pretend that I had complete self-confidence.

I hid my nerves as best I could, because, after all, I was to all intents and purposes the supervisor of the proceedings. Lance with his boys, bassist Maxwell Smith and drummer Clarence "Tootsie" Bean, walked into one room, which I presumed was where they were going to play, so I walked into the room next to it. This turned out to be the control room, which suggests you are in control of proceedings. I waited for something to happen, not saying much so as not to give away that I didn't know what to do. This was actually a lesson that served me well later on, when I actually knew how to make records. Let things evolve, keep the mood cool—the best things that happen in a recording studio never occur in an orderly fashion, or because you expect them to.

The band played a tune, Ken did whatever he needed to do to get it on tape, and then they all looked at me to see what I thought. I sat there looking, I hoped, thoughtful—and then Lance said, "Shall we play it again?" That saved me from having to say something relevant.

"Yes, please do," I said with as much authority as I could muster. They did what I asked. The second take was possibly better than the first. My advice to play it again had worked! I was now a record producer, whatever that was. From that moment, I decided, *This is what I want to do for the rest of my life.* I'd gone from the outside to the inside in a flash. I was in heaven.

I wouldn't call the Hayward recording a great, groundbreaking jazz album. It's a souvenir of a time and place and will take you to sunny, easygoing 1959 Montego Bay in an instant. I don't suppose it sold as many as 200 albums, mostly in the hotel itself as a holiday souvenir. But now I was eager to make more records, immediately. My next album featured a guitarist I'd come across while working some shifts at the Half Moon Hotel, the twenty-seven-year-old Ernest Ranglin, a son of Manchester Parish in west-central Jamaica.

Ernest had played on some of those mento records recorded by Stanley Motta and was already working on special not-for-sale ace-tates for Coxsone Dodd, who had taken to recording his own exclusives for his sound system. One such single, entitled "Easy Snappin'" and initially credited to Clue J and His Blues Blasters, is of historical significance. Clue J was the double bassist Cluett Johnson, and the story goes that he liked to greet friends and colleagues with a rousing, nonsensical call of "Skavoovie!"—which is as plausible an origin story for the word *ska* as any other told in Jamaica.

Another suggests that Johnson declared that, in a certain part of the song, he wanted a sound "like some jazz scat." The band misheard him and started referring to the style in which they played as ska. Whatever the reality, it's true that Jamaicans like to make up new words and tell tall tales, bringing new meaning into the world.

The writer of "Easy Snappin'" was a self-taught pianist and vocalist named Theo Beckford, who, like Ranglin, had played on some of the mento records for tourists. Beckford, Ranglin, Johnson, and crew were seasoned players who nimbly switched between jazz, calypso, and mento, and from this mélange of influences emerged the ska beat. The song was a big hit for Dodd's sound system, and the Jamaican public wanted more.

Having logged a few years hunting for records, I was now hunting for musicians to record. For a brief period, I ran my own little restaurant and nightclub to get close to musicians: the Ferry Inn, on the road that linked Kingston to Spanish Town. The tavern had been built in 1684 next to a swamp, a convenient stopping point for travelers waiting to cross the river on a ferry before there was a bridge. On one occasion I had the pleasure of showing my mother and Ian Fleming to a table when they came to see how I was getting on. But running the place pinned me down too much; I needed to get out and about to find what and who I was looking for. My career in hospitality would come later down the line.

But Ranglin presented himself right on my doorstep, a stroke of good fortune. He was a versatile and melodic guitar player influenced by the early masters of electric guitar, Charlie Christian, Les Paul, and Wes Montgomery. He was also a skillful arranger. Over time, Ernest turned into my secret weapon, someone I could call upon to add virtuosity and Jamaican realness to any record.

The album he made for me, *Guitar in Ernest*, was a blend of melodic jazz and ska-in-the-making. I gave it the catalogue number CB23. It's another fine souvenir of a time and place, a sonic blast of optimism, the sound of Black Jamaican musicians breaking free of the colonial grind.

As I was pressing my two early instrumental albums, I realized that I was a little out of touch—most Jamaican vinyl was coming out in the form of singles, songs to be played on the radio and the sound systems. I changed course and decided that singles with vocals were where I needed to put my energy.

Jamaica boasted a wealth of amazing homegrown singers at the time, many of them showcased on the talent show Opportunity Hour, which was produced and hosted by a newspaper columnist and radio personality named Vere Johns and held at various movie theaters in Kingston. Opportunity Hour's roots dated back to the 1930s, when it was conceived as a stunt to draw larger audiences to the cinema. But it really came into its own in the late 1950s, when fledgling record producers and the sound-system guys were looking for ready and willing vocalists.

These contests had a real carnival atmosphere, with the winners chosen by raucous crowd reaction. Every winner received a small cash prize, which was exciting given that most of the contestants were from poor families. You received maybe two pounds for winning, and in those days two pounds was serious money—but the real prize was getting the attention of the new breed of record producers.

Just about every Jamaican singing star of the 1960s and '70s came through Opportunity Hour, including Bob Marley, Jimmy Cliff, John Holt, Millie Small, and Derrick Morgan. The first singers I raided from the talent show were Wilfred Edwards (whom I later renamed Jackie Edwards because "Wilfred" didn't seem like a show-business name), Laurel Aitken, and Owen Gray.

It was almost too easy to find singing talent. I would be talking in front of a theater with Wilfred, and would immediately be approached by young hopefuls pleading, "What about me, what about me? I can sing, I can sing!" Most of my early singles came out on an Island subsidiary I named R&B—I wanted a label that clearly identified itself with what was happening: Black Jamaicans doing their take on American R&B music.

My first R&B release was "Boogie in My Bones" by Laurel Aitken. He was a Cuban-Jamaican singer I'd met while we were both doing the rounds of the Kingston clubs. An argument can be made that "Boogie in My Bones" was the first indigenous Jamaican pop record: a midtempo rhythm-and-blues track with a local accent and some lingering traces of mento. Backed by a "my baby left me" song of lamentation called "Little Sheila," the single went to number one on the Jamaican charts and remained there a few weeks. Feeling that I was now up and running, I soon thereafter opened the first Island Records office on South Odeon Avenue in Half Way Tree, a commercial suburb of Kingston, just opposite the new offices of the Jamaica Broadcasting Corporation.

*   *   *

THE HORNS ON "Boogie in My Bones" had a Jamaican feel but were not actually played by Jamaicans. The only Jamaicans involved with the track were Laurel and me. I kept this quiet at the time, because I didn't want to have anyone question the single's authenticity, which would have been fatal, especially for a young label run by a privileged white Jamaican kid.

The musicians I hired to back Aitken were an Australian group called the Caribs. Their story is yet another example of how mixed-up and polyglot the Jamaican music scene was, drawing participants of Cuban, Panamanian, Trinidadian, Lebanese, Chinese, Indian, and European origin. But even by Jamaican standards, the Caribs were an anomaly. And Errol Flynn, their fellow Australian, had something to do with their migration to our island.

The Caribs were not remotely Caribbean. They started out as the house band at a tourist hotel in Surfers Paradise, a suburb on Australia's Gold Coast. Because their stage was fringed by palm trees and the band played a lot of songs with Latin rhythms, they arrived at the name the Caribs. A couple of the group's members actually traveled to the Caribbean and a made a friend in Abe Issa, the owner of one of Kingston's most celebrated nightclubs, the Glass Bucket Club, in a perfect spot on the border between uptown and downtown. Errol Flynn was a regular at the Glass Bucket and knew Abe well. He mentioned that he knew a crack band in his homeland called the Caribs, and how great they were playing calypso and mento. Abe remembered meeting the guys and got in touch, saying that if they were ever passing through, they should give him a call. En route to England after some shows in Miami, the Caribs told Abe they were on their way. They never made it to England.

The Glass Bucket catered to tourists and the local upper class, and featured such top-line American acts as Sarah Vaughan, Sammy Davis Jr., and the Cuban king of mambo, Pérez Prado. Many of these artists used local musicians, including the great trombonist Don Drummond, to back them. The versatile Caribs became the club's house band, working there six nights a week until the club folded in 1959. Established in Kingston, or just stuck there unable to get back home, they moved on to the elegant Myrtle Bank Hotel, where Ian Fleming stayed when he first visited Jamaica in 1942.

The Caribs were used to playing live and playing tightly, which was important in the early days of recording, when we had only a single-track machine. I trusted them to be the backing band on many of my records, and when I needed a great guitar solo with authentic Jamaican flair, I brought in Ernest Ranglin to play with them.

The Caribs were friends with another Australian transplant to Jamaica named Graeme Goodall, a young sound engineer. He had come over to help Radio Jamaica set up their studios after developing his expertise working for broadcasters in Melbourne and London, where he worked with such singers as Petula Clark.

I met Graeme at a wedding under dubious circumstances: we nearly got into a fight after I chatted up his beautiful Chinese-Jamaican girlfriend, Fay. Once we smoothed that out (Graeme and Fay eventually got married), we took an immediate liking to each other. Like me, he was a white kid at ease amongst Black Jamaicans, a fosterer of mutual respect. Graeme emerged as an incredibly important figure in Jamaican music. In 1961, for Ken Khouri, he put together Federal Records' first custom-built studio, complete with an echo chamber. Coxsone Dodd, Duke Reid, and Prince Buster all cut records at the new, improved Federal as soon as it was open, with Graeme acting as chief engineer.

The studios that followed in Federal's wake, opening up and down Orange Street on the western edge of downtown Kingston, were all influenced by Graeme's innovative sound practices. Orange Street became the Jamaican Tin Pan Alley, where Jamaicans of all manner of backgrounds were now in the business of buying and selling songs. Dodd built Studio One inside an old nightclub around the corner, on

Brentford Road. Reid opened Treasure Isle Studios above his liquor store.

Graeme loved how music sounded in the open air as it pumped from the sound systems, affected by such factors as humidity and echo. He worked quickly to translate the systems' in-your-face, in-the-red sound and bass-heavy bottom end onto records. Jamaican recording was now not only about faithfully capturing live performances but about picking up ambience and mood. Graeme taught me how crucial the engineer was in making good records; accordingly, I made him a director of Island Records, holding 24 percent of its shares. Another 24 percent went to Leslie Kong, an unlikely figure—a friendly young Chinese-Jamaican guy who ran a record shop and ice-cream parlor on Orange Street called Beverley's.

THE ICE-CREAM PARLOR, started by Leslie and his older brothers, Fats and Cecil, had come first. But soon enough, the Kong brothers took an interest in Kingston's burgeoning recording scene and started selling records on the side. One day they were approached by an ambitious teenager named Jimmy Chambers, who hoped that they would sell his records—even though he had yet to make any. He had written a pining, pleading love song entitled "Dearest Beverley," clearly trying to ingratiate himself with the brothers. (I never found out where the ice-cream shop got its name from.) He sang it to them, a cappella, as they were closing up for the night.

Fats and Cecil didn't like the kid's voice, but Leslie did. He sent Chambers to see the singer Derrick Morgan, whose records had sold well at Beverley's. Morgan was impressed by Chambers's talent and told Kong the youngster had promise. Which was all well and good, but, as Leslie explained to Jimmy, he wasn't in the business of producing records. "Well, you *could* be! I know people," the kid said. He had some brass neck.

Kong decided, *Why not?* and took a flier on producing his own records for the shop on top of selling other people's. It was a time when such thoughts seemed to make sense in Jamaica, when a family that owned an ice-cream parlor could think that going into the recording business was a perfectly rational idea. Leslie didn't care for Jimmy Chambers's name, though. He wanted something that evoked the late-1950s pop idols who'd had hits in England, people like Billy Fury, Marty Wilde, and Tommy Steele. So Jimmy Chambers became Jimmy Cliff.

Leslie paid for the newly named Cliff to record some songs at Ken Khouri's Federal, also allotting some of the studio time he'd booked to Derrick Morgan, to get a bit of value for his money. All of a sudden, Kong had a record label, Beverley's, and was now a record producer. Leslie was a man of few words in the studio, but he knew what he liked and had a knack for putting out great records. Like Dodd and Reid, he was another prime example of a Jamaican entrepreneur who came from a business outside music and found he had a special gift for recognizing talent.

He put "Dearest Beverley" on the B-side of a catchier, more upbeat Cliff song, "Hurricane Hattie," which told a topical tale that Jamaicans could relate to, and fifteen-year-old Jimmy made it into the charts. Soon Beverley's was attracting all sorts of ghetto urchins and would-be stars milling about outside the store, looking to follow in Jimmy's footsteps. Some of them turned out to be the real deal. As I had found, once you're producing records and people know you exist, singers start to find you. And if you know vaguely what you are doing, and firmly what makes a good song, you can achieve wonders.

Kong was the first to record Desmond Dekker (after he'd been turned down by Dodd and Reid), Toots Hibbert and the Maytals, and John Holt. Derrick Morgan broke away from Prince Buster to record exclusively for Beverley's. This caused a hip-hop-style public beef, with Buster and Morgan chucking insults at each other through song; Buster voiced his displeasure that Derrick would want to sing for a "chiney-man" instead of him. In the end, the dispute provided great publicity for both artists.

Beverley's also put out the first single by Bob Marley, "Judge Not," in 1962, when Bob was just another scrappy seventeen-year-old from off the streets, years from making a wider impression. It must be noted that everybody wants a piece of the action when there is a story to be told in Jamaica, and several people have identified themselves as the person who "discovered" Bob Marley. Jimmy Cliff, Derrick Morgan, and Desmond Dekker have all claimed to be the one who introduced Bob to Leslie, urging the former to audition for the latter.

It's complicated. Certainly, Desmond worked with Bob at a welding shop on the docks, and he encouraged Bob to audition a second time for Leslie after not passing his first time out. Jimmy probably was the one who drew Bob to the Beverley's scene. But truthfully, no one really discovered Bob Marley. He discovered himself.

I have sometimes been credited as the man who discovered Bob Marley, but, as Bob himself used to say, he discovered me. We wouldn't work together until the early 1970s, a decade after his first record with Kong and well after he had formed a vocal trio with Peter Tosh and Bunny Wailer that initially billed itself as the Teenagers.

Bob, Pete, and Bunny had each received informal singing lessons from a master of harmony by the name of Joe Higgs, who brought them together as a group. "They weren't singers until I taught them," Joe liked to say, and he too can lay a partial claim to Bob's discovery. Joe taught them to harmonize in his tenement yard in Kingston's Trench Town ghetto, and he himself was one of the first Jamaican singers to sing of everyday troubles and suffering. Bob took notes.

Coxsone Dodd produced their first album as the Wailers, 1965's *The Wailing Wailers*. It featured some Marley originals, the seminal Marley-Dodd collaboration "Simmer Down," an early version of "One Love," and some unlikely covers, such as their take on Burt Bacharach and Hal David's "What's New Pussycat?" They were not yet Rastas. Under Dodd's cool, disciplined tutelage, the Wailers dressed sharp in skinny suits and had short hair like the Coasters and the Temptations. There was nothing yet to distinguish them from their peers and contemporaries; they weren't yet the Wailers transformed by their religious beliefs who, when they toured America in the early 1970s, were described by American musicians as looking like something out of the Old Testament.

I put out several Bob Marley songs and Wailers songs in the UK, where I had a deal with Leslie Kong to distribute some of his records via Island. I was living in London in 1963 when I first heard "Judge Not." Looking back, it's a remarkable, inspirational record, especially when you think about what Bob would go on to achieve. He recorded it the very month that Jamaica gained its independence. It was as ska as anything at the time, quite modern, a sign of the Jamaican self-determination that was gaining momentum by the minute. You can hear young Black Jamaica's hope and optimism, the kind of spirit and power the British had consistently tried to suppress for centuries.

But at the time, "Judge Not" didn't strike me as anything major. It was just another of those records beginning to pour out of Jamaica. In fact, it came to me in a jumbled box of various imported records from Kingston, misattributed to "Robert Morley"—an especially rich misprint given that, at the time, there was a plump, foppish English character actor of that name. Mistakes like these were fairly common in those days, with proofreading not a particular priority at these upstart record companies frenetically rushing out seven-inch singles to keep up with demand.

I later learned that Leslie Kong had tried to rename Bob the way he had Jimmy Cliff—he wanted Bob to go by Bobby Martell. But Bob, true to character, stood his ground.

BEFORE I MOVED to London, I tried my best to hold my own in the booming Jamaican scene. I produced and released a couple of Wilfred

"Jackie" Edwards records, "Your Eyes Are Dreaming" and "Tell Me Darling." As you can tell from the titles, these singles were gentle and pop-ish, well over to the softer side of ska. Jackie was a ballad man in the mold of Nat King Cole and Johnny Ace, and there was a romantic Latin feel to his records, not least because of smooth playing by the Caribs. In a way, the records were too polished, Jackie sounding a lot older than his twenty-one years, because Graeme and I cared more about getting a balanced sound than the other producers, who were letting instruments bounce all over the place in their pursuit of a new, freely Jamaican style. Distortion was an intentional part of their flavor.

For a brief moment, Jackie was the most popular Jamaican singer on the island, with four number-one hits and a boss nickname, the Cool Ruler. I also had some success with Owen Gray, a convincing soul singer who scored a number one with "Please Let Me Go," and with the Downbeats (featuring Count Prince Miller) and the Rhythm Aces. But these weren't normal times for Jamaica, which was on the cusp of major social and political change. You could feel it in the air and started to hear it on the radio—the British influence melting away and a new, exuberant sound of Jamaican independence.

The changeover to self-rule came in 1962. It was a joyous, celebratory occasion for the island to get rid of all the Brits who had fucked everything up. I never felt personally threatened, and indeed was on excellent terms with my peers. But however much I loved Jamaica and its music, my accent put me on the wrong side of history. The story of 1962 was a Black story, and I didn't fit in it.

It made much better sense for me at that point to move to England. I was already selling more records there, to homesick transplants from the Caribbean, than I was in Jamaica, where you could have a number one yet still sell only 4,000 copies.

Furthermore, a lot of the records I was releasing in Jamaica were being pirated in the UK. And let's face it: to some extent I was losing touch with the latest Jamaican trends, which were defined by the funkier, flashier sounds being made for a new Jamaica by Sir Coxsone Dodd, Duke Reid, King Edwards, Prince Buster, and Leslie Kong.

I enlisted Leslie as a partner in Island Records because he knew what he was doing and was an honorable man. At one point in 1962, he and Beverley's had seven songs in the top ten. He had overtaken me in getting to talent first, using Derrick Morgan and Jimmy Cliff as his scouting representatives. It was a clever tactic, using musicians to lure in other musicians, who trusted their peers more than businessmen. I would adopt this method myself in my next phase of life, letting my artists serve as my recruiters—if you had Steve Winwood, Nick Drake, Roxy Music, John Martyn, Grace Jones, and Bob Marley on your roster, you had a head start with promising new acts.

Leslie was as straightforward as anyone was in those freewheeling days, when copyright was a moot point and everyone was running rings around everyone else to get records made, paying no heed to contracts or royalties. He was generous and paid his musicians more than most. He put his favored artists on a weekly wage so they could concentrate on their music, another strategy I took from him and implemented at Island Records.

Because Leslie and the sound-system guys gave me the green light to distribute their records in Britain, when I opened for business in London in 1962 I had a ready supply of incredible records. On top of that, my arrival in England was a classic case of right time, right place. I landed in the middle of exciting times, being given an instant soundtrack because of songs that were being released as 45 rpm singles. Great songs instantly reflected and created a very different way of life for liberated postwar young people and the quickly forming fashion tribes they belonged to. And for those Jamaicans now living in colder, rainier parts of a strange new land, these records I was getting my hands on brought a welcome slice of home into their lives.

*   *   *

SHORTLY BEFORE MY move across the Atlantic, though, I very nearly got out of the music business entirely. In 1961, I received a request from Ian Fleming, via my mother, asking if I wanted to work as a production assistant on the very first James Bond film, *Dr. No*. It was based on the sixth Bond novel and was to start filming on location in Jamaica at the beginning of the following year.

I was already kin, of sorts, to Bond. By the time he wrote the novel in late 1957, Ian was friendly enough with my mother to use her first name, Blanche, in *Dr. No* as an inside joke for an "aged tanker of around ten thousand tons." The Bond franchise had become a lucrative one for Ian, but the novels had yet to be adapted into feature films. Fleming knew that film rights were where the money was.

Dr. No didn't have much of a budget, because the powers that be in Hollywood feared that the source material was far too British to have widespread appeal, never mind that the story was set in the backwater of Jamaica.

I was asked to look for some locations, source various items that would be required for scenes, and generally help out by using my access to the various musicians and personalities I knew. Choosing good locations for the first Bond film was a significant task. At the beginning of *The Man with the Golden Gun*, Fleming writes, "The first law for a secret agent is to get his geography right." I was determined to help get the geography right. I knew the island inside out from the thousands of days and miles I had logged updating my jukeboxes, all over Kingston, around the whole coast, up in the mountains, and into some of Jamaica's most obscure rural areas. I could use the map of Jamaica I had in my mind to make the map of Jamaica that featured in *Dr. No*, which was one of the first mainstream films to ever give an idea what it was really like, strangely timed to appear when Jamaica separated from Britain.

In some respects, the film served as a deluxe visual tourist brochure for the sights and delights of the island, as well as hinting at some of the seductive, disconcerting dangers—the parts the tourists usually never get to see. Jamaica might not have been British anymore, but it was fascinating and magnetic, a place you surely had to visit. *Look at what you once had*, it seemed to say to its British viewers, *but through tourism, this island can still be yours.*

You can definitely see my map of the island in the finished movie: the mangrove swamp at Falmouth where Sean Connery's Bond and Ursula Andress's Honey Ryder are captured; the governor's mansion, King's House on Hope Road, where Bond is briefed by UK intelligence officers; and Laughing Waters, the beguiling, secluded beach a few minutes outside of Ocho Rios where Honey famously emerges from the water. It was a private beach at the time, but I cashed in on a family connection. The property's reclusive owner, Minnie Simpson, was a distant cousin of mine.

I got as many of my musician friends as I could jobs on *Dr. No* as grips and gofers. Then, when the soundtrack composer Monty Norman flew into Jamaica in January 1962, I met with him and gave him some guidance about the local music scene and the best places to go. Monty hadn't read any Bond books and had written only one film score before, for a Hammer Films horror picture. But he had cowritten the songs for the English stage musical *Expresso Bongo*, which had been turned into a 1959 film starring Cliff Richard that became a cult hit. The movie was a satire of Britain's brand-new rock and roll scene, and *Dr. No*'s producers, Harry Saltzman and Albert R. "Cubby" Broccoli, were impressed by Monty's knowledge of pop music and his versatility in mimicking various musical idioms.

When he was asked to do the job, he was initially a little reluctant. To warm him up, he was told he could bring his wife out to Jamaica to get a sense of the island, all expenses paid, and he imagined it would be more holiday than work. In the end, he was required to write the soundtrack in Jamaica, because some of the scenes being filmed there required local music. The producers decided that as the story was based in Jamaica, it was important to feature as much local sounds as possible.

I found Monty a shady room with a piano, away from the hot sun, where he could concentrate and write. We went on a tour of Kingston nightlife so he could get a feel for the variety of music in Jamaica. I took him to see a talented, very enjoyable ska and calypso band called Byron Lee and the Dragonaires, whom the producers ended up using in the film for a scene set in a nightclub, shot at one of the group's regular venues, Morgan's Harbour Hotel in Port Royal. At one club we went to on the edges of Kingston, Monty was taken with how the dancers jumped up and down with their hands in the air, so for the nightclub scene he wrote a song called "Jump Up." An immaculately attired local entertainer I brought in, Count Prince Miller, really grabbed his moment in the scene, hopping up and down like a madman in his loud checked shirt. I'm in the scene too, very briefly, dancing in a blue shirt. Blink and you'll miss me.

Monty also used Byron and his band to record the Jamaican parts of the score, at Ken Khouri's Federal Studios, with my stalwart Ernest Ranglin on guitar, because how could I not have Ernest play? Ernest also played on Monty's first attempt at a Bond theme, "Dr. No's Fantasy," which wasn't used in the film but did appear on the album soundtrack.

The film was made at such a furious pace—the location shoot wrapped inside of five weeks—that every day was a riot, even as the production had to deal with the slow pace of the locals working on the film, who operated on a different clock than the British and American crew.

Ian Fleming regularly paid visits to the set with his pal Noël Coward. These two great English wits had made themselves so at home in Jamaica that they were considered honorary Jamaicans, much to the surprise of the cast and crew. A major celebrity in his own right, Noël took a shine to Connery and gave him advice about how to deal with the press. As it happened, Noël had been Ian's personal choice to play the nefarious title character in the film, but when the producers offered him the role, he sent a telegram that read simply: DR NO? NO. NO. NO.

Working on the film up close, none of us Jamaican locals could really see any rhyme or reason for it to exist. We never glimpsed the eponymous villain, a Fleming take on Fu Manchu with metal hands and an exotic lair; Joseph Wiseman, the gifted actor who played Dr. No in Coward's stead, filmed all his scenes on a soundstage in London. We didn't see the very first Bond villain, but we saw plenty of the very first Bond girl. Ursula could barely speak English and would be overdubbed later by another actress, which made things seem very flimsy when we heard her say her lines on set. Not until we watched the rushes of Ursula's first scene, sensually walking out of the surf soaking wet, singing a Monty Norman arrangement of an old Jamaican folk song called "Underneath the Mango Tree," did we crew members think this picture stood a chance.

Nonetheless, and despite not getting a credit, I thoroughly enjoyed working on *Dr. No*. It was fantastic hanging out with the actors, getting to know Sean and Ursula, especially at the wrap party, where she danced with total abandon. I loved the feeling of belonging to a team. I reveled in the challenge of fulfilling seemingly impossible tasks.

Near the end of one shooting day, I was ordered to get hold of a green tractor by seven o'clock the following morning. I protested: "How on earth am I expected to do that overnight?" In no uncertain terms, I was admonished to make it work out. Somehow, some way, I did, proudly delivering the green tractor to the desired location right on time. The tractor ended up playing a key role in the film: it formed the basis of the Dragon Tank, the frightening flamethrower fitted with a long dragon's neck and dressed up with painted teeth and eyes that Dr. No uses to keep curious locals away from his Crab Key island headquarters; in the movie, the gullible islanders believe it to be a mythical beast.

Dr. No was released in the UK on October 5, 1962, two months after Jamaica became independent and the same day that the Beatles put out their first single, "Love Me Do." Though thematically it was a hangover from the dying British Empire, the film, in its stylishness, sexiness, and self-awareness, seemed utterly modern, a part of the flashy new future. And it was a surprise hit.

The film also left an impression on Jamaican culture. Bond's no-nonsense womanizing tough guy resonated with the rebellious sound-system ruffians and shantytown gangsters known as rude boys, who were dealing with the pressures of downtown Kingston in the early '60s. You had to have a certain kind of toughness to thrive in Kingston, living off your wits, on the edge of your nerves, exploiting the kind of smartness you don't get at school, and Bond had signs of that toughness.

The rude boys were getting up to no good to try to escape the trenchant pressure of poverty, always on some sort of mission, fighting for space, hustling each other, and looking for a break. They were celebrated and condoned in songs like Stranger Cole's "Rough and Tough," Duke Reid's "Rude Boy," the Wailers' "Simmer Down," Jackie Edwards's "Johnny Gunman," Count Lasher's "Hooligans," Derrick Morgan's "Court Dismiss," Clancy Eccles's "Guns Town," Alton Ellis's "Cry Tough," the Slickers' "Johnny Too Bad," Desmond Dekker's "Rudy Got Soul," and of course his "007 (Shanty Town)." Some of these singers had been rude boys themselves, making the charts and offering hope to the up-and-comers, who could see and hear a way out. Ten years after *Dr. No* revealed one kind of Jamaica, I helped put a version of these rude boys into *The Harder They Come,* because juvenile delinquents had *Rebel Without a Cause*, hippy dreamers had *Easy Rider*, and American Black Power had *Shaft.* The swindled, conned, victimized, targeted underdogs can win; they can beat the system.

The music used in *Dr. No*, especially the "James Bond Theme," which emerged from a collaboration between Monty Norman and the chart-topping arranger John Barry, was making an impact of its own, and would reach into ska. Dodd's Studio One specialized in James Bond–related songs, quick to embrace the Cold War Spy Boom in the 1960s. Their great house band the Soul Brothers, formed after the breakup of the immense Skatalites, took on the theme itself in "James

Bond Girl," produced by Dodd. They also did a great ska-jazz version of "Thunderball" and a reversion of John Barry's "007" with Dodd.

Lee "Scratch" Perry's lighthearted yet sinister "Pussy Galore"—a song celebrating a character Ian Fleming based on my mother, played in *Goldfinger* by Honor Blackman—features the Wailers on harmony from their Studio One days. Lee issued a grim warning about how a beautiful woman might steal your rights as a bachelor: "She's got charms! Lovely arms!" Seven, eight years before I started working with Bob Marley and the Wailers, there is already a discreet link, suggesting we were destined to get together one way or another.

Harry Saltzman was impressed enough by my work to ask me to stay on with him as his personal assistant. It was a tempting offer. In the late 1950s, he had worked on some of the great social-realist films that had come out of Britain, such as the film version of John Osborne's *Look Back in Anger* and the 1960 adaptation of Alan Silli-toe's *Saturday Night and Sunday Morning*. I liked Harry and believed I'd have a lot of fun working with him. And, as I gave the matter more thought, I wondered if my time in the music business had passed. Maybe I had gone as far as I could.

I genuinely couldn't make up my mind which path to choose. There was only one way to come to a decision. When I was a child, my mother had taken me along on her visits to the fortune-tellers of downtown Kingston, an activity she loved. (I had become a bit of a gambler a few years earlier when I met some slick Egyptians in London who had this tremendous feel for beating the odds and an essential addiction to the rush. For a while, I was a regular in gaming rooms and at racing tracks, convinced a big win was always just around the corner. Convinced, actually, that I was never going to lose. I'd get to the point that I was so sure I would win that I had to start betting such large amounts that when I did lose it really hurt.)

I went downtown and called upon a Lebanese soothsayer. I had convinced myself that there was . . . *something*, a deeper truth to her craft, even as I recognized it to be a con. I guess I thought that fortune-tellers were healers of a kind, there to sort out your destiny.

I told the psychic in her colorful turban, in a candlelit room that could have been a set in a Bond movie, that I had a problem: Should I choose music or film as my future?

Slowly, patiently, she laid out some cards on the table between us, as if she were making some deep connection with me. She stared dramatically at the cards for a few minutes as though something magical was happening. She was so intensely solemn, I really believed in her divining powers. I decided that whatever she said, I was going to do.

It was a toss of a coin, in a way, but I truly did believe that it was more mysterious than that, connected with some great tide of fate. Eventually the psychic smiled to herself, raised her eyes to mine, and announced her decision. She calmly announced that I should choose music. "The cards don't lie," she murmured.

And that's how I made up my mind to stay in the music business.

—CHAPTER THREE—

THE SIXTIES, LONDON:
MAKING CONTACT

When I arrived in London in 1962 to establish the next stage of Island Records, the English music scene was in a twilight zone between the lively, clean-cut pop-idol era of Cliff Richard and the arrival of such blues- and R&B-influenced beat groups as the Beatles, the Rolling Stones, and the Kinks. It was more of a pop world than it would become, still emerging out of an old-fashioned Britain of variety shows and music halls. In London's recording studios, the technicians still wore white lab coats, and producers dressed in suits and ties. Most of them were salaried employees of the major record labels, working strict, union-mandated shifts that were totally counterintuitive to the idea of recording as a creative process.

Joe Meek and Mickie Most, and then Shel Talmy and Andrew Loog Oldham, were amongst the first independent producers to break free of the corporate system, beginning to take control of the recording process more as freelance artists than as employees. Meek got around the lack of independent studios by developing ways to record at home in his kitchen. By 1965, even George Martin, still working at EMI's in-house studios on a staff producer's salary, went independent.

Independent producers hungry for new facilities meant progress was made in the design and capability of recording studios. Initially this had been much slower than in America because Britain's major record companies didn't appreciate the impact recording technology could have on the commercial potential of records. Even by the mid-1960s, the Abbey Road studios were relatively primitive, because there had been no innovative independent producers demanding the latest updates in order to match the sound being achieved in American studios—and the success of the Beatles made EMI with their prized Abbey Road think there was no need to change their methods.

Britain was behind Jamaica in many ways, certainly in terms of how that intensification of influences was leading to a singular local style and various new kinds of music, and in terms of how collaboration amongst artists, engineers, entrepreneurs, and musicians, the sheer joy of discovery, was creating new sounds and a prolific new kind of business.

In Jamaica, I had operated as a producer in a way that would have been difficult in the British system. This worked in my favor: when I arrived in London, I carried on as I had in Kingston without thinking about it.

The first musicians who got in touch with me when they heard I was in town were Black musicians from Jamaica or Africa, some working in musicals, some trying their luck in the music industry. The funny, vibrant Lord Kitchener had come over as one of the first wave of West Indian workers brought over as cheap labor to alleviate the postwar labor shortage. Known as the "king of calypso," Kitchener worked hard in pubs and clubs all the way through the 1950s singing the kind of typically naughty calypso about British events and characters that connected with the British sense of humor.

By this time, calypso was losing out to pop and rock and roll, but Kitchener was still trying to make a living, and he contacted me from Manchester a few weeks after I'd been in Trinidad, where I had a romance with a Trinidadian girl. I thought of two songs I liked the idea of him doing—a risqué calypso called "Love in the Cemetery"

and a road march, which would be the tune everyone ended up playing whenever there was a carnival in Trinidad. When I went to Trinidad the following year for the carnival, I asked the cabdriver taking
me to my hotel from the airport what that year's road march was.
He said, "Well, some guy called Kitchener has just come back from
England, and he's done this year's road march." I was thrilled—it was
like having a hit single. It was the kind of thing that got me addicted
to making things happen.

I was constantly on the lookout for opportunities and alliances,
checking what was happening in the clubs and pubs, seeking out
those who could help me work out manufacturing and distribution.
Once I had my bearings, I focused on the parts of London and greater
England where Jamaicans were starting to create local communities.
That was my initial target audience.

The first single released on a UK-based Island Records, with the
catalogue number WI001—WI for West Indies, replacing CB, which
made it previously seem like the label was perhaps a hobby—was Lord
Creator's "Independent Jamaica," a jaunty, old-fashioned calypso
song that reported the news of the independence, as if Jamaica's
future was now tidily sorted. It wasn't quite the first Island record
to make the shops—that was the Leslie Kong–produced and Beverley's Music–published "Twist Baby" (WI002) by Owen Gray, with
the B-side "Patricia," both songs a little more ska-aware than Lord
Creator's. Island's original orange sun logo was now part of a cheaper,
more basic red-and-white design, with the address of the label given
vaguely as Island Records, London, England. This label design would
last for a good five years.

I leased my early Jamaican releases to a label called Starlite, itself
a subsidiary of the independent jazz label Esquire. Esquire was owned
by the drummer and bandleader Carlo Krahmer, who, beset by vision
problems, quit playing to concentrate on his label, aided by his wife,
Greta. Launching a label straight after the war, in a period of austerity
and privation, had been a bold, even foolhardy move, but Krahmer

was a dreamer who saw those dark times as the perfect opportunity to make something joyful happen with the music he loved.

As well as building his impressive jazz list, Carlo was always on the hunt for interesting sounds. He set up Starlite in 1957 to capitalize on the current skiffle boom. Skiffle was a sort of UK answer to American rock and roll, a homegrown DIY music that incorporated such homemade instruments as the washboard and the washtub bass. But Starlite had little success with skiffle and pivoted in the late fifties to concentrate on music popular in the West Indian communities then emerging in Britain.

The postwar era had seen an influx of immigrants from the Caribbean known as the Windrush generation, so named for the *Empire Windrush*, the giant passenger ship that ferried some of the first West Indians over in 1948, Lord Kitchener amongst them, to help with the labor shortage. Enticed from their island homes by the promise of steady work in England, they presumed that they were essentially moving from one parish to another. They imagined they would be made to feel welcome. After all, they had grown up under British rule, governed by British law, treated as British.

Then they arrived and discovered how different England was— not just in its cold, damp weather, but in the bleakness of the gray, bombed-out areas of London where they were permitted to live. A naturally friendly and curious people, the Jamaican immigrants were stunned by how indifferent and even hostile the British people were towards them. Rather than receiving a warm welcome from a thankful populace, the Windrush generation was confronted with appalling racism, discrimination, and ghettoization. Far from treating the Jamaicans as fellow citizens of a common empire, many white natives were flagrant in their bigotry.

Naturally, the West Indians in London craved the sounds of their homelands. Krahmer heard from some of his clients who ran record shops that their Jamaican customers were asking for "blues" records. They weren't referring to American blues but to the music the sound-system operators were starting to make, which had somehow acquired that unlikely name. Krahmer duly built up a strong West Indian catalogue through Starlite. I made a deal with him to put out Laurel Aitken's "Boogie in My Bones," which was the first Jamaican record Starlite ever released and the first official release of a ska record in the UK.

For about a hundred pounds, I bought a list from Esquire of the record shops to whom they supplied Jamaican music. From there, I followed the same strategy I had in Jamaica. I spent my days driving around the ghetto areas of north and south London, neighborhoods such as Peckham, Brixton, Lewisham, and Harlesden, where the Jamaican immigrants lived. I could fit about a thousand 45 rpm discs in the boot of my dark-green Mini Cooper, and I sold them straight from there, on the streets. I kept a little portable Dansette record player in the car so I could advertise my wares as I drove. I measured my journeys by how many times I played a certain record—from central London W1 to Harlesden NW10 would be about ten plays of James Brown and the Famous Flames' "Night Train." Nothing says the sixties to me more than driving through an increasingly run-down north London in my Mini with the windows open, shouting "Oh yeah!" over the saxophone of J. C. Davis and the drums that Brown himself played while his drummer was on a break.

I loved flying around London like this, getting a hands-on feel for the demand for certain records. It was a lot like when I serviced my jukeboxes in Jamaica. I liked finding out what was happening on the street, and even after I'd leased a proper office, I was never keen on sitting in it.

In those early London years, I lived a double life. By day, I was careening through the streets from record store to record store. By night, I went out to nightclubs favored by white people—some of them posh places where the old Harrovians went, others dark, mysterious dives where new musical trends were emerging. I was in a position of privilege: I received a steady monthly stipend from my prosperous family, enough to cover the rent and living expenses so I could carry on pursuing my efforts to establish Island.

I really enjoyed meeting people and giving them records they were hungry for. My fiercest competition was a label called Blue Beat, which proved so successful that *bluebeat* became a genre term, used to describe the new, Jamaican-influenced pop music that was gaining in popularity in Britain. I was a small-timer by comparison: a door-to-door vacuum-cleaner salesman going up against Hoover. But I could lavish my customers with personal attention in a way that Blue Beat couldn't. And they responded in kind, trusting me.

Blue Beat was run by a music publisher named Sigmund "Siggy" Jackson, who gave the label its name because he thought the music he put out sounded "bluesy but with a great beat." He was smart and prescient and had gotten a head start on me, releasing records by Duke Reid, Coxsone Dodd, and Prince Buster before I arrived in London. I had a lot of catching up to do. I found myself in a running battle with Blue Beat for ska talent. I invited Owen Gray to sign with me after releasing his singles "Twist Baby" and "Jezebel," only to find shortly thereafter that Blue Beat had gazumped me, nabbing him from under my nose.

I traveled home to Jamaica a few times a year to pick up new releases and keep up on emerging new artists. One of my trump cards was my ongoing connection with the laid-back, gentlemanly Leslie Kong, who supplied Island with a steady flow of singles such as Jimmy Cliff's "Miss Jamaica" and what counted for a hit in my area of southeast England, Derrick Morgan and Patsy Todd's "Housewife's Choice" (WI018), one of those sparky man-woman call-and-response songs that signaled ska's development from an easygoing shuffle to a faster, harder-edged sound.

For my first couple of years in London, I mainly concentrated on record shops that catered specifically to the Jamaican community. At the time, white Britons had less than little interest in this music. I had virtually no luck in central London because few West Indians lived there, though I had high hopes for one place, the record department of the Covent Garden location of W. H. Smith, a chain of high-street shops. The person in charge of ordering the store's records was a young blond guy who liked to order as many obscure blues records as he could get away with. I'm not sure how he ended up with his position—he was just a kid, really. But Brian Jones patiently listened to me as I raved about my latest singles. I tried hard to make him fall for the Jamaican boogie-woogie man Errol Dixon's "Morning Train" (WI023), but he didn't bite like I thought he would. Anyway, as it would turn out, Brian had ambitions for the new band he was in, the Rolling Stones, and was not long for W. H. Smith.

I noticed that there was a new-music boom going on in white Britain that reminded me a lot of what I had witnessed in late-fifties Jamaica: an inventive response to the great new music coming over from America, which involved a cross-fertilization of genres and the emergence of a few leading tastemakers. The two big ones in London in the early 1960s were Alexis Korner and Cyril Davies, who formed bands that launched the careers of several young white musicians who played an amplified, British version of the blues.

At first, this music was the province of a select few, swapping records and going to shows in tiny, sweaty venues. All sorts of chance reasons took me to see certain groups at just the right time and place, just when they were starting. I'd come across four South African girls who had been in a musical, and I managed to get them a gig at nights Cyril Davies was putting on at the Marquee when it was on Oxford Street. I went down, and one of the other acts was Brian Jones's band, the unknown Rolling Stones. I told Cyril they were fantastic, but he wasn't so sure.

At one show I stood close enough to the young Stones to bear witness to the moment when they found their new drummer, Charlie Watts. I overheard Brian, Mick Jagger, and Keith Richards talking with Davies, their mentor, and his drummer about whether Charlie was better than their current drummer, Tony Chapman, who had trouble keeping time, forcing them to speed up or slow down and seem very ragged. It was obvious that Charlie was the far better musician, even though at the time it seemed a risk to have a jazz drummer play the blues. Cyril Davies's drummer could have been the Stones' drummer—he was good enough—but he went out of his way to recommend his friend Charlie Watts. He knew how great the Rolling Stones could be with the right drummer.

A few years later, when the Stones were a big success, I saw Cyril's drummer working in a hot dog stall at Wembley Stadium. It's a tough world, pop music.

As confident as I was in my knowledge of jazz, this new blues-influenced rock wasn't my area of expertise—at least, not yet. For the time being, where Island was concerned, I concentrated on what I knew.

AT FIRST, IT seemed unrealistic for me to make records in London.

Another label targeting British West Indians called Planetone had been set up in 1961 by a tall, slim, very gentle Jamaican carpenter, Clinton "Sonny" Roberts, who'd arrived in the UK as a twenty-six-year-old in 1958, and his friend and fellow music enthusiast Lloyd Harvey. Inspired by the Busters and Dodds, Roberts didn't want to merely import and sell Jamaican records; he wanted to record them. With homegrown enterprise, he got hold of a one-track recorder and some disc-cutting equipment and set up a makeshift studio in his flat off the Edgware Road.

I couldn't keep Island going as a one-man band, so I enlisted some help. First I hired Francine Winham as my assistant. Francine was a former debutante who was rebelling against her parents' wishes for her to settle down with a rich husband. That said, Francine used her parents' Mayfair home for swinging parties at which she danced to the latest jazz records with such soon-to-be-famous friends as Michael Caine and Terence Stamp. She and I did Island's accounts together, and whenever we needed a photo for a record that had come over from Jamaica but didn't have pictures of the original artists, Francine, a resourceful woman, rounded up some friends and took a photo of them, and we pretended that they were the act.

For the cover of an album called *Keith and Enid Sing*, we enlisted a Jamaican actor living in London, Winston Stona; and my girlfriend at the time, a beautiful model and fellow Jamaican named Esther Anderson. Winston later appeared as a cop in the movie *The Harder They Come*. Esther, who also worked in Island's makeshift office with Francine and me, went on to act in *The Avengers*, dance on *Ready Steady Go!*, and take an iconic photo of Bob Marley smoking a giant spliff. They looked great together, Winston and Esther, standing in for Keith and Enid. I got one or two angry letters from fans who noticed the switch.

We worked out of my flat in Rutland Gate Mews, a cobbled cul-de-sac near Marble Arch. Technically, I was violating the terms of the lease with my landlord, the Anglican Church. Furthermore, I had all sorts of people staying there: musicians, girlfriends, Jamaican visitors. Jackie Edwards, one of my first signings, moved in for a while. I persuaded him to come to London to help me out. Sometimes he found himself delivering copies of his own record to stores, a model of vertical integration: make the record, import the record, deliver the record. For a time, our sales force consisted of me in my Mini, our colleague Dave Betteridge in a small van, and Jackie stoically carrying some stock on a packed, smoky red London bus.

Dave was someone I managed to poach from his secure job working for the record distributor Lugton. He liked the music I liked and had the knowledge of the stores and clubs I needed to be in touch with. We canvassed new venues that were promoting and playing Jamaican music, like the Roaring Twenties on Carnaby Street, the Ram Jam in Brixton, and El Partido in Lewisham. We were keeping up to speed with the nascent genre of ska and getting to know our audience.

Needing more floor space, we soon moved Island out of my flat and into an office at 108 Cambridge Road in smoky, cluttered Kilburn, in northwest London. Our landlord was Lee Gopthal, a Jamaican accountant of Indian heritage. We were doing more business and releasing more records but still not making money—we needed to up our game. I asked Lee if he would help us out. He was initially reluctant to give up his steady, respectable business in accountancy, but he relented and proved himself to be an excellent businessman. With his help, I set up a distribution company called Beat & Commercial Records Limited to sell records to retailers, maybe produce our own records here and there, and perhaps even open up our own outlets.

But what I really needed was a hit. Something more mainstream than what I was usually putting out, that I could get played on the radio. Even Blue Beat records didn't get much airplay. So I decided to look outside my West Indian comfort zone, to Denmark Street in Soho, London's Tin Pan Alley, where the big labels and studios were, along with the clubs and hangouts where musicians and machers hung out.

Soho was a darker, dodgier, and more dangerous place in the early sixties than it is now, a square mile tightly packed with clip joints and strip clubs. In some respects it was closer than the rest of London to the melting-pot nature of downtown Kingston, with all sorts of punters, pimps, prostitutes, tourists, sailors, gangsters, early mods, and teenagers looking for action and the right kind of music.

Everyone was busy looking for the next big thing. Everyone was learning on the spot. The rules and strategies of a new business were being made up on the go. Not just with the musicians, but with the managers, promoters, talent scouts, producers, publicists, journalists, assistants, general dogsbodies—everyone was breaking new ground, because there had never been anything like this before.

There was an improvisational quality to it all that I really loved and which my Jamaican experiences had prepared me for. Even the bigger companies, the Deccas and Parlophones, for all their dominance, were not yet as corporately minded as the major labels would later become.

The music business old boys knew enough to give the younger new heads a certain amount of freedom, to see what was out there, what they could come up with. Who knew what the hell was happening?

This was when Decca and EMI had about 95 percent of the business, Philips had about 4 percent, and the rest, the independents, fought over the remaining 1 percent—this was a near monopoly that certainly needed to be challenged, and within a few years it would be. When I started, there were a lot of barriers to entry, but a few of us took it as a challenge. The way to break down those barriers was to find the talent that the majors needed at a time when, by the beginning of the sixties, they didn't have the know-how to find.

I made the acquaintance of two industry insiders, Harry Robinson, a Scottish bandleader, songwriter, and scenester, and Chris Peers, a shrewd, hustling, old-school promotions man who represented various disc jockeys and musicians and seemed to know everyone in the business. The three of us formed a production company called BPR—Blackwell Peers Robinson—and made it known we were looking for unsigned talent: musicians, songwriters, the lot. We assembled a backing band for our planned projects by tapping into the wealth of young talent available in the blues clubs. Amongst my recruits were the crack R&B organist Graham Bond and an ornery force-of-nature drummer with red hair named Ginger Baker. One day Graham and Ginger brought in a teenage bassist to play with them. His instrument seemed far too big for him. I dismissively asked him, "Are you sure you can play that thing?" The kid took umbrage; I had made an enemy of Jack Bruce, who in a few years was winning Best Bass Player polls as a member of Cream.

Harry, Chris, and I were told about a promising female harmony duo, Lois Wilkinson and Andrea Simpson, two eighteen-year-old white girls with cute, very fashionable bouffants. They had demoed a middle-of-the-road country song from 1950, "You Don't Have to Be a Baby to Cry," which was whispery and as light as air, the very opposite of the Jamaican music I adored. But maybe I needed to try something with more obvious appeal, because I was having no luck getting my imported singles played on the radio or covered in the press. Harry thought he could tighten up "You Don't Have to Be a Baby to Cry," and we took his shiny, politely swinging arrangement to Decca with a plan to package the girls. They picked it up for release on one of their subsidiary labels, Ritz, which was a vehicle for a producer, writer, and promoter named Bunny Lewis.

Bunny was one of those figures making the rules up as they went along. He rechristened the girls the Caravelles. With the combined hustling pizzazz of Bunny, Harry, and Chris, who got the record distributed by Decca in 1963, the girls were very quickly singing "You Don't Have to Be a Baby to Cry" on *Juke Box Jury*, *Thank Your Lucky Stars*, and *Ready Steady Go!* Without having much say in anything, I had my first British hit record.

It was the whitest, fluffiest record I have ever been involved with, completely lacking in the kind of rhythm and punch I love. But there it was at number three in the summer of 1963, a chart position it would duplicate early the following year in the US, making the Caravelles the first British act to chart in America in 1964, ahead of the Beatles.

Brian Epstein, the Beatles' manager, invited the Caravelles on a package tour he was putting together with Billy J. Kramer and the Dakotas, Johnny Kidd and the Pirates, and the Fourmost. I was getting closer to the inner workings of the music business, but with a record that didn't mean much to me. There was a chance of a follow-up written by Burt Bacharach and Hal David, then at their hitmaking peak with Dionne Warwick. Bunny found himself in Bacharach's spectacular flat in New York, and, being Bunny, casually asked the master pop composer what he had on the hob.

Burt said he had a track he was about to send over to Dusty Springfield, who was about to have a massive hit with Bacharach and David's "I Just Don't Know What to Do with Myself." On his piano, he played the new song "Wishin' and Hopin'." Bunny pounced, blagging on about the hot new girl duo he had, and somehow persuaded Burt to let him have the song for the Caravelles. He sent it over to us with the message to get the record done quickly, "before Burt changes his mind and sends it to someone else."

But the Caravelles didn't like the song. They'd been on television and cracked the top ten, and they decided that now they knew best. They turned down Burt Bacharach and Hal David. Bunny couldn't believe it. Neither could Blackwell, Peers, and Robinson. The song went to Dusty and became one of her staples and a pop standard. The Caravelles, offered fame on a platter, floated off into obscurity.

It was a good lesson for me in how young artists can get delusional, to their detriment. After a bit of success, they are suddenly experts about their careers, even though they often haven't got a clue. And sometimes, as hard as you try, you just can't help them.

This experience taught me a lot, and I vowed to do things differently the next time. With records piling up at the Island offices in Kilburn, I set out to work with another teenage female artist, but one who had the kind of energy I loved and understood. A Jamaican energy.

I HAD DISCOVERED that when I played my Jamaican records to my white London friends, far from being put off, they *loved* what they heard—the infectious ska rhythms, the unexpected variety of voices. Yet these records weren't available in the shops that they usually went to.

There was one record my friends particularly loved, "We'll Meet" by Roy and Millie, a fantastic boy-girl duet produced by Sir Coxsone Dodd. Roy, a smooth baritone, sang his verse first. Then Millie sang hers in an incredible high-pitched voice, almost Alvin and the Chipmunks–like. But it worked. There was no one who sang like Millie, with such wonderful little-girl earnestness.

My friends burst out laughing at Millie's entrance every time I played "We'll Meet." But then they would immediately want to hear it again. It was intriguing to me that they responded so positively to Millie's voice, and that they moved so easily and intuitively to the ska music, which was unfamiliar to them. I was convinced that I could break Jamaican pop into the mainstream, in a way that even Blue Beat, the market leader, couldn't.

I decided to get in touch with Millie. She was born Millicent Dolly May in 1946 in Clarendon, a largely agricultural parish in the Jamaican south that is also where Toots Hibbert, Linton Kwesi Johnson, Derrick Morgan, and Leonard Howell, the father of Rastafari's, were born. She was the youngest of twelve siblings who were raised in a small shack on a plantation where her dad worked as an overseer. The family loved to sing, and even though they didn't know anyone in the entertainment business, Millie came through the talent-show route, winning one of the Vere Johns amateur shows at the Palladium Theatre in Montego Bay in 1960. She was all of twelve years old.

This put her on Coxsone Dodd's radar. He renamed her Millie Small and partnered her with Samuel Augustus "Roy" Panton, who had done the rounds singing for Dodd, Reid, and Leslie Kong but gotten nowhere until he sang with Millie.

I had to persuade Coxsone to let me manage her. This took a bit of sweet-talking, but I sensed he felt he had gone as far as he could with Millie in Jamaica, and he had plenty of other singers to work with. I called my engineer friend Graeme Goodall in Kingston and told him to send Millie over. He wasn't so sure about her squeaky voice, but Leslie Kong heard what I heard about her potential, so Graeme got the process in motion. Millie was only fifteen, so we needed parental permission for her to come over to London. They had trouble finding her dad but managed to track down her mum.

At first Millie's mother said no, which was entirely reasonable—why should she send her sweet teenage daughter thousands of miles to England after hearing from some slick stranger who told her over the telephone he could make the girl a star? Eventually, though, she relented, after I told her again and again, in all sincerity, that of all the singers in Jamaica, Millie was the one I thought had the greatest chance of success in the UK.

I promised her that I would look after Millie and that no harm would come to her daughter. Graeme got all the paperwork together, helped Millie with a passport photo, and booked her on a BOAC flight. She left the warmth of the sunshine and her loving Jamaican family and landed in London on a chilly, foggy morning, wondering what on earth she had let herself in for. On the bus into London, she later told me, she couldn't believe the number of chimneys she saw. They stretched for miles, and there were no mountains in the distance, and no inviting blue sea at the edge of everything to soften the sights and smells of poverty.

As was the trend at the time—think of Brian Epstein with the Beatles, dressing them in neat suits and ties—I put some time into preparing Millie for what I hoped would be stardom. Pop was to some extent still an extension of music hall, of variety, and a manager or promoter was expected to train his performers and design their image. I wasn't trying to whiten Millie or tidy up any rough edges, though her impish Kingston patois needed a bit of massaging.

This was a serious business for me, because I had learned that to have a hit in Britain, you had to take its show-business mores seriously. And why shouldn't Millie receive the attention usually paid to the white singers? Berry Gordy at Motown was clearly grooming his artists to ensure that there could be no chance that the reason given for not playing his records on the radio or booking his acts on television was that they were unprofessional.

I enrolled Millie at the Italia Conti Academy of Theatre Arts for speech training and intensive dance study, so that she would be ready for the television pop shows I was hoping to book her onto once we had the right record. My girlfriend Esther looked after Millie with a couple of her friends from Jamaica, the sisters Martine and Lorelei Beswick— Martine would soon play the crazed gypsy girl who fights with another girl over James Bond in the follow-up to *Dr. No*, *From Russia with Love*.

Jackie Edwards, with his own experience of relocating to London, also helped Millie settle. I had to become Millie's legal guardian in England, as she was too young to sign contracts, so I had a real sense of responsibility for this trusting girl whose life I had turned upside down.

At first, I approached Millie from the point of view of BPR and the team that had worked on the Caravelles. We made a first single with Millie, a song she had cowritten, called "Don't You Know." It was a conventional beat pop song, more Cliff Richard than Jimmy Cliff, backed by a jaunty jazz band led by Harry Robinson. It sounded far too anonymous and ordinary, with no Jamaican rhythms, and it barely sold. I had let my love for jazz and Harry's light-pop sensibility take Millie too far from Jamaica and who she really was. I needed to give Millie a rethink.

I turned away from BPR and looked to my own contacts. I had brought over another of my Jamaican compadres, the guitarist Ernest Ranglin, initially to see if I could get him some work at Ronnie Scott's Jazz Club; I always thought of Ernest as a jazzer more than anything else and felt he should be playing at London's hottest spot for jazz. I reached out to Ernest to ask his advice. He, Millie, and I sat around one evening in my flat trying to think of a follow-up song for Millie.

In the late 1950s and early '60s, when I went to New York to visit the great record stores, there were lots of little ones along Sixth Avenue between Forty-Second and Fifty-Third Streets. I was particularly interested in the 78s put out by Atlantic and Mercury, along with a smattering of odd, wonderful labels based in the South and Texas. If I made a sale of one of these records to Duke Reid or Coxsone Dodd, I sold them the one vinyl disc I brought back—but before I turned it over to my buyer, I would make a copy of it on a big reel-to-reel tape recorder, so I had a record of the songs that I had sold. This was like my filing system—a way of keeping a reference of all the rare discs that had passed through my hands. In those days, if you didn't have the record, you had no access to the song. This was long before cassettes.

One of the songs I bought was called "My Boy Lollypop," written in 1956 by Robert Spencer of the doo-wop group the Cadillacs and originally recorded by a white fourteen-year-old singer named Barbie Gaye. I suspected it wasn't right for the sound-system guys, and I was right, because there were no takers amongst the Big Three. But I still thought there was something about the song.

I sold my only copy to one of the less dominant sound systems and then forgot all about it. But when we were trying to find a song for Millie, I unearthed the tape that held my recordings of the songs I had bought in New York and sold in Jamaica, and on it was the original version of "My Boy Lollypop." It was a great piece of luck, as without this discovery, I wonder if we would ever have found the right song for Millie to sing.

As soon as we all listened to it, with its engaging Professor Longhair– Rosco Gordon shuffle, we knew it would work with a ska beat. Millie loved it, and Ernest instantly locked into the music. We knew that Millie would be perfect singing it, and I wasn't unaware of the suggestive sauciness of the lyrics, and even their connection with "On the Good Ship Lollipop" by Shirley Temple, especially as sung by the teenage Millie, who was all cheek and charm, viewing her time in London as a great adventure. A few days later we went into the original Olympic Studios on Carlton Street, off Regent Street, to cut the record.

Ernie did the arrangement, wrote out the charts, and helped the white session musicians understand the exaggerated bouncy rhythm he wanted, encouraging them from his special vantage point as one of the originators of ska. I coached Millie on her vocal phrasing. Keeping things in the family, another of my lodgers, the Jamaican singer Tony Washington, wrote the B-side, "Something's Gotta Be Done."

After a bit of finessing of the arrangement, replacing the original's intrusive saxophone solo with a harmonica part, the song came out exactly as I had heard it in my head. (Contrary to some rumors I have heard, the harmonica solo was not played by Rod Stewart.) It had all the brashness of ska, but not in a way that would trip up the untrained ears of white listeners. I saw to it that the record lasted only 1 minute

52 seconds, because Millie's high-pitched voice had the potential to wear out its welcome. I had done the same thing with her first single, which was five seconds shorter. The idea was to make the song short enough to leave people wanting more, but not so long that it started to get on people's nerves. Nobody ever said a word about the shortness of the song. We packed a lot in, for sure, even a few seconds of fade. I thought it best that it was in and out, and after it was over you wanted to hear it again. And one of the things I had noticed selling music for jukeboxes was that you needed to grab people's attention with a song. *Bang*, and you're in—which is how we made the record. You are straight into the song, no time to catch your breath. *Bang*, you're in a different world. In this case, in Jamaica, which until then was thought of as the land of calypso, if anything.

When I heard the finished "My Boy Lollipop"—by accident or design, we replaced the "Lolly" with "Lolli"—I knew it was a hit. And because it sounded like a hit, I also knew that it was way beyond what Island and my Mini could handle at the time. Millie's first single had been released on Fontana, but we didn't need their muscle for that one, which barely sold. We did for the follow-up, now that I had gotten the sound right.

Fontana, which had been set up in 1958 as a UK subsidiary of Dutch company Philips, signed romantic crooner Matt Monro and the Greek singer Nana Mouskouri, released the winner of the 1962 Eurovision song contest "Are You Sure?" by the Allisons (arranged and conducted by Harry), and had a strong folk and jazz list as well as the clean-cut middle-of-the-road and hopeful novelty records that were clogging up the early sixties.

They were slowly breaking away from the pre-Beatles crooners and comedians. By 1962, they were releasing records on the Tamla Motown label (founded, like Island, in 1959), including the Marvelettes' 1961 "Please Mr. Postman," which had inspired the early sound of the Beatles.

I licensed Millie's records to Fontana because I had learned something from observing the American independent-record business. If an independent label scored a hit, perversely, it was pretty much guaranteed to go out of business, because most of the time these small labels lived hand-to-mouth and couldn't collect their money from the stores fast enough to pay the pressing plant to make more records to keep up with the skyrocketing demand. If we had a hit record on our hands, we needed outside help.

"My Boy Lollipop" was indeed a huge hit—not just in the UK, but everywhere in the world. One country after another fell for its charms. I brought Millie over to England in summer of '63. The record came out in February '64, entered the British charts in March, reached as high as number two (behind the Searchers' "Don't Throw Your Love Away"), and then entered the American charts in May, this time kept from number one by the Beach Boys' "I Get Around." It sold over six million copies worldwide.

It was selling to a white audience, because, as I had anticipated, when you contain a certain sort of captivating energy inside a dynamic pop song, all sorts of prejudices can fall away, even if only for the two minutes of the song. And Fontana, along with the Mercury subsidiary Smash in America, was very good at selling the single and Millie herself.

When Millie first arrived in New York, straight from promoting the record in Germany, she was presented with a giant lollipop by the record company there, whipping up some Millie-mania. I accompanied Millie around the world, getting caught up in the hype, believing that Millie's success was only the beginning of something Beatles-like. My assistant Francine came along for some of the American dates, both to photograph Millie and to act as a chaperone. It was so exciting. One of my favorite sixties memories is of Millie sharing a dressing room with the Supremes at a show whose bill also had Dusty Springfield and Little Anthony and the Imperials.

Even though some newspapers got it wrong and called Millie "the Blue Beat girl," I became known as the architect of her ascent. Interviewed for the *London Evening News* by Maureen Cleave—to whom John Lennon, two years later, would describe the Beatles as more popular than Jesus Christ—I was called a "rather handsome 26-year-old with reddish hair." Flattering, but I didn't savor the attention. This was when I started to become wary of coming out from behind the scenes and being a part of the story.

Maureen's article explained to her readers that the Mini I had been using to flog my records around London had been replaced with a white Jaguar, which might well have been true—as soon as some money came in, it would be time for a new car; Miles Davis had trained me well. Like Ernest, I was calling the music ska, which it had become, and *bluebeat* was no longer the way the press denoted the genre.

Suddenly I was catapulted into the middle of a scene—from a Jamaican nobody driving around derelict immigrant areas of London to a recognizable impresario in the pop-music business, as if I knew what I was doing. Of course, I was totally making it up as I went along.

THE RELEASE OF "My Boy Lollipop" coincided with a big change in British radio. Before 1964, the BBC played only two hours of pop a week, as if there were no such thing as teenagers; and its chief alternative, the erratic, unreliable Radio Luxembourg, was controlled by a few self-serving record companies. It was a struggle for Island and other upstarts to get our records heard, and even while pop music was changing at lightning speed, a lot of great music besides mine was struggling to break through.

Fortunately, a charismatic twenty-three-year-old maverick named Ronan O'Rahilly came along in '64, fed up with this unchallenged monopoly. O'Rahilly ran the Scene Club in Ham Yard, off Great Windmill Street in Soho, and managed such Scene regulars as Alexis Korner, Graham Bond, and Georgie Fame. But despite his acts' growing local following and hipness, he couldn't get them onto the BBC

Light Programme or Radio Luxembourg. He reacted to this situation like it was a form of censorship, which, in many ways, it was.

On Easter Sunday of 1964, O'Rahilly sailed an old passenger ferry he had acquired and fitted out with studios and a 180-foot-high transmitter into international waters. It was called MV *Caroline*. It was an act that was somewhere between a very shrewd piece of business, a generous act of philanthropy, and a wildly defiant form of performance art. In the North Sea, three miles off the coast of Essex, the first record the new station played was "Not Fade Away" by the Rolling Stones. So began the adventures of Radio Caroline, which broadcast its eclectic playlist to millions of listeners. Suddenly, great new records were getting the kind of constant daytime play that they never got from the BBC, half the country getting addicted to hearing pop music changing by the week. In some ways, the so-called Swinging Sixties started out there in the sea. Millie and my other Island acts would be amongst Radio Caroline's many beneficiaries.

I accompanied Millie to various TV studios where she appeared on the pop shows and gamely mimed "My Boy Lollipop." For all the dance training she'd had, and the choreographer I'd commissioned to teach her some steps, she ended up doing her own thing, alive in the moment, and the results were incendiary.

I found myself hanging out backstage with the Beatles, the Stones, the Who, and the Kinks, and, more interestingly from my perspective, their managers, Brian Epstein, Andrew Loog Oldham, Kit Lambert, and Shel Talmy. I learned from them simply by watching them in action. They did things their own way. They didn't have a boss to please. They had freedom. That's what I wanted. And thanks to "My Boy Lollipop," I was starting to get it. I was also proud that my Jamaican experiences and alliances were what had differentiated me and made me break out in London.

People were now taking my calls and reaching out to me. I'd gotten my foot in the door. On some level, though, I didn't feel a great amount of satisfaction, because I couldn't sustain Millie's success.

She adored the experience of having a hit and did everything that was asked of her, sometimes to the point of exhaustion. At one point she was so depleted by the endless promotional work, a bout of food poisoning, and some injuries sustained in a minor car accident that I had her take a few days' rest.

Millie felt a weight of responsibility to her family now, as their breadwinner. Just in case her mother was concerned that Millie was not able to work, she cabled her with the assurance: **DON'T WORRY! CAN STILL SING "LOLLIPOP."**

The problem was that her single was being treated like a lot of records were at the time, as a novelty, a one-off. Millie was seen as adorable but replaceable rather than as a serious musician. She was a blast of something new and exciting, but there were constant blasts of something new and exciting, and we couldn't come up with a follow-up half as electric.

Ska would go on to have a huge impact on pop music, especially when it crossbred with the English punk scene and mutated into two-tone. But the Millie record was an anomaly, ahead of its time. Its follow-up, "Sweet William," climbed no higher than number thirty, which was another big lesson for me: no matter how big a hit you have, for your next single, you have to begin again, and be as clever (and as lucky) as you were with the original hit. I thought I had been a genius when Millie was at the top of the charts, but I realized that to be a genius, you have to keep doing it. Otherwise, you're just a lucky idiot.

Millie kept touring and making records, for us and later for the label that Graeme Goodall formed, Doctor Bird. But she never again came anywhere near that heady "Lollipop" level of attention. This totally changed how I viewed the music business. I would never again chase hits so aggressively and single-mindedly. After Millie, I would be interested in original talent that I could work with over a long period of time, building success block by block. Years later, I was talking with Tom Waits about hit records and commercial success. He mentioned someone who'd noted to him how strange it was that he had never had a hit single. "Well," Tom replied, "I have had a hit life." After Millie, that became my kind of thing. Hits would be a bonus, not the be-all and end-all.

The other thing that convinced me to move away from pop music was Millie's grand return to Jamaica after she had become, temporarily, world-famous. She appeared in a concert in her hometown where Otis Redding, Patti LaBelle and the Bluebelles, and Inez and Charlie Foxx all took second billing to the local success story, Millie. She was driven as Jamaica's "Little Queen" through the streets of Kingston in an open-top car, surrounded by cheering, flag-waving crowds. When she finally got a chance to visit her family in a rough, poverty-stricken neighborhood of the city, the car she was in was mobbed by neighbors. Millie was being received as an all-conquering hero.

She got out of the car and ran towards her mother, whom she hadn't seen for months. Her mother looked at Millie, who was now the most famous person in Jamaica. She took a couple of steps backwards as her daughter got closer, as if she were now a stranger, and said, "Hello, Miss Millie." Then she curtsied. I was mortified. In her family's eyes, Millie had become someone else, almost royalty. What had I done?

I vowed then and there that I was finished with straight pop music and the idea of making and marketing stars. I didn't want to be a pop Svengali.

OVERNIGHT, BECAUSE OF this big hit I helped make happen, different people started calling me with songs and musicians they thought I would be interested in. I apparently had the magic touch. I was asked to go to Birmingham to see a well-known local group called Carl Wayne and the Vikings, who would become the Move. I got to see them after Millie recorded an episode of *Thank Your Lucky Stars* at the ABC Studios in the city on March 28—other guests included the Swinging Blue Jeans, the Merseybeats, Frank Ifield, the Bachelors, and Alma Cogan, which tells you how white pop music was then.

The Vikings wore uniforms, slightly ridiculous shirts, ties, and velvet-collared suits—the Beatles wore uniforms at the time, even the Stones did—and they were very polished but didn't mean much to me, being a jazz fan. After I said they didn't interest me, I got taken to a pub in the city center, on the second or third floor of this old building. The people taking me there said they didn't know if I would like the next thing—it was a bit different, they warned.

Walking up these steep stairs, before I even saw anything, I heard a powerful soul voice that sounded like Ray Charles on helium with a swinging blues backing that suited my taste much more. There were recognizable blues chords, but with this incredible, swinging musicianship. There was no way for me to know if the person singing was black or white, young or old.

Then I walked into the club, and onstage was this skinny white kid with floppy hair, about sixteen, the same age as Millie, playing guitar and sometimes amazing keyboards as well, like it was all second nature. The kid's name turned out to be Steve Winwood. He was part of a group unimaginatively called the Rhythm and Blues Quartet. They weren't wearing any kind of pop uniforms or grinning inanely, because it was clearly the music that mattered and they concentrated on the playing of their instruments the way jazz musicians did. They were just wearing the clothes they usually wore. They looked like they meant business, and the crowd was absolutely loving them. I'd never heard anything like it—white boys playing the blues like it meant the world to them.

Steve and his brother, Muff, older by five years, had grown up with music, playing in their father's jazz group in Birmingham pubs near their house. Steve had started out learning thirties and forties dance music to play with his dad, and he was a High Anglican chorister as well; so when skiffle and early rock and roll came along, he was only ten but already taking to this new music, and to the new soul sound of Ray Charles, as a highly skilled, technically very adept, and versatile musician. By the time Steve was fourteen, he was playing with Muff in pickup bands for visiting blues players like Sonny Boy Williamson and Memphis Slim.

Spencer Davis was a Birmingham John Mayall or Cyril Davies, a total jazz and blues nerd beginning to organize local gigs and find musicians. Scenes were erupting all over the country, and Spencer was one of the leading members of this one tucked away in the Midlands. It was like the lights went on in England in the early sixties, because up until then nobody you heard on the radio had anything other than a BBC-type voice or accent. It was impossible for anybody with a Cockney accent or a Liverpool accent or a Manchester accent to get on the radio, much less have a decent job. But then, with these bands, influenced by American music but not copying the accent, bringing into the music their own sense of urgency and urban nonconformist English appetites, that all started to change.

Spencer had come across the Winwood brothers playing as part of the Muff Woody Jazz Band, Steve, he said, singing like Ray Charles and playing piano like Oscar Peterson—two for the price of one. He was in urgent need of good musicians and quickly drafted them for a gig he'd booked that was playing with jazz drummer Pete York. They started a regular Monday night spot at the Golden Eagle with their own noisy, disciplined, totally contagious R&B energy, and word quickly spread and the queue outside started to grow. Steve started to play organ because there were so many bad pianos about, and then he played organ like Jimmy Smith. This made him a triple threat. It came to him so easily, but never superficially.

Steve became my first British signing, as part of what became known as the Spencer Davis Group. My first act working with them was to suggest they change their name, and they decided to name it after the musician who'd started the group, who was reading German at Birmingham University and could speak a handful of languages. As the most articulate member, they thought, he would be better at handling any interviews they might be doing. Steve especially was very shy, and not the type ready to be any kind of spokesman.

Later it would look odd that it wasn't the Steve Winwood Group, but at the beginning he was so young that, when the group started to tour Europe, I had to become his legal guardian to get the paperwork done, as I had with Millie. And as with Millie, I licensed the group to Fontana, anticipating the sort of success Island wouldn't have been able to cope with, and also because they didn't fit in with the music we released there.

That first night I heard them, I went backstage as soon as they were finished and crammed into a tiny, scruffy room, and within minutes, it seemed, we had made a deal—Muff taking charge—and sealed it with a handshake.

Decca had been vaguely interested in signing them, but on the back of my hit with Millie and the sheer enthusiasm I had for them, I soon talked them into signing with me, as manager, and, in the way you did things then, to a label deal. This was proof that the power of Decca was crumbling.

We also promoted gigs as part of a whole package—which, depending on your point of view, was either convenient and practical or a conflict of interest. It seemed convenient in the sense that, with no other factors involved, we were in the studio recording them inside a month making their debut single. We made the decisions amongst ourselves and could move fast.

We chose one of the best crowd-favorite songs in their set as the first single, a cover of John Lee Hooker's "Dimples" that they had been doing for quite a while. We had it in the shops by the end of May 1964, a couple of months after I had seen them in the Golden Eagle. I produced the record as though I were in Kingston, and it sounded raw and aged in the best sense.

I got very excited, because prodigy Stevie Winwood singing John Lee Hooker like he'd learned direct from the master seemed a sure thing, but the timing was bad. John Lee Hooker himself started a British tour, now that these previously obscure blues legends were more known and in demand because of their influence on Mayall, Korner, and Davies and their protégés.

What seemed fresh and new when you couldn't easily get hold of it didn't seem so fantastic when the real thing was in the country. Three Spencer Davis Group singles quickly followed, all brilliantly chosen and played covers of blues and soul standards. They all made the lower reaches of the charts but stalled tantalizingly outside the top forty. Around the band's home city and the rest of the Midlands they were selling like they should be in the charts, but despite an intensive UK tour they weren't breaking through. After a few months the Spencer Davis Group was being thought of as the best group in the country without an actual hit. It was very frustrating.

Their rival beat groups having the hits—like the Stones, the Beatles, the Who, the Animals, Small Faces, and the Kinks—were writing their own songs, leaving behind the days when most of their songs were cover versions of their favorite American tracks. The Spencer Davis Group was only just beginning to come up with their own material, so their first album was filled with these superbly performed covers. They needed something of their own to show they were moving with the times. I turned once again to my secret weapon—Jamaica.

The liquid-voiced Jackie Edwards had developed into a very fine and versatile songwriter, and he had released on the West Indies Records Limited label (founded by Edward Seaga, who later became a prime minister of Jamaica) a self-composed, beguiling late-ska song, "Keep on Running." The group loved it when I played it to them; they loved Jackie when they met him, always neat, tidy, and chatty in his porkpie hat; and we did a version of it that combined all their eclectic influences and everything they were great at—Steve's emphatic soul voice and a charged, fuzzed-up guitar sound nabbed from the Stones' "Satisfaction," using an American fuzzbox called the Big Muff; Spencer with a punchy Motown guitar; Muff with an eloquent, buoyant bass line. I pushed that bass up in the recording in a way that wasn't done so much in Britain. It was my Jamaican training. Bass obviously to the front, as would become clear with reggae.

Like Millie's "My Boy Lollipop," "Keep on Running" was the kind of record you could play again and again, because you never got sick of it. There was enough of a hint of its ska roots to separate it from the British groups influenced by the usual soul and blues, and you could already hear British beat music splintering into new genres. The group played it like they'd written it and they owned it, and I think it helped them come up with their own songs and a dynamic, yearning sound that was all their own. They wrote the B-side, "High Time Baby," and that was like everything they were good at, with that 1965 fuzz guitar, the soul of Steve and his nimble, percussive piano, the confident rhythms, without there actually being a distinctively structured song.

Jimmy Cliff was in the studio when we were recording "Keep on Running," and he got caught up in the spirit, and brought his own spirit, and you can hear him shouting and whooping in the background and at one point you can hear him go, "Hey, come on."

Even though it was on the Fontana label, "Keep on Running" marked the birth of a new Island Records: out of Jamaica and now very much part of the new English scene. It's amazing what can happen because you find yourself in Birmingham on a Monday night in May because you met some people you didn't really know, and you climb up these stairs in this dark city-center pub and come across something that will change your life.

The Spencer Davis Group made their first *Top of the Pops* appearance singing "Keep on Running" on December 16 along with P. J. Proby, the Kinks, and the Shadows, their second the week after with Herman's Hermits, the Hollies, and the Walker Brothers. They were now officially part of a British beat invasion, to such an extent that their faithful, purist fans in Birmingham—craving a new future featuring their kind of sound but strangely wary of change—were moaning they had sold out.

They kept climbing the charts over Christmas and New Year, and by January 1966 the single was chasing down, of all groups, the Beatles, replacing "Day Tripper/We Can Work It Out" at number one on January 18. In Britain it was the fifteenth-biggest-selling single of 1966, in between the Beach Boys' "God Only Knows" and the Beatles' "Paperback Writer."

Stevie Winwood was seventeen and looked boyish but didn't sound it; by the time he was eighteen in May, the Spencer Davis Group had achieved their second number one with another ska-bruised Jackie Edwards composition that sounded so perfectly sixties, "Somebody Help Me." With wonderful, blues-soaked nonchalance and a voice that sounded like he'd paid his dues a few times over, Steve was singing how "When I was just a little boy of seventeen, I had a girl" as though he were looking back at a long-ago time. It was two minutes long, which was brisk ska timing, all you needed in a pop song to make your point and then get out of the way before you outstayed your welcome.

After a third hit with a song Jackie wrote with Steve, "When I Come Home," which didn't make the top ten, I decided it was time for the group to write their own songs—in the way that Andrew Loog Oldham had urged the Rolling Stones to compose their own material, which had led almost immediately to "Satisfaction." And the writing of songs, bringing some real life into this new music, led to the development of the album as the prime vehicle for what were now rock bands more than pop groups. Being merely a "covers band" started to have a different, not so positive meaning, even if the songs you covered were expertly chosen and played.

I didn't want Spencer Davis to fall behind, so I set them up in a rehearsal room round the back of the Marquee on Soho's Wardour Street and told them to work on some songs of their own. I could be firm and businesslike about these things. I wanted them to work in all senses of the word.

CHAPTER FOUR

HITS, MISSES,
AND THE HUMAN HOST

After the success of Millie and now with Spencer Davis, I'd moved my offices into the West End, where the music business was mostly based. It was the beginning of a move away from Island being a label that mainly released Jamaican music. Island and the B&C sales and distribution company had moved for a short time to the much larger Music House offices in Neasden.

I was now based at 155 Oxford Street near the Oxford Circus Tube station, in a building used by the hit record producer Mickie Most, where his friend Peter Grant had set up his growing management company. After a few years as a performer, Most began as an in-house producer for Columbia and produced the early Animals, including "House of the Rising Sun," which he recorded in fifteen minutes, and was soon producing million-sellers for Herman's Hermits and the Nashville Teens.

Grant had been a jobbing actor in the early sixties, and because of his menacing shape as an ex-wrestler had been a stand-in for the portly actor Robert Morley, the very man with whom the label-pressers had confused Bob Marley. When it got tough landing acting roles, he had started driving pop groups to their gigs, and by 1963 he was tour-managing visiting American acts like Little Richard, Chuck Berry, and Bo Diddley.

A year later Grant was managing Terry Reid, the Jeff Beck Group, and Stone the Crows, on the way to looking after the Yardbirds. These were serious, thoughtful musicians, and Grant realized how much the business was shifting away from the perky post–coffee bar pop. He was always a lot shrewder and more strategic than his hard-man image suggested.

The pop music that came out of the coffee bars was being replaced by a more progressive and even conceptual rock music, album-based rather than singles-based. Grant saw that the future was rock—and hippie, and countercultural, even intellectual—in the way Brian Epstein and Andrew Loog Oldham five years before had seen that the future was mod, a world of teenagers finding for the first time a way of inventing their own identity and constructing their own image.

He took this thinking into his management of Led Zeppelin, whose extraordinary success meant he couldn't concentrate on the label he had set up with his old friend Mickie Most in 1969, RAK, which, driven by Most's commercial instincts with the addition of Mike Chapman and Nicky Chinn, became a nonstop pop machine with Suzi Quatro, Mud, and Sweet.

When I later set up a recording studio inside an old deconsecrated church in Notting Hill to record Island acts and those on other labels, you could really see this split between the efficient, very familiar commercial pop of Mickie and the heavyweight album sound of Led Zeppelin when they both recorded there: Mickie's hits were produced by day in tightly run shifts, almost to a formula, while the denser, stranger, often purposefully more formless album music was produced at night into the early hours. Funnily enough, the snappy pop of Mickie Most would usually feature the hired-hand guitar of Jimmy Page and the bass playing and arranging of John Paul Jones, who would form half of Led Zeppelin. By day, Sweet's "Funny Funny"; by night, Led Zeppelin's "Stairway to Heaven."

As I went to see how the Spencer Davis Group was settling in on their first day writing songs down Wardour Street, I was now sharing a building with two ambitious industry activists helping to change the shape of rock and pop. London felt at this time as though it were at the center of the universe, or at least at the center of what was being talked of by journalists as the Swinging Sixties, where those designing, composing, managing, singing, modeling, photographing, writing, and running clubs and studios were becoming pop culture aristocracy. My group now needed to move in the album-oriented direction people like Grant were taking, even as, I hoped, they came up with a hit single that could rival Most's catchy million-sellers.

When I got to the rehearsal room, just down the road from my new offices, there was no sign of Steve, Spencer, Muff, and Pete. No two ways about it: I was absolutely furious. I thought they were skiving or hadn't even made it into work. I charged around their usual haunts in Soho and found them in a café nearby, laughing and fooling about. I laid into them, accusing them of not taking their task seriously. They might have had two number ones, but pop was increasingly competitive and groups like them could come and go in a flash.

They protested, claiming they had come up with an idea, and were just taking a lunch break before they went back and finished. That afternoon they played me what they had done, and you could tell they had processed all their favorite music and paid attention to how the songs were written. They had come up with something terrific that from the very first bars instantly sounded good enough to be played amongst all the great American gospel–influenced R&B tracks of the mid-sixties.

Although Steve Winwood got the writing credit at the time and improvised the title and chorus as they messed around with the riff, between them Muff, Steve, and Spencer had come up with "Gimme Some Lovin'." As they performed it for me, already very at home with it, Steve particularly ecstatic, the song sounded like a hit, positively trembling with energy—the energy I was after—but also throbbing with a rhythmic cool. Here were white kids who'd listened to soul, jazz, and the blues and, thinking it over, came up with their own take. I immediately let them off for taking an early lunch break.

I dared think it might give the Spencer Davis Group their third UK number one, but the sound of pop, and the genius of its greatest musical thinkers, was moving at such a pace at the time that it got no higher than number two. "Gimme Some Lovin'" was destined to be a sixties pop classic that would bring with it the excitement and adventure of the times fifty years later, but it was stopped from reaching number one by another timeless pop classic, the Beach Boys' "Good Vibrations," which demonstrated what you needed to do to keep up with the visceral sound of modern pop music in the mid-sixties, if not the songs or performances. Even though the SDG failed to get their third number one, their first self-written song was still something of a moment.

I was the producer again, and as a producer I wasn't a musician, a technician, an engineer; I didn't place the microphones or arrange the songs. I came from the Jamaican world, where as a producer you worked as a listener, the first listener for the music, the first listener the group had for their music. That's how it began for me—the Lance Hayward Trio played, and I listened, and they wanted to know what I thought.

You had a sense of what you thought the record should sound like and helped the group to achieve it by passing on suggestions to the engineer. I didn't know how to create the sound, but I had in my head an idea of what the sound should be.

I wanted to break the Spencer Davis Group in America, and "Gimme Some Lovin'" seemed like the up-to-date British take on rhythmic American music that could work there. I knew, though, that the song needed a different kind of sound, another level of groove, to be a success in the much bigger and harder-to-crack American market. It needed another pair of ears—another listener. On a recent trip to America looking for new music, I had heard a great track, "Incense" by the Anglos, and released it in the UK. It was produced by music addict Jimmy Miller, whose dad was an entertainment director in Las Vegas who later booked the Elvis Presley comeback performances at the International in 1969. Born in Brooklyn, Jimmy had been a cabaret crooner in upstate New York, then a drummer. When he learned that the producer's job was to take care of the sound of everything, he knew that's what he wanted to do. He started out working with New York– and New Jersey–based acts mixing up R&B, gospel, folk, and jazz—the perfect training.

"Incense" sounded like one of those tracks that if I had put it into my jukeboxes in Jamaica, I would have been mobbed by a pack of hungry music lovers shouting, "Tune!" It's so good and fast—swerving around all kinds of corners, a pure, funky celebration of movement—that it's almost funny. The singer sounds like he's listened to a lot of James Brown, but also to some Steve Winwood—there are those who thought it was Winwood, for some sneaky reason, but it was a singer called Joe Webster.

I asked Jimmy over to do some work for me, and his first task was to remix "Gimme Some Lovin'." The great American specialist had landed in London at the right time, when it was going through a tumultuous, experimental period of transition, just like Jimi Hendrix did. (Hendrix saw what the likes of Jeff Beck, Eric Clapton, Peter Green, and Steve Winwood were doing with blues guitar, and took it to the next level and beyond.)

What Miller brought to his version of "Gimme Some Lovin'" is a kind of wild magic. You can hear how he speeds it up slightly, adds backing vocal, percussion, and some live ambience, but the result seems to be about something much more than those decisions. He somehow intensifies the sheer noise of everything, turns up the heat, threatens some kind of chaos, piles up the drums, without losing the groove. It takes Steve's vocals, and his organ, to a higher place. And Jimmy certainly played the role of producer, the creator of the vibe, more visibly and obviously than I did, sitting on the studio floor and manically pounding on a big drum. He loved to make the toms go boom and the crash cymbals sound like skyrockets, and his mix of the song did what it was meant to do and got to number seven in America.

Jimmy wrote the next single with Steve, "I'm a Man," and produced it, emphasizing that carefully achieved combination of noise and control. Here he's given the group a new sound, something that spins around inside your head, and sets the outside world spinning. You can hear something materialize, and what it grew into was the sound of the greatest Rolling Stones songs between 1968 and 1973, after Steve left the Spencer Davis Group, and Jimmy produced his more free-flowing, jazzier, folkier, freakier, sometimes even poppier group Traffic.

Steve was starting to think the Spencer Davis Group didn't have enough of its own identity and wanted to play in the kind of group that incorporated the different types of music he was interested in. His bandmates were older than he was, and at his age three or four years was a huge gap. There were those who thought he was mad to leave Spencer Davis when they seemed on the verge of being really big, but once Steve had made his mind up there was no stopping him.

He wasn't quite nineteen when he formed Traffic with Jim Capaldi, Chris Wood, and Dave Mason. He based the lineup on the sax, organ, guitar, and drums of Junior Walker and the All Stars, but ended up exploring how cosmic rhythm and blues could get, and how progressive and even experimental traditional music could become. Traffic also carried on ideas Jim Capaldi was having in his previous group, Deep Feeling, about introducing exotic international rhythms into rock.

Their very eclectic and almost willfully anticommercial music symbolized how what in 1965 and '66 had been about dancing all night in clubs and interacting with reality was now in 1967 about expanding the mind and taking realism in different directions. (You could hear Winwood's out-of-hours jamming mates Jim Capaldi,

Dave Mason, and Chris Wood of Traffic on Jimmy's remix of "Gimme Some Lovin'" as they added to the new backing vocals. They would be guesting on "I'm a Man" as well, helping with Miller's signature propulsion.)

The Spencer Davis Group was an Island Records Production on the Fontana label, but Traffic would be signed to Island Records, influencing the emergence of a very different label. Steve had developed the confidence to start something himself from scratch and felt he had done all he could with the SDG format. If British beat music was changing into something stranger, deeper, looser, slipping away from its tight R&B roots and throat-grabbing three-minute songs, he wanted to see where that would take him.

"Dear Mr. Fantasy" symbolized the segue between the Swinging Sixties and the Summer of Love and became a signature song for Traffic, and for Island. It was like the music for the opening credits of a new era of Island Records, as the Jamaican years and the red-and-white label we'd used gently segued into the British progressive rock years and the new pink label. We chose pink because it created a clear break with our Jamaican years, because pink was the color that felt most removed from ska and reggae. You didn't associate pink with Jamaica. The spirit of the island is captured in colors that are usually connected with African greens, reds, golds, and blacks, and its own vibrant spin on those reflecting the coastline, the high hills, the bright sun and the hard shadows it created. Anything pink wouldn't really register, or would melt away in the sun.

The WI catalogue number was now WIP—the *P* perhaps for pink, or progressive—and slowly the progressive music on the label was replacing the Jamaican. In 1968, my erstwhile landlord Lee Gopthal and I formed the joint venture Trojan Records to concentrate on the music that was evolving from ska into rocksteady and then what would be called reggae. Trojan formed around a series of record shops in places like Brixton, Ridley Road, and Ladbroke Grove markets, licensing records to the label from the Jamaican producers for general sale rather than importing records. Lee was very much the leader of the new enterprise, and I could feel my attention drift to what was changing in British music, and how Steve Winwood and Traffic fit into that.

It seemed London was not the best place for Steve and Traffic to work on new music, so I had the idea of sending them out to the country, away from the city and its pressures, and away from people. It was something I liked to do, change scenery, see new sights, keep moving so that I never felt stale or at a loss for what to do next. I was always traveling, even if I seemed to settle down, and I felt that musicians worked best if they were traveling, even if just a few miles into the country, into another time.

Traffic would get a chance to think about nothing but their music and feel the peace and inspiration of being in the middle of nowhere. No distractions. That was the idea anyway, although in the end you do get the feeling that distraction follows certain musicians wherever they are.

I had an Old Etonian friend called Sir William Pigott-Brown who had inherited his title and the equivalent of £16 million when he was twenty-one in the early sixties, and in some way seemed quite happy to spend liberally until the money ran out. He was a classic sixties rich bachelor playboy, searching for a role in life, looking enviously at the seemingly self-confident new pop culture celebrities who were living the kind of racy, glamorous lives that used to be the exclusive territory of the rich and the aristocratic. As the sixties peaked, hipness was replacing the old class divisions of breeding, schooling, and wealth.

He was always very intrigued by my lifestyle, working in music, moving amongst the new makers and shakers in the music business. I sometimes think he wanted to be me, or at least who he thought I was, hanging out with Mick Jagger and Marianne Faithfull, spending eight hours a day in the recording studio, eight hours a day in nightclubs, and eight in New York or Jamaica or the South of France.

It was actually Pigott-Brown who moved easily between the fashionable young and high society, linked to a never-ending series of models and heiresses. He was profiled in the *Daily Mail* in 1964 as a notable single man. He opened a Mayfair nightclub called Sibylla's, persuading George Harrison to become a director, and founded Browns, a boutique on South Molton Street, but somehow he was always convinced he was missing out.

I had asked him for a loan in the autumn of 1965 before we released "Keep on Running" because I needed an injection of cash to help me get proper support for the single. I was convinced it was going to be a hit, and it was another example of the gambler in me—the kind of gambling Pigott-Brown appreciated, as a high-stakes gambler himself. The deal was that he would give me the loan, but if I couldn't pay it back within a certain amount of time, he would receive a substantial number of shares in Island Records.

I was confident that "Keep on Running" would be a success and I would be able to pay back the money. Luckily, all went well, and I didn't have to hand over a large percentage of Island to one of the decade's great roisterers.

One of Pigott-Brown's adventures was as a fearless champion amateur jockey, and when he lost his nerve in 1964, he started to breed racehorses on Sheepcote Farm, his 1,800-acre country estate near Aston Tirrold, tucked away at the foot of the Berkshire Downs. There were various properties on the land in secluded settings that seemed perfect as locations for Traffic to get inspired. We rented a white-brick cottage down a muddy lane surrounded by overgrown trees and bushes for a few pounds a week, starting from mid-April 1967. I settled into the gamekeeper's bungalow a mile or so away, so I could keep an eye on everything. I was married at the time to my first wife, Josephine, but it was already clear I wasn't going to be the type to be house-trained and live the life of a conventional husband. I was always looking for new adventures, and different situations to put in place to see what might happen. I had places to live, and offices to base the label, but mostly I liked to be on the road.

Away from the industry noise and convoluted social tangle of London, the cottage had a weird stillness about it, and the combination of the isolation, the surrounding land's ancient history, and the drugs being taken generated a definite sense of there being ghosts in the house. Some sort of spirits, anyway, usually sensed in the early hours after a hard night's play.

The band were there to "get their heads together in the country," as it was soon to be known clinically as a thing that rock groups did. But they were also a little rattled by their new fairy-tale surroundings— just as local villagers were rattled by the oddly dressed long-haired weirdos wandering around their quaint, sheltered community sharing jokes and making themselves at home in the local pub.

Pigott-Brown was in his element, having a rock band staying on his land, inviting them up to his big house to show them off to his friends. He was running out of money by then and would soon sell up and move to South Africa, so this was like his last hurrah, a chance to hang out with visitors like the Who's Pete Townshend, the Animals' Eric Burdon, and Steve Marriott of Small Faces and feel as though he'd found himself.

Traffic soon settled into a musical routine, which involved a lot of aimless jamming through the day into the early hours, whoever was in the mood, with any musicians who happened to visit them to check out this new way of doing things. There was an exposed concrete patio in front of the house where they could set up using a rigged-up generator and send music out across the fields as the evening light lasted longer and the Summer of Love approached. Traffic probably played some of their best shows when there was no one to hear but some sleepy friends and a few sheep.

Clapton came by a few times. Ginger Baker turned up, so even as Traffic was coming together there was the ominous shadow of something dark that lay ahead, one of those apparitions the more sensitive ones present were detecting. We had put another new Island band, Spooky Tooth, in a cottage a few miles away, and they would pop in and play with Steve, Chris, Jim, and Dave, four multi-instrumental masters, each of whom could have been the leader of Traffic, feeling out what kind of group they were, learning to play with each other. Steve, the soul fan, on guitar and organ; Chris, the cerebral jazzman, on flute and sax; Jim, the fan of music from around the world, on drums—the combination letting them move their music around in many different directions—Dave slightly on the outside, never fully connecting.

Stephen Stills of Buffalo Springfield was in England and he came to see what was going on, beginning a campaign to poach Steve, his favorite singer, for what would become Crosby, Stills, and Nash. When the trio started to tour as an electric band and needed a fourth member, Stills would dream of an organ player who could sing the blues better than most, and that inevitably pointed to Steve. Winwood, he would say, was even shyer than he was, and they communicated best when they played music together, just for the heck of it. Crosby, Stills, and Nash would sing a version of "Dear Mr. Fantasy" as their homage to a member who got away.

Young lads living together in a manner somewhere between soldiers in their barracks and students living away from home for the first time meant that their cottage was always scruffy, sometimes bordering on the squalid. It was all quite basic: they had to get water from a well, and build fires on cold mornings, and their diet was usually jam sandwiches and cornflakes. The house rapidly filled with beer cans, cigarette butts, empty milk bottles, dirty plates, burnt pans, and a constant smoky haze; but they could set up their gear, make a racket at two or three in the morning, and spread their wings, and that was the main thing. To clear their heads after a long night, they'd take walks through the downs after they finally got out of bed, doing a spot of bird-watching.

There were plenty of ancient myths and sights nearby that found their way into the music: old Iron Age forts, numerous burial mounds, Dragon Hill (named after its association with dragon slayer St. George), and the 400-foot-long stylized prehistoric White Horse of Uffington carved out of the chalk bedrock under the earth. They seemed happy, and I didn't have much chaperoning to do, give or take the odd visit to the local police station to bail out a visitor who had gone back to the house at three in the morning to fetch his bongos and got arrested by an alert local bobby. (Though not alert enough to notice the constant running of a couple of willing mates between the estate and London to pick up vital illicit substances.)

Mr. Fantasy, the record that came out of all this, could be seen as a concept album about what it was like to write songs in this isolated candlelit cottage in an obscure corner of southern England—summed up by "Berkshire Poppies," which is on-the-spot psychedelia right on the knife edge between inspired and indulgent, the nutty and the supernatural. They made themselves at home, and then worked out a soundtrack for the nature of this home and the way they could let their minds wander.

Linda Eastman, later Linda McCartney, visited the cottage to take the first photographs of the group. She brought with her an advance copy of the Beatles' just-released *Sgt. Pepper*—it was very like the twisted, irreverent, carnival English rock and roll that Traffic had in their heads, and the band members were both annoyed that the Beatles had gotten there first and inspired that the most popular group in the world had entered similar territory. In its own less-celebrated way, Traffic's ancient and modern out-there country rock was as much a blueprint for what was to come over the next few years as the landmark Beatles album.

"Dear Mr. Fantasy" was inspired by a cartoon character that Jim Capaldi, emerging from an acid trip, had doodled in his well-worn ideas notebook, alongside a letter he wrote to his creation, which turned out to be the song's mysterious muse. The character had a spiky sun hat, which seemed important to Jim. He'd flaked out and woken up to hear Steve and Chris musically bringing his fantasy to life.

It was a great time for the collective interactive swapping of ideas, skills, and experiences. Discoveries found in one setting would have an unexpected, greater impact elsewhere. You'd be working with people in the studio on one project and they would have some thoughts about musicians they'd like to work with, and I was always ready to try new things if there was enough enthusiasm and vision. Eddie Kramer, an engineer at Olympic Studios working with Jimmy Miller, told me about various tremendous improvising jazz musicians who were working with the drummer John Stevens. He had helped found a collective of some of the finest jazz musicians in the country called the Spontaneous Music Ensemble. By 1967 Stevens was the leader, working closely with the saxophonist Evan Parker, whose music was becoming increasingly free.

It was a jazz music inspired by revolutionary improvised music from America, both jazz and classical, but also caught up with the same exploratory tendencies that were leading British pop musicians into the optimistic, joyous, and playful freedoms of psychedelia. In that sense, it was a form of spiritual psychedelic jazz, and needed a new name, as it was definitely a progression beyond even the most extreme American jazz. It was part of a general musical era of wanting to break out of pigeonholes.

Eddie had started out assisting at Pye Studios on records by Petula Clark, the Kinks, and the Searchers, and in 1967 would be engineering the Beatles' "All You Need Is Love" and working with the Rolling Stones, Small Faces, Jimi Hendrix, and Traffic with Jimmy Miller. In those few years, the role of the engineer had changed considerably, as multitrack recording developed and options increased. Engineers were required to learn a new kind of concentration and ability to conceive the new shape-shifting architectural possibilities of a track. Even though Eddie's day job was as a pop and rock producer, he was still interested in working with the Spontaneous Music Ensemble, with that impressive engineer's attitude of valuing all music the same once you were working on it, knowing that all sorts of solutions and breakthroughs happened when you blended various forms of music.

I was interested in having a jazz arm to Island, and Eddie seemed an ideal person to help organize it. We met John and Evan in the Oxford Street offices, and they said they would ask radical guitarist Derek Bailey, trumpeter Kenny Wheeler, and double bassist Dave Holland to form a quintet. Eddie had access to after-hours studio time at Olympic, which was perfect for such a project, which wasn't exactly going to be a commercial proposition.

They had never played as a group before, but these musicians would work together in various combinations for years to come, so it was a quiet landmark album in that sense. They decided to call the label Hexagram, and in the end the record they made, *Karyobin (are the imaginary birds said to live in paradise),* was the only album released on the label. It was as though everything that needed to be said and done was said on this one record. It also didn't sound as such like jazz, although there was still a lot of jazz in the rhythm and in the heat of the playing.

I think it was an important record, both for the five musicians and for this kind of intangible improvised music—and it taught me the value of using the recording studio as a kind of research and development department. That was very much a Jamaican factor as well. Discoveries in one setting that might not be heard by many people would be used on records that would become hits. The hit records relied on the experimental attitude of studio technicians, looking to broaden the possibility of sound. It's all about looking for a sound.

Alas, the label quickly dissolved because my attention was increasingly taken up by Traffic and new rock acts we were signing. *Karyobin* was at the margins of things that were happening at the time, but it was also at the center, and in its own energetic but withdrawn way influenced a lot of the policy of Island Records, a way of trying things just to see what might happen and allowing people to follow an idea as far as it would go even though you didn't necessarily know where you were going. My role was to listen to an idea, hear a plan, and say, "That sounds good, let's do that." Sometimes I didn't say anything at all. I just nodded and waited to see what would happen.

*   *   *

JIMMY MILLER STARTED working with Traffic in the autumn after their summer spent improvising songs at the haunted Berkshire Downs cottage, at what became his favorite playground, the new Olympic Studios building in an old movie theater in Barnes. Traffic was in Studio Two at the same time that the Rolling Stones were working in Studio One, amongst the first bands to work there, still at the time one of the few independent studios in London. You could tell how much things had changed in terms of how at home artists now felt inside recording studios. Studios had started to become more like social clubs, places to hang out and relax and meet other musicians and swap ideas as much as places to work. You would see Lennon's Rolls-Royce outside Olympic even if he wasn't doing a session. With its mood lighting and comfy leather sofas, Olympic was more like a nightclub than the old, austere studio workhorses of the late 1950s and early '60s.

As music trended away from singles and towards coherent albums, Mick Jagger and Keith Richards with their usual animal cunning knew they needed new outside musical input. Their engineer, Glyn Johns, suggested they check out Jimmy. Mick slid into the control room and—gathering intelligence—watched Jimmy at work on Traffic. Liking what he saw and heard, a way of experimenting with sound and capturing a spontaneous feel without sacrificing precious groove, he got him to work on a new song he'd written with Keith. It was called "Jumpin' Jack Flash," and Jimmy passed the audition with flying colors. Jimmy being American helped, because the Stones had been raised on American music, and he had much more rootsy musical know-how than Loog Oldham. He gave them a real boost, both back to their roots but also into their future, taking something of Traffic with him.

He stayed with the Stones for what was their greatest run of albums, possibly the greatest run of rock albums, period: *Beggars Ban-*

quet, *Let It Bleed, Sticky Fingers, Exile on Main Street,* and *Goats Head Soup.* He gave (almost) everything to those records, and spending so much time close to the insidious, ever-accumulating intensity of the Stones—repairing them, making them whole, reading their minds, setting up situations, channeling their desires, taking the same drugs, showing them the way—eventually cost him dear. Keith could cope with the heroin. Jimmy couldn't, and was dead at fifty-two.

Jimmy was a loyal man, and even as he headed into the dark, messy heart of their own legend with the Stones, he didn't desert Steve or Traffic. He set to work on Traffic's second record, helping to establish Island Records' own transition from releasing mostly Jamaican pop singles to releasing progressive British rock.

He went with Steve when, still only twenty, out of a combination of innocence and inspiration, he set up Blind Faith with Cream's Eric Clapton and Ginger Baker and bassist Ric Grech of Family. There was no warning that Steve was going to leave Traffic, and he made so little fuss he didn't even tell Chris and Jim that he had left or why. I had to give them the news. Ric neglected to tell Family as well.

Traffic's story was wrapped inside Steve's constantly provisional nature, which he shared with the other members. Dave Mason left soon after *Mr. Fantasy* was completed, leaving the basic Winwood-Wood-Capaldi trio, where the real chemistry was, all three of them firing off each other's current musical infatuations, whether it was delta blues or classical. Mason rejoined when they recorded their second album, and then left again. It got to be a bit of a joke—one week there were three of them, and the next week there were four. You had to keep diving in the dustbin finding the photos you'd thrown out. Then the next week you'd throw them out again.

Blind Faith was intended to be a quiet, intimate, and deliberately low-key backing away from sixties pop fame and the excesses of Cream, making and exploring music for its own sake, but quickly got hyped up as a Second Coming. The word *supergroup* was coined to describe the combination of talent, which was where some of the trouble started, a level of anticipation that could never be satisfied. Cream had already been a kind of supergroup, and Eric always had his eye on Steve to make them a quartet. Musicians from Hendrix to Bob Dylan were enthralled by how on earth a wide-eyed teenage Brummie had ended up sounding like he did. Dylan once asked Spencer Davis where he'd found this incredible wunderkind. In a pub, he replied.

Eric never got him for Cream, but he eventually got to play in a group with his man. They would have been happy playing for the sake of it in out-of-the-way houses a little like Dylan and the Band had done on the material that ended up on *The Basement Tapes*, but they wound up crashing into another, messier world.

Blind Faith playing their first, nervy show—closer to Traffic's eclectic drift than Cream's explicit virtuosity—in front of an expectant 120,000 at Hyde Park didn't help. And Eric had tried to distance himself from the tiring antics, brutal eccentricity, and offstage drama of Ginger, who somehow ended up pushing his way into the group. Ginger loved playing with Winwood, calling him the best musician he had ever worked with, and Steve loved playing with Ginger, having no idea how difficult and even dangerous he could be. He was used to much gentler—let's say *normal*—musicians with an approach to drug-taking that was less cataclysmic, in a way a little more innocent and childlike. He persuaded Eric to let Ginger in, so the problems Eric was trying escape from in Cream seeped into Blind Faith from the very beginning. Baker was a great drummer, but a crazy, often obnoxious human being.

I remember when we were on tour, driving through customs from America into Canada in a Pontiac Thunderbird, which certainly drew attention to us. Unbeknownst to me he had stashed his drugs, including heroin, in a camera box and almost gleefully presented the box to the border agents, possibly just to see the look on my face when he told me after what he had done. Amazingly, thank the Lord, they didn't look inside, Baker got the reaction he wanted from me, and I felt like giving him the kind of punch Errol Flynn would have appreciated. I think, like Flynn, he liked the danger. I liked my danger to be less dangerous, and Baker might have found a way to survive jail, but it wasn't for me. I might still be locked up now, and I still get angry thinking about it.

I came in as the band's co-manager because of Steve, alongside booking agent and Cream manager Robert Stigwood looking after Eric, which also caused some friction, as we had very different ideas about what Blind Faith was. I brought in my vibe, which was very much a casual "let's see what happens, let's see where we go, even if it's weird folk, or free jazz, a group that isn't a group." Stigwood, however, was anticipating a Beatles–style scenario of spin-offs, film rights, and merchandising, seeing arena-sized rock music as a fast-developing corporate business. He was thinking big money. I wasn't averse to big money, but not at the risk of damaging the musicians.

It was more education for me about how not to do things. Don't fly too close to the sun. I began recording some Blind Faith sessions, but that went horribly wrong when Ginger Baker lost his temper over some small incident, which was fifteen minutes of pure fury you never wanted to experience. Jimmy came in as producer to calm things down, but the positive, open-minded musical mood that Steve and Eric were seeking was already tainted. They were the sort of musicians who often lost interest in a project fairly quickly, and that should have been a clue as well that Blind Faith was destined to be a temporary alliance that ended up stranded between Traffic and Cream.

When Blind Faith inevitably broke apart after a few months of uncontrollable supergroup highs and lows, crashing from disaster to disaster, Jimmy Miller stayed loyal to Eric and even to Ginger, who took Steve and Ric for a few torrid months into his suitably mad Afro-rock big band Ginger Baker's Air Force. Jimmy produced Air Force's live debut album, the only person on the planet who could have handled the job. Ultimately, it was all as punishing on his sensibility as working with the Rolling Stones. Aiding and abetting these intense musical artists as they searched for inspiration took its toll.

After the one album and tour, and the one season in hell with Blind Faith, Steve decided enough was enough and started a solo album. But Wood and Capaldi couldn't resist his gravitational pull and it became—after we released *Last Exit,* a collection of odds and sods after their first breakup—the fourth Traffic album, *John Barleycorn Must Die,* which as a speculative hybrid of prog and folk straying into R&B and jazz was probably what he had in mind for the Blind Faith album.

Things shifted around like Traffic was more a fluid, interchangeable jazz collective than a rock group. Its members were all resisting the routines, expectations, and schedules of the business, an attitude that, as they were effectively the very first white rock group signed to Island, influenced the DNA of the label itself. They helped stretch the shape of pop into a new eclectic underground style, which helped define Island's identity.

Steve would never be happy settling in one place, even when he eventually shook off troublesome groups and went solo. It could be hard to keep the group together even when it was a one-man band. He just wanted to play, but that meant making records, and the business and relationships that got caught up in the playing—the success or the failure—were never what he expected.

When Steve left the Spencer Davis Group, so did older brother Muff. Liking his temperament and taste and liking working with him, I offered Muff a job at Island, with no particular title, because I never liked to pin people down. This was a sign of the change in the kinds of records Island was now releasing, because success with Spencer Davis became a kind of invitation for different types of acts to approach me and the label. And I started to like the new musicians who were interested in Island, because by their very nature they were the sort who would not necessarily interest the mainstream labels.

Muff was to some extent working in an office, but essentially involved with making records, signing bands, running studios. I always felt that, while signing the label's artists was vital, just as important was who worked for the company, what their vision was, what the attitude to music was. I had started to put a team of people in place as soon as I hired Dave Betteridge, and then Tim Clark, who started in the mail room at Cambridge Road in Kilburn and would go on to become, if I had to describe his role in a title, director of marketing and art and then managing director.

Somehow the way Traffic worked in their cottage and then with Jimmy Miller in the studio influenced not only the music on Island but also how people worked *at* Island—in production, art, marketing, sales, A&R—a sense that everyone could have a say and contribute ideas and concepts. I moved about as the label developed, New York, Jamaica, the Bahamas, and I suppose as each period had its own team; it was a little like Miles Davis changing his band, changing personnel and sound, and leading in a certain enigmatic way, with his solos having the last word.

Those working for Island also had ideas about the types of artists we should be signing, which meant the label moved on from special- izing in Jamaican music. It was someone who had just started working with me—and would be with me for years—who early on brought Elton John to my attention. Actually, Lionel Conway brought a short, mild-mannered, obsessive, music-loving songwriter called Reg Dwight to my attention. He had studied classical music at the Royal Academy of Music and been around awhile trying to get attention. One of his jobs as a working session singer was supplying backing vocals on the Scaffold's "Lily the Pink," and he supplied the vocals on cheap-label versions of hit records—he deftly imitated the lead vocals of Stevie Wonder, Art Garfunkel, and Robin Gibb.

Reg also played keyboards in Bluesology, who'd backed visiting American acts like the Ink Spots and Patti LaBelle—and Little Rich- ard, giving Reg some ideas. In 1967 Bluesology became Long John Baldry's backing band. Saxophonist Elton Dean was in the band as well, inspiring Reg's new first name. His new surname was pinched from John Baldry.

Reg auditioned to be a replacement for Steve Winwood in the

Spencer Davis Group but lost out to someone with a voice more like Steve's, Eddie Hardin. SDG also went on to use what would become by 1970 Elton John's rhythm section, Dee Murray and Nigel Olsson.

When I met Reg to talk about signing him, I thought he was far too shy and even staid. He'd come to see me in my flat above the studios in Notting Hill and seemed a little winded after climbing the spiral stairs to reach me. I asked him to take a seat, and he sat on the floor. I had decided to see him because I had played a couple of his songs to Joe Cocker, who didn't write and was always looking for new songs, and who said he was very good singer.

I could understand his worth as a musician, perhaps as a songwriter, but he seemed far too insipid to be a performer. Reg was very different from Elton. Reg was clearly a music fanatic and was a big fan of one of Island's labels, Sue, which was releasing the latest trendsetting American R&B, but he didn't make me feel he had much of a future as an artist.

I passed on signing him, and I don't think Elton John spoke to me again for over fifteen years—although a few years ago, for no reason at all, I received a bunch of flowers from him. Perhaps he was eventually saying thanks for passing, as Island wouldn't have been right for Elton and Elton wouldn't have been right for Island. Maybe if he'd signed to Island, he wouldn't have needed to change his name, and Elton John would never have existed.

WITHIN A FEW years of starting pink-label, rock-oriented Island, I was mainly concentrating on artists I felt personally close to. If I didn't like something, I would have to be persuaded, as I didn't want the label to stray too far from my own standards. The majors had to imitate Island by setting up "artist-friendly" subsidiaries, and many of them copied our ideas, as though our role was to test the market. EMI had Harvest, Phonogram had Vertigo, Pye had Dawn, and Decca had Deram, and that was their way of trying to compete with

Island's potential to monopolize the best new progressive talent. But the more interesting, wild acts still fancied singing on Island. The big labels' faux-independent subsidiaries could never quite work out how to re-create the kind of organized chaos that true independence embraced.

After a little gentle persuasion, Muff ended up producing the furiously irresistible "This Town Ain't Big Enough for Both of Us" for Sparks, adding, Jimmy Miller–like, the gunshots at the beginning. It was very Island to decide that it was going to be their first single with us when even Muff wasn't sure it was a very commercial decision. He played it to Elton, who knew his stuff, and although the mischievous Mael brothers liked to put out the story that Elton bet Muff it wouldn't be a hit, Elton's pop instincts were getting stronger by the year and he recognized it as a winner. He bet Muff it would make the top three, and it did. Island didn't have many pure pop groups, but when we did, we had in Sparks the most wonderfully warped.

Sometimes it would be the other way round, and I would be interested in signing an act when no one else at Island was, from the press and marketing departments to the A&R team. When the pressure internally was on me to give the green light to U2 in 1980, I was taking an interest in a group who were causing a scene in the West End of London as part of a new tribe being dubbed the New Romantics. I might have been nostalgic for nights out in the sixties in the clubs of Soho, as they were now the latest club-going inhabitants of the building that used to be called the Flamingo, and which was now the Wag.

The group I had come across was called Spandau Ballet, the dandy opposites of U2, who were the kind of plain, dressed-down, serious-faced four-piece rock that didn't immediately inspire me. Spandau Ballet seemed influenced by soul, and their club nights were dance nights that reminded me of all-nighters in the sixties. I was seduced by the scene surrounding Spandau Ballet, but Island staffers thought they were just a flavor-of-the-month pop group, with none of the perversity, wit, and intelligence an Island group traditionally had. They could see something in U2 that I wasn't yet seeing, and I think they thought I was nuts when I invited Spandau Ballet's very cocky manager for a meeting about a contract.

The guy was acting very much like the big deal, which was fair enough as they were one of those hot bands of the moment feted in the press and being chased by all the main labels. (U2 wasn't.) Spandau Ballet had cocktail-drinking fans queuing up around the block to see them. I admit it now: I was attracted to the shiny object, the lights and noise. It happens. Sometimes the lights and noise mean something—and sometimes they're all there is.

Spandau Ballet fancied their chances and weren't keen on our offer, nor on the fact they wouldn't be dealing with me day-to-day. Thinking I should spend all my time attending to their needs, they went elsewhere. What was interesting was that within Island, those who supported the signing of U2 were amping up their advocacy during my brief Spandau Ballet dalliance. Which I really noticed. People were prepared to fight for U2, with the first person they needed to fight being me. I thought I better look closer.

On the surface, even on the balance sheet, Spandau Ballet might have seemed the correct choice and would have given Island a nice run of hit records for a couple of years. But under the surface—which, after all, was where Island was used to looking, finding the underdogs, misfits, and rejects, seeing things no one else could—U2 was the correct, music-changing choice. In the end, it was meant to be. When you think of Island Records, you think of U2. And when you think of U2, you think of Island Records.

ISLAND'S IDENTITY RIGHTLY rests upon its greatest artists, chief amongst them Bob Marley, U2, Grace Jones, and Traffic. Some might say the greatest signing was Bob, for so much more than the music. Island, though, was as much about those "behind the scenes" as it was the musicians and acts, and I sometimes considered that the greatest, most significant signing after Bob Marley was the incredibly talented Guy Stevens, although it's debatable how much he was behind the scenes.

Guy was a wiry little mod and an energetic writer about music whom I had first come across in 1964, when I saw him spinning records at Radio Caroline founder Ronan O'Rahilly's Scene Club in Soho. It was set in a little yard off Great Windmill Street and it quickly became the place to be seen. You went down some stairs, got your hand stamped, and you were in with the in crowd.

The twenty-one-year-old Guy ran their R&B Disc Night on Mondays, traditionally a dead night, and brought the club alive with his enthusiasm. He played the latest, hardest, fiercest Black American soul records that no one else seemed to be able to get. He haunted the dustiest shops to find his treasures and built up contacts across the Atlantic by writing letter after letter to record distributors in the deepest American South. And he packed that dance floor.

Along with the rock visionary Andrew Loog Oldham (eight months Guy's junior and the manager of the Rolling Stones by the time he was nineteen), Guy was one of the main engines of the mod youthquake and an inventor of modern music marketing. His record collection was considered to be the best in the country. He was a music fan essentially—perhaps one of the greatest—and he was incredibly musical even though he couldn't play an instrument and incredibly visual even though he wasn't trained as an artist. He reminded me of Duke Reid and Coxsone Dodd in their early days, when they started out simply as die-hard music fans, evolved into DJs who hunted down fresh sounds like detectives, and then finally became impresarios with a deep understanding of what makes a great sound.

I was keen to bring Guy's enthusiasm to Island. My opportunity arose in 1964, when I brokered a deal to distribute the Sue Records label in the UK. Sue was a pioneering Black-owned label in New York, founded in 1957, a couple of years before Berry Gordy launched Motown. Its owner was a man named Juggy Murray, another non-musician who just intrinsically knew what a great record was and how to produce and promote it. He'd book the very best New York musicians, including ex-Basie sidemen and King Curtis on sax, which meant a Sue record always sounded tremendously tight and potent.

Sue and Juggy had caught my attention on one of my periodic trips back to Jamaica, when, while driving down Orange Street in Kingston, I heard this sensational record blasting out of the speakers of a shop: "Mockingbird," by the girl-boy brother-sister duo Inez and Charlie Foxx. (The song became famous some years later when the then-married Carly Simon and James Taylor sexily covered it.) I had to stop my car to take the song in, and then I decided that, before I flew back to London, I had to detour to New York to meet with the guy who had released "Mockingbird": Juggy.

I met him in his "Sue Building" offices on West Fifty-Fourth Street, not far from the legendary Brill Building. Juggy was a smiley, passionate man who was very proud of what he was doing. Sharing pure passion for the mystery of a great record, we got on famously.

He already had a UK distribution deal with Decca through London American, but I won him over with my enthusiasm. We hatched a new deal wherein I would license Sue product and properly launch the label in the UK, including the records he put out through Sue's companion labels, Broadway, Eastern, and Crackerjack.

I was friends with Charles Saatchi, a bright young adman, who, with his brother Maurice, was soon to launch their legendary firm, Saatchi & Saatchi. Charles had helped us come up with the original red-and-white Island logo, and for the UK version of Sue, he and I came up with a bolder, brasher yellow-and-red label, the yellow of the sun with a flash of red across the middle. The fluid way *Sue* was written was connected to how *Island* was written on its label, but this was meant to demonstrate a very different world of rhythm.

By December 1963, we were rushing out "Mockingbird"; releases planned for 1964 included songs by Ike and Tina Turner, Ernestine Anderson, Baby Washington, and Jimmy McGriff's high-powered instrumental version of Ray Charles' 1954 "I've Got a Woman," where gospel and blues first got together as soul. The Jimmy McGriff single had been a top twenty on the US charts, and here I was with this access to such great music, like I was still packing my jukebox with crowd-favorite tunes, but instead it was now on a subsidiary of Island.

Juggy was pleased that Sue had such a pioneering visual presence in the UK, but I knew what I needed next was someone with the right kind of energy to run the label's UK operation. As much as I loved the music Sue put out, I didn't have the personality or the bandwidth to make the label my cause.

Guy was clearly the guy. He wasn't just on the beat-group scene; he'd helped make it. It was his taste in music that helped the early blues boys like the Rolling Stones, the Animals, Small Faces, the Kinks, and the Yardbirds learn their trade. They would carefully study Guy's rare imported seven-inch singles, copy and perform the cover versions, and then begin to crack the code, which they would twist and turn to come up with their own original songs. The Who, when they were still known as the High Numbers, based their first attempts at original songs on the R&B and soul tunes they heard Guy play. When Pete Townshend was asked what it was about Guy's curated playlists that so electrified him, he looked to the heavens and said, "I can't explain"—which became an electrifying song in its own right. Those first Spencer Davis covers we released before we got Jackie Edwards to write for them came from the Guy Stevens collection. It's one of the places where British rock music started.

He was exactly who I needed to take charge of Sue, and if I hadn't grabbed him, Rohan would have for his brand-new Radio Caroline. I reached out to Guy, who, naturally, already knew all about Sue Records—he had ordered singles directly from Juggy. He started working for Island in April 1964 for something like £12.50 a week, and while Dave Betteridge looked after the day-to-day details and I kept an eye on him as much as you could, Guy did what I hoped he would do, as though he were a pop culture reincarnation of Errol Flynn, and set about selling and representing Sue.

It was still tough to get Black music onto mainstream British radio and into the high-street shops. "Mockingbird" was a top ten hit in America, but Guy couldn't get it to be much more than a cult hit in the UK, even after we got Inez and Charlie over to England to tour their wild, eccentric show with the Rolling Stones and the Spencer Davis Group.

As it turned out, the UK Sue wasn't the hit machine I'd hoped it would be, and Guy soon felt restricted by representing the Sue repertoire when his tastes in music were so much more wide-ranging. He started to license records from America that didn't come from the US Sue and released them on the UK Sue, much to Juggy's annoyance. Hurt, Juggy renewed his deal with London American at Decca. Sue continued without Guy's central involvement, run more sensibly by the editor of *Blues and Soul*, running out of steam in 1968, about the time I started Trojan with Lee Gopthal, the soul and R&B sounds of Sue now reaching the mainstream charts through labels like Motown and Stax.

But though I had misjudged the viability of the Guy-Sue marriage, Guy's time at Island was only just beginning. Guy was getting frustrated, but still valuing his knowledge and expertise, I didn't want to lose him. In 1965, thinking of how Reid and Dodd had moved from playing records to producing them, I encouraged him to start producing. In the mid-sixties, as Island was morphing into the kind of label that specialized in albums—where, after all, I had begun in 1959 with Lance Hayward and Ernest Ranglin—Guy jumped into the role of LP Man with total enthusiasm.

Guy was one of those mods who, by 1967, went full-blown hippie. His neatened curly mod hair grew out into a frizz that jutted out horizontally from the sides of his head. He developed a love for psychedelic togs and florid, J. R. R. Tolkien–like verbiage. His whole angle of attack had changed after Keith Moon introduced him to speed. He'd resisted the pills throughout his tenancy at the Scene, and his relatively disciplined running of Sue, and any craziness was all channeled into his love for music and his beloved record collection. Now that things had gone wild and punchy three-minute songs were being replaced by longer, weirder songs, Guy went wild and weird to keep up, and sometimes set the pace.

You can hear Guy's tastes changing on a self-titled album he produced for us by the pop-art collective Hapshash and the Coloured Coat, who were responsible for the ultra-vivid, deeply trippy posters for the new psychedelic clubs like UFO and Middle Earth. The music was credited to the Heavy Metal Kids, one of Guy's dream names for a band, years before heavy metal was a genre. The album featured a congregation of joyously stoned pals, including Brian Jones; Guy produced it and played the role of Human Host, like he fancied himself as an English Frank Zappa, or P. T. Barnum on acid. Pressed on red vinyl, it was some sort of hypnotic nighttime bongo freak-out somewhere between the droning repetition of the Velvet Underground and the droning repetition of such German rock bands as Amon Düül II.

Guy and rock and roll had come a long way from Chuck Berry, and you could see what was coming next. He was photographed for the *Sunday Times* with the chief Hapshash artists Michael English and Nigel Waymouth of London's first psychedelic boutique, Granny Takes a Trip. They had explosive hair and rococo wardrobes, and stood at the vanguard of the next phase of conspicuously weird, unapologetically mind-altering music. They looked like they were quite aware that at that moment they were the Lords of the then-British dominance of Western pop culture. As Guy liked to say, he and his mates were the people your parents warned you about.

Around this time, Dave Betteridge, Muff Winwood, and I moved the Island offices to Basing Street in Notting Hill Gate, back when it was a rawer-edged place than the ode to gentrification that it is now. I felt we needed our own studios, our own Olympic, with our own engineers and producers, so that we were more in control of the making of our records. I wanted to be close to our bands as they recorded, and quickly give them comments and thoughts even when I wasn't the official producer.

To get that energized Olympic rock sound, the one I was hearing on the ever-improving albums of the Rolling Stones and the Who, I poached the pioneering, wonderfully eccentric engineer who had built the studios there, Dick Swettenham. Olympic wasn't keen on letting him go, but I got around that by offering to finance Dick's own business so he could supply a range of studios, starting with mine. By decade's end, we had two fully equipped studios on Basing Street: on the second floor, the large Studio One, which could hold eighty musicians if necessary, and on the first floor, the more intimate Studio Two.

Guy joined us there as Island's freewheeling A&R man, image-maker, talent scout, and font of inspiration. I always liked to have meetings about a round table, so that no one was ever at the head of the table—this way, ideas circulated with no sense of hierarchy. I installed such a table at Basing Street. On Guy's first day in the new building, he scrambled onto the table and did a little war dance in front of us. "This is going to be the best fucking label in the world!" he shouted. Then he dismounted and handed me a huge joint.

Guy's first signing was the VIPs, a band from Carlisle who originally sounded like they had done a lot of listening to hard-core Sue Records R&B. In 1965, they were neatly suited and mod-looking. A year or two later, however, they were all Guyed out: their hair was growing, their clothes were ballooning, and a name like the VIPs seemed hopelessly old-fashioned.

After two singles, they changed their name to Art. Guy produced their first album, *Supernatural Fairy Tales*, whose opening track was tellingly entitled "I Think I'm Going Weird." The album didn't sell, but I had already learned a trick: when faced with lack of sales, think of a solution. While I was on tour with the Spencer Davis Group in Europe, I met an American singer and organist named Gary Wright who was studying psychology in Berlin. He had a band called the New York Times and turned out to be an old friend of Jimmy Miller's. A recording deal for the New York Times didn't work out, and the band broke up, leaving Gary on his own. I introduced him to the members of Art, who were disappointed with the reaction to their debut and on the verge of splitting. Gary and the Art guys hit it off and, with renewed enthusiasm, emerged as a new band called Spooky Tooth, a name Guy Stevens invented for them.

Their debut album, *It's All About*—with Jimmy Miller producing alongside the engineer Glyn Johns—didn't sell many copies, but that didn't put me off. There was some sense of a new "Island sound" materializing: soul and blues mixing with prog and psychedelic experimentation. I was interested and patient enough to see where that would go.

Spooky Tooth made a few more albums with their lineup constantly in flux, perfecting a soulful heavy-rock sound that eventually did make it into the mainstream, but not under their name. One of their later members was Mick Jones, who commercially perfected the formula of hard-rock, pop, and white soul with Foreigner. There was something quite Island about their story: Spooky Tooth would watch others take off using ideas that they originated, forethoughts in a bigger story.

Guy was smitten with Gary Wright's organ playing, along with Al Kooper's similarly soulful work on Bob Dylan's "Like a Rolling Stone," and started fantasizing about putting together a new pop group based on this type of sound. Right around then, a hustling young kid named Keith Reid paid me a visit. He was a lyricist looking for someone to write music with. I wasn't interested initially and passed on signing him. But he had something about him, so I told him to go see Guy. Maybe Guy would know what to do with him.

Guy took a liking to Keith and commissioned him to write some sleeve notes for a Sue compilation he was putting together. He also introduced Keith to a musician named Gary Brooker, whom he'd known as part of an R&B group called the Paramounts. I think Guy had the idea that Brooker and Reid might work well together as a songwriting duo.

Gary Brooker had a nice, yearning, English-soul voice, a little like Steve Winwood's, and he decided he wanted to sing the songs that he and Keith were writing. Guy started to assemble a group around them with that organ-y, *Blonde on Blonde* sound in mind. Keith had come up with an intriguing lyric after going to a party and hearing a very stoned Guy tell his wife that she looked a little worse for wear— "a whiter shade of pale," to be specific. Keith seized upon this phrase and built a song around it.

Gary Brooker made Keith's words fit to some music he had based on a jazzy arrangement of Bach he'd heard and liked. Using the musicians he had assembled around Gary and Keith, including Matthew Fisher on Hammond organ, Guy recorded a demo and presented it to me as "A Whiter Shade of Pale," by a group that didn't really exist, though Guy had come up with a characteristically barmy name for them: Procol Harum.

I was not moved at first. The song struck me as one of Guy's indulgent follies, like the Hapshash album. It seemed too long and aimless, the word *fandango* didn't help, and I felt I had already recorded the best possible version of that white-soul voice with Steve Winwood. Guy was devastated when I told him my opinion, and he ended up not working with the group.

Feeling let down, Procol Harum, which now considered itself a real group, signed to the Deram subsidiary of Decca. The producer Denny Cordell cleverly recorded the song at Olympic Studios using Bill Eyden, a fine jazz session drummer. Bill genuinely made the track swing a little, which is frequently missed as one of reasons it was such a hit. "A Whiter Shade of Pale" wanders about lyrically, but musically, it absolutely sticks to the point.

It rose up the charts and reached number one in May 1967, the same week the Beatles went to number one in the album charts with *Sgt. Pepper*. In some ways, "A Whiter Shade of Pale" was a one-off, a novelty song; but in capturing both the whimsy and the melancholy inherent in that year's psychedelic pop, it became a key part of the soundtrack to the so-called Summer of Love.

Traffic made their own trippy contribution to the charts that summer with "Paper Sun," written in their rented Berkshire cottage with plenty of acid-inspired input from Guy. It was their debut single. "Paper Sun" reached number five, but I couldn't help but notice that the song I had turned down without a second thought was a blockbuster, on the way to a million sales. It stung a little, but I had learned from my gambling days that you have to live with your losses. There are always going to be hands that don't go your way, no matter how good a poker player you are.

Before Traffic, the first British rock band to release an album on Island was called Nirvana. Years later, Kurt Cobain and company were compelled to pay the first Nirvana $100,000 and promise never to stray into the earlier band's symphonic psychedelia, which wasn't going to be a problem anyway. Muff had brought these guys in, and they gamely auditioned for us at Basing Street on acoustic guitars. We made up our minds that we would sign them. I asked them a few questions—how they imagined their sound, did they want to do what we'd done with Traffic and work in the country, did they think they needed an orchestra—and was abrim with optimism, eager to get their first album out as soon as I could.

Jimmy Miller had a listen to their songs but wasn't keen, so I produced their debut album. *The Story of Simon Simopath* was one of the very first concept albums. It wasn't as accomplished as the Who's *Tommy* or the Pretty Things' *S.F. Sorrow*, but it was by a few weeks the first rock album that linked songs together following a character from life to death. The album made little impact in Britain and zero in America. Guy Stevens hated it because he said he couldn't dance to it.

The original Nirvana finally became a revered cult band years after the fact, when the Seattle Nirvana raised awareness of their back catalogue. The confusion reigns to this day: when Island's greatest signings are listed in articles and books, they often add the second Nirvana to our roster, right after Bob Marley and U2.

AT THE END of 1968, I came very close to signing Led Zeppelin, looked after by my old office neighbor Peter Grant. We had a deal for the UK almost finalized, but I lost out when Atlantic, which was signing them in America, offered Peter a monumental sum for world rights that I couldn't get anywhere near to matching. Peter did acknowledge some Island influence by telling me that he had put into the contract a provision that Atlantic had not previously allowed: no singles; albums only.

I could accept losing Led Zeppelin with a certain calmness, even though I knew they were going to be huge. Having a group that big would have distorted the label and created a kind of force field around it. They would have dominated everything and distracted us from the kind of artist's artists we liked to work with.

It was the same with the Rolling Stones. In 1970, when the Stones were thinking of leaving Decca, Mick Jagger spoke to me a few times about the possibility of the band signing to Island. On paper it seemed promising, and there was a definite Island connection in their adoption of one of our original in-house producers, Jimmy Miller, and their occasional use of our studios. But as with Led Zep, the Stones would have been too much of a circus for Island. We were used to building something from scratch, not being handed a massive mansion to maintain. It was fun to talk things out with Mick, but it was never meant to be. The Stones also ended up going through Atlantic, with their own bespoke label. I didn't think of that one as a loss, more a game I never chose to join.

That said, Island's own Guy Stevens was the one who gave the Stones' first Atlantic album its title: *Sticky Fingers*. He was clever that way, if volatile. In 1968 he served eight months inside Wormwood Scrubs, the infamous west London prison, for drug possession. If nothing else, this gave him a lot of time to dream up an ideal new band, one that would sound like the Stones with Bob Dylan as singer, Jerry Lee Lewis on piano, and the soul-jazz master Jimmy McGriff on organ. He was obsessed with that combination of piano and organ in the same band.

Guy was even more manic after coming out of jail, not helped by having a breakdown upon discovering that his legendary record collection had been stolen from his mum's house, where he had stored it. His mother didn't like him much, so you have to wonder what really happened to that extraordinary information center. He came back to Island with both renewed vigor and a desperate need to impress.

He started channeling his energies into creating the dream band he had thought up in prison. Guy being Guy, he already had a name for them, lifted from a novel he'd read in jail: Mott the Hoople. His prime recruit was a twenty-nine-year-old singer and pianist named Ian Hunter, who had logged a lot of time working in factories and never seemed to take off his dark glasses. I think it was Guy who told him to keep them on at all times, because that's what Dylan was doing in the late sixties. Hunter was almost ten years older than the rest of the band, which created a warped dynamic that only Guy in all his grandiosity could have engineered. As he once declared in all sincerity: "There are only two Phil Spectors, and I'm one of them."

Ian Hunter's piano playing turned out to be basic at best. But we let Guy keep going, and over time, he allowed the group to work out what exactly they were. Their second album revealed them to be a collage of proto–heavy metal, proto-glam, proto-punk, and proto–power pop, with Hunter turning out to be as sensitive and defiant as Guy was. Guy supplied the album's title: *Mad Shadows*.

Exhausted by Guy's antics, Mott didn't want him anywhere near their third album, *Wildlife*. But after it flopped, they realized they missed what they had to admit was his magic. They persuaded him to come back for their fourth album, *Brain Capers*. Mott had quite a loyal following for a band that didn't really sell many records, but they seemed doomed to never break through. The group thought I was about to drop them, and they may well have been right. In any event, it didn't hurt to make them think this was their last chance and they had better do something special. I gave them Island's basic four days in the studio.

Mott and Guy pushed each other to the limits, with Mott now giving as good as they got. Guy's overall concept for the record seemed to be to destroy the studios they were working in, which just happened to be our studios. He dressed up in a Zorro mask and cape and waved toy pistols in the air. At least, I hope they were toy pistols.

Ian called me one day when they were nearly finished to inform me that there was a fire in the studio. I presumed this was some stunt that Guy was using to get a performance out of the group. I thought about it for a moment, then asked Ian if it was totally necessary. He said yes. Which seemed fair enough. If the record was good, the pyrotechnics would be worth it. We'd clean up the damage later.

Brain Capers was indeed a very good album, Guy's dream coming true of an ideal rock group mixing danger and angst, noise and melancholy. But it too failed to sell. The members of Mott the Hoople had been right: Island dropped them.

Defeated and disappointed, feeling the world was against them, the group decided to split up after a shambles of a show in Zurich. They were unexpectedly given a second life when David Bowie, a superfan who owed an artistic debt to them, wrote them a stomping single, "All the Young Dudes." Released on CBS, it became the hit they needed—and for Guy, another generational anthem, alongside "A Whiter Shade of Pale," for which he had essentially laid the groundwork but gone unrewarded for his efforts.

Mott's glam-rock success made Guy bitter. He ranted to anyone who would listen about what pathetic sellouts they were and mocked their ill-fitting sparkly outfits. So began his downward spiral. Guy's drinking got worse and his erratic behavior less charming. He was no longer a playful presence at Island but a disturbing one. We had to let him go.

He drifted throughout most of the seventies before he went out with one wonderful, unexpected final flourish. To the initial alarm of CBS, the Clash declared that they wanted Guy to produce their third album, *London Calling*, in 1979. They revered him for his formative role in shaping British rock music. They were his students and he was their mad professor. His job was to bring the emotion to the studio and make sure it was audible on the finished record.

London Calling is a great rock album and a fitting climax to Guy's career. It wouldn't have been the same without him. Its success gave him the chance for a second act, but just a couple of years after the LP's release, he died from an overdose of the pills he was taking to treat his alcoholism. He was only thirty-eight. For all the havoc he wreaked, Guy taught me so much about production and creating situations where great music emerged. My sessions were comparatively orderly, but I took from Guy the notion of creating a specific atmosphere in the studio to help find out where the magic was. His was an extreme version of how to get the best out of an artist.

Guy was crucial to establishing rock-era, pink-label Island, a magnet for talent and always overflowing with ideas. Letting him have his way in the mid to late sixties meant that at the time he came up with the brilliant idea of putting together a budget-priced Island sampler in 1969—cheap enough to make the top-twenty albums chart when long-players cost today's equivalent of £20 each—we were still a small, almost family label, still relatively obscure, but we were already showcasing Jethro Tull, Spooky Tooth, Free, Traffic, Fairport Convention, John Martyn, the Spencer Davis Group, and the first Nirvana. We had such a family vibe going at Island that we persuaded all of these bands to turn up in Hyde Park one cold morning after a late-night party to have their photo taken together. The sampler, entitled

You Can All Join In, after a Traffic song, flowed together like it was a coherent piece of work: one out of many.

A sampler album we released in 1970 called *Bumpers* was indeed a bumper collection of eclectic Island music generously spread over two LPs. I called it *Bumpers* because my wife at the time, the beautiful model and actress Marilyn Rickard, spotted all over London at the time on posters for swimwear, had been shopping. She had found a boutique along the Kings Road specializing in very trendy sixties items. They were selling a series of prints in multiple bright colors of high-top sports shoes that were then nicknamed bumpers. She told me I should go and have a look.

I liked them a lot and bought a hundred prints, not immediately sure how to use them, and they turned out to be the work of the artist Tony Wright. We paid him £200.00 and used a selection on the cover of *Bumpers*. It was his first work in the music business, and as an imaginative designer of record sleeves and logos he would make a significant contribution to Island's visual style throughout the seventies.

CHAPTER FIVE

FOLK: NEW ALLIES
AND NEW SOUNDS

It was a big, agreeable folk singer in his thirties who traveled around on a tiny scooter who introduced me to John Martyn. Theo Johnson was an ex-navy man from Northumberland in his mid-thirties who liked to collect songs from around the world. He was doing a bit of unofficial scouting for me, mainly for the Blue Mountain publishing company I was running alongside Island. You might be the one who first signs an artist, or is said to discover them, but there is always someone who first brings them to your attention. Theo would make an under-the-radar album, *Bawdy British Ballads*, for an Island subsidiary called Surprise Records; it originally came to me from a gangster loan shark in New York I took a shine to, or who took a shine to me. He was a terrible, dangerous guy, the kind of operator who'd chuck you out of a high building if you got on his wrong side, but I never saw that side of him.

As a front for his true, highly dubious activities, the gangster dealt in risqué records by the likes of the comedy poet Nipsey Russell, the foulmouthed comedian Belle Barth (who inspired Bette Midler), and the raunchy stand-up Redd Foxx. We launched a version of the label in Britain in 1964, responding to an adult-only niche market we thought we'd spotted, which we hoped would be good for cash flow.

Bawdy British Ballads contained the kind of dirty songs you'd hear sung in rugby clubs, and it created a nice bit of controversy when a clergyman from Coventry in central England said it should be banned, which helped us shift a few copies and boosted our finances when we were in real trouble. There is a world where Island Records might never have happened without the grievances of a provincial priest. There wasn't any strategy; chance was the name of the game.

There was also a record called *Music to Strip By* that came with a free G-string, which was a nightmare to manufacture. Lee Gopthal would sit around hand-stitching them. We also made a comedy dramatization of the Profumo scandal, in which the conservative government of twelve years was brought down by a very British sex scandal, now that "British" included a Jamaican element.

One "surprise" result of this record was personal: Aloysius "Lucky" Gordon, one of the minor players in the affair between the Tory secretary of state for war John Profumo and young model Christine Keeler, began hassling me for money. Gordon, a Kingston-born jazz singer and drug dealer and one of Keeler's lovers, had been involved in a fight with yet another of Keeler's lovers outside the Flamingo Club in Wardour Street during one of their all-nighters. The vicious knife fight, which left Gordon needing seventeen stitches in his face, set off a chain reaction that led to the most infamous political scandal of the times, Profumo's resignation, and the eventual toppling of the government.

I'd played Lucky Gordon on the record, and he was outraged not so much at my terrible impression but more because he hadn't got paid. I didn't give him any cash, but despite his dodgy background there was something about him and his insider knowledge of the Notting Hill area I thought would be helpful. His Jamaican food and general demeanor were popular with Bob Marley and Traffic, so I hired him as a cook at Basing Street Studios, where he remained a fixture long after I sold it, constantly patrolling the Notting Hill area. His presence in the kitchen became very important in helping to establish the vibe at the studio.

Before we got to having our own studio, we needed to sign some interesting British acts. It was enthusiastic, unaffiliated characters like Theo with their own contacts and specialized knowledge that helped Island start to release records not sourced in Jamaica. We could move away from producing ad hoc albums that were more about helping us survive than making great music.

Theo was a regular at the folk clubs in and around London, such as the Kingston Folk Barge, where Paul Simon, Al Stewart, Maddy Prior, and Jackson C. Frank regularly performed in their younger days. So too did John Martyn, an angel-faced, curly-haired singer whom Theo pressed upon me as a great potential signing. John was a roguish hippie with a bit of attitude. When Theo tried to sell himself to John, claiming he could make the young man a star, John replied nonchalantly, "Go on, then."

John had come to London from Scotland to seek his fortune, or at least to play all the folk clubs that were opening, like Bunjies on the fringes of Covent Garden and the more adventurous Les Cousins in the basement of a Greek restaurant a couple of streets away. Soho was the hothouse center of the acoustic universe at the time, the folk equivalent of the Scene Club—during just one week, it might feature Davy Graham, Bert Jansch, John Renbourn, Ralph McTell, Sandy Denny, Roy Harper, Van Morrison, Cat Stevens, Donovan, various members of Fairport Convention, and, from America, Paul Simon and Tom Paxton.

John Martyn was an amazing, robust guitar player and had a combative Glaswegian swagger, which immediately made him something more than just another "new Dylan." The problem was, it didn't seem to make sense to sign this Scottish singer to a label known really for Jamaican music.

I was vaguely considering the idea of expanding the breadth of Island's roster, though not as far as signing a Scottish folk singer. But

I did, because I couldn't resist the fact that it didn't seem to be what I should be doing. And I liked John's personality. He struck me as a warrior, a good type to have on our side.

John was technically the first white artist we signed to Island, at the vanguard of our becoming another kind of label, one that would be of interest to folk and rock fans. To me, he was like a jazz musician, brilliant at improvising, be it with his voice or on his guitar, with a very free sense of timing. All kinds of musicians have declared themselves John Martyn fans over the years—from Johnny Rotten to Eric Clapton to Talk Talk to Massive Attack—and they're responding to him not as a folk artist but as a fearless sonic explorer.

The first album we made together, *London Conversation*, was recorded on a two-track at Pye Studios off Marble Arch and released in October 1967. It featured the rattling acoustic guitar, harmonica, and earnest, dreamy, and uncluttered songs that John was playing in the clubs, plus a little sitar, some flute, and the inevitable Bob Dylan cover, a fine, muted version of "Don't Think Twice, It's All Right." It cost about £150 to make in glorious mono, so it wasn't much of a roll of the dice, and the low-key do-it-yourself quality was emphasized by the album's sleeve, which featured a photo of John, taken on the roof of my flat, playing his guitar surrounded by chimney pots. He was so proud of that album and would walk around Soho carrying it under his arm. These were the days when he would get angry if he came across anyone smoking dope near him. He wasn't yet experimenting with substances and was trying to be careful with his drinking, worried about following his father into alcoholism.

We quickly made a second album, and that's when the transformation of John began. His accent started to slip and slide between tough-nut Glasgow and a weird, slippery mock-Cockney. Still working out how to produce a John Martyn album and believing that he needed a little more studio polish, I enlisted Al Stewart, a fellow Scot and a folk singer with a distinctive, plaintive voice who hosted the regular all-nights from midnight to 7 a.m. at Les Cousins. (Ten years later, Al would become well-known in the wider world for his hit song "The Year of the Cat.")

All that said, Al knew nothing about recording. This didn't necessarily seem a problem, as everyone was experimenting in their own way with studios, and Al and John were good friends. When Al came to play me the resulting album, *The Tumbler*, a little nervously, it seemed exactly how I thought the second John Martyn album should sound. There was some progress from the first record, the addition of a second guitarist and a bass guitar, and it was a bit more playful. His voice was beginning to slur bluesily through the words, and John's fast, precise guitar had taken an incredible leap.

I still wasn't sure Island was the right record company for him in terms of where we were at the end of the 1960s, though. Meanwhile, I had been developing a close working relationship with Joe Boyd, an American well-liked in the folk world as a producer, manager, and all-around musical savant. Born in New Jersey, Joe had arrived in Soho in the sixties to work as Elektra Records' emissary to London. Elektra had for many years been strictly a folk label, with singers such as Judy Collins and Tom Paxton, but had grown hot with its kaleidoscopic rock records by the Doors and Love. These records inspired Joe to seek out new sounds and genre combinations that could not be pigeonholed as simply folk, rock, or confessional singer-songwriter fare. The result was a flourishing career as a producer for the likes of the Incredible String Band, Fairport Convention, Nick Drake, Richard and Linda Thompson, and Fotheringay: folk music produced in a rock-and-roll way.

Joe and I connected easily, as we were both record-company men who also happened to be obsessive music fans. That meant we mixed passion with pragmatism. As producers, we were not avoiding the fact that our work, in the end, was about selling records, but we were most keen on capturing moments and making records that sounded like nothing else. As soon as I met Joe, I could see that he had what a lot of musicians don't have: a sense of where music becomes history, and how and why it will eventually be listened to.

After the Incredible String Band, Joe had other acts that he wanted to sign to Elektra, such as wild pop group the Move, whom he saw playing live in Birmingham. He was there in the first days of Pink Floyd, noting how their then-leader and cultural magpie Syd Barrett randomly found the group's name from a list of blues musicians Joe had recommended to him that included Pink Anderson and Floyd Council. After producing Pink Floyd's first single, "Arnold Layne," Joe expected to continue working with them through Elektra.

But Jac Holzman, Boyd's boss at Elektra, balked at signing Pink Floyd and resisted many of Joe's other recommendations, assuming his charge had become overexcited upon being set loose in London. He was let go by the label. Thus liberated, Joe set up a management, production, and booking company called Witchseason Productions, which was initially going to sign Pink Floyd through Polydor. Polydor was on a great run at the time, having just signed Jimi Hendrix, Cream, and the Who. Then the personnel at Polydor changed; Joe wasn't dealing with the person who had initially wanted to work with him, and even though he had been offered a lot of money, he lost interest in the deal.

I bumped into Joe one day and asked him why he had taken Fairport Convention to Polydor and not brought them to me at Island. I was a bit put out by that, but the result of this conversation was that, because he was uncomfortable with the changes at Polydor, we did a deal for his production company to come to Island.

Even Joe still thought of us as a West Indian label until I told him about Traffic and Spooky Tooth, and said I thought that Fairport Convention would fit with them. Blues musicians had responded to the Bob Dylan of *John Wesley Harding*, the Band of *Music from Big Pink*, the bootleg Dylan and the Band *Basement Tapes*, and the grand sonic eccentricities of *Sgt. Pepper*, and folk musicians had in their way too. Joni Mitchell's unadorned but captivating 1968 debut *Song to a Seagull*, with its stately melodies, alternate tunings, and abstract story-telling lyrics, was also having an effect on British musicians, both folk and rock.

Joe as an American didn't have a purist's sense of what British, often particularly English, folk should sound like. He encouraged a modernization of traditional music that didn't compromise its roots and was a zealot about selling folk music to a wider audience in much the same way I was keen on getting Jamaican music to as many people as possible.

Fairport Convention came to Island after all, which made me very happy. This also meant Island could work with one of the great voices of the times, the extraordinary Sandy Denny, and later with her brief but beautiful Fotheringay, as well as the immensely gifted guitarist Richard Thompson and therefore the classic 1970s records he made with his then-wife, Linda Thompson.

In 1974 the Thompsons made one of those quiet, captivating spiritual masterpieces, *I Want to See the Bright Lights Tonight*, proof that one of the great benefits of the way Island worked was the space and time—if not necessarily the budgets—we gave musicians, allowing them to come up with music and stories that came from their very own space and time. We didn't tell musicians like Richard and Linda Thompson what to do. In fact, we did whatever the opposite of telling them what to do was. In many ways our job was to be the first fans of artists like Richard and Linda, and then try to find as many other fans as we could.

Island became associated with all these other wonderful musicians and groups that Joe was working with, which could only have happened because of Joe's experience, connections, assertiveness, and musical instincts. Here was something else Joe and I shared—in the middle of all his hedonism and all this shifting cultural chaos swirling around us, we were always efficient and organized. Really, just making the decision to work with Joe—well, from that point, the rest followed, and Island became something else that was like nothing else.

Witchseason was great for Island, and vice versa—I don't think Joe could have found a better spiritual home for what he was doing. His adventurous artists were a natural fit with the artists we were beginning to sign; when you look at those Island samplers from the late 1960s and early '70s, everyone fits together in their eclecticism and energy: Fairport Convention, Free, Nick Drake, Mott the Hoople, Dr. Strangely Strange, King Crimson, Blodwyn Pig, Quintessence, John Martyn.

NICK DRAKE HAD come to see me one day in 1967 in the office I kept in Oxford Circus. I think it was John Martyn who suggested that he do so, after seeing him sing at Les Cousins—a little out of place in his shyness and quiet presence, but possessed of a batch of elegantly structured songs that seemed to suggest he knew a lot about falling into and out of love.

Nick was eighteen or so when I met him, all in black, very tall but seemingly keen to look smaller, as if he didn't quite want to be noticed and might flee at any moment. This wasn't so unusual at the time. I was used to young musicians who were utterly confident as performers or players but barely said a word in conversation. Just about all the early young British rock musicians I was meeting were like that, however impressive they were onstage, whether that was Steve Winwood lost in his own world or wild-haired, virtuosic lead guitarists. Usually you could loosen up these types with a couple of drinks down the pub or a joint while listening to music. For a while, that did the trick with Nick. To be honest, compared to how he was later, when he would be almost completely paralyzed by any social interaction, he was quite jovial and straightforward, if very serious, and outward enough to be visiting music businesspeople (me) and playing his music with no apparent qualms.

I can't deny that I felt a public-school, old-boy affinity for Nick. There was an unspoken thing where if you shared that background and experience, you had a natural connection. Nick was one of those public-school boys who found unusual, individual ways to deal with the experience and assert his individuality—in Nick's case, coming up with strange, bewitching open tunings on his guitar and writing mesmeric, melancholy songs. He was just starting at Cambridge University, studying English literature and playing on the Cambridge folk circuit, which simultaneously put him in contact with many people and fostered a sense that he didn't belong.

He played me some songs, never daring to look at me while I listened. The songs were delicate and tentative but confident in their idiosyncrasy—they came across like magic spells he had created as a defense against the world. I suppose the songs were everything he had at the time, and he'd worked hard on them and knew they were strong. I liked them very much, but compared to Traffic and Spooky Tooth and the other rock stuff I was focusing on at the time, they seemed a little flimsy.

I told him, "I love what you're doing, but I'm not sure whether we're the right people credibility-wise to sell your music. That said, why not come back in six months and see where we're both at?" So he did come back, but nothing had really changed—I liked his music a lot but didn't feel I could do anything with it. We were used to mixing our acts on tours, but I thought that if I included a solo singer as understated and confessional as Nick, it would get lost.

But when we started working with Joe Boyd and Witchseason, Nick Drake had joined as one of their artists. Island was now in a better position to work with Nick, and we allowed Joe the freedom to follow his instincts. The combination was the perfect one for Nick to be able to write and move at his own pace.

There were many reasons why Nick Drake's music didn't sound like any other, not even like Fairport Convention when its members were backing him. One of the main ones was that Joe saw to it that

Nick's songs were always arranged with care and in service to Nick's dulcet, otherworldly voice, melodically filling in the gaps, the strings serving almost as another vocalist. Joe had imagined strings being something that could elevate the songs without sinking them.

It was a dangerous idea, because folk at the time was meant to be abrasive and rustic, and strings can often become schmaltz, a background sweetener, but this was an idea to use the strings for added emotion and texture. Joe didn't necessarily consider Nick Drake to be folk music. It was a set of indefinable songs that needed recording in the most appropriate way.

On Nick's debut album, *Five Leaves Left*, Robert Kirby, a classically trained Cambridge friend of Nick's, arranged the strings, using just an intimate string sextet. His work was exquisite, a perfect accompaniment to Nick's soft, righteous voice. But there was one song, "River Man," Kirby couldn't get to grips with—he couldn't work out the indefinite jazz timing. It was Harry Robinson, of all people, from my Millie Small days, who came up with a solution. He had gone on to write some brilliant orchestral scores for Hammer Film Productions that were so smart in distilling the essence of classical composers into his short-form arrangements.

Harry could hear the influence of Ravel and Debussy on "River Man," the radical blurring of textures, and Nick loved the beautiful, sinuous chord structures and intense Englishness of the composer Delius. He held Harry rapt talking about how he imagined the mood of the song, and Harry imaginatively arranged it for fourteen string instruments.

Nick sang it live amidst the string players while Harry conducted, just like Frank Sinatra had sung live in the studio with Nelson Riddle's orchestra. The results were gorgeous, with the whole performance a haunting blend of classical and jazz influences. I consider it one of the greatest string arrangements ever on a pop record. Richard Thompson has said that "River Man" is even better than "Eleanor Rigby," and I concur.

Five Leaves Left was released in September 1969 and barely caused

a ripple in the outside world—which was never anything to particularly concern Island, although it's astounding to think now that such
a masterpiece of an album was barely noticed, or badly misjudged. It
was what I was worried about when I didn't initially think I should
sign him to Island, that such sophisticated but indirect music wouldn't
stand out in what had become a noisy world.

The lackluster response to the album caused Nick to start with-
drawing further into himself, and it took a few months for John
Wood, the proprietor-engineer of Sound Techniques, the London
studio where Nick recorded, and Joe Boyd to get the next record,
Bryter Layter, into a form that the increasingly fastidious Nick was
comfortable with. The second album came out just over a year after
the first and was much more a representation of Nick as a pure studio
artist. Because he didn't like performing live, his later songs made no
concessions to engaging beer-drinking punters in the front row.

The arrangements became more ornate and the dynamics more
emphatic. There were further contributions from members of Fairport Convention, as well as from the Velvet Underground's John
Cale, who would later record a short series of albums for Island. Cale
happened to be in the studio working on the mixes for the German
singer Nico's *Desertshore* album and was besotted when Joe played
him what he was up to with Drake. He immediately wanted to meet
Nick; when he did, they instantly bonded, although no one was ever
quite sure where and how.

The songs on *Bryter Layter* were timeless, but the pop-friendly
production was of its time, when folk and blues entered a baroque
stage because of studio techniques and the use of unusual instruments. Perhaps if we had released a couple of tracks as singles, there
might have been an increase in awareness, but we never did, not even
"Northern Sky," where Cale adds to the song's beauty by playing
Hammond organ, celeste, and piano.

Like Bob Marley, albeit not on the same scale, Nick is posthumously so revered that it's hard to come to grips with how much of

a struggle it was to find his listenership. Maybe a single could have been the hook that was needed, or we should have devised some sort of marketing strategy to sell Nick Drake to the masses. But such strategies seemed blasphemous for such fragile music. And we were prepared to take our time, and let Nick take his. It was a rhythm we were used to at Island.

Bryter Layter sold modestly, enough for us to be happy to continue the relationship. But Nick was frustrated that the amount of love and care he put into the music seemed to be going nowhere. James Taylor was selling millions of albums. Island's own Cat Stevens was dominant in the charts. Neil Young's *Harvest* proved there was a large audience for pensive, delicately wrought songs.

Nick started to take it personally. He was only twenty-one, which is easy to forget because his songs had so much wisdom and perspective, and Joe's enthusiasm for his music and belief that he would be a success made Nick think it was going to happen. When it didn't, he was confused and even angry. He didn't want to be famous, but I think he wanted to feel his songs were reaching people and in some way helping them. There had to be a *reason* for what he was doing.

In 1970, Joe Boyd was feeling burnt out from his own bewilderment that Nick wasn't more successful and was also being uncooperative when it came to publicity. The following year, he sold Witchseason to Island. He moved to Los Angeles to work for Warner Brothers, coordinating the soundtracks for films such as *Deliverance*, *McCabe and Mrs. Miller*, and *A Clockwork Orange*. He made a feature-length documentary about Jimi Hendrix and had the idea that he would become a film director in Hollywood. It was too good an opportunity to miss, but it certainly changed things for the musicians who were used to being looked after by Joe. In a way, he had been the leader of a movement, and now he had bailed on it. Nick took Joe's move especially badly.

There was no difference to Nick financially; we paid him a weekly stipend to cover his basic living costs. But Joe was his main point of contact, someone who gave him the stability that helped him deal (sometimes) with the promotional side of the music business.

Nick did one interview in total with a music paper, a short piece in *Sounds* that inevitably began, as though this were all there was to say, "Nick Drake is a shy, introverted folk singer who is not usually known to speak unless it is absolutely necessary." Sometimes a myth forms whether you want it to or not.

Joe and Nick would talk on the phone, and Joe offered advice and help, but it wasn't the same. I personally didn't have what Joe did in terms of being able to provide the emotional and psychological support Nick needed. We loved Nick at Island, but we didn't do a very good job of understanding what he was going through and how we could help. In my English (as opposed to Jamaican) way, I believed that it wasn't my business to ask Nick about his feelings.

It wasn't an era when people discussed or even acknowledged mental-health issues or depression. The unforgiving music business regarded such issues as a weakness, or even as self-indulgence—which made Nick's suffering still more difficult and necessary to hide. Nick was ashamed of his fragile state, fearful that Joe and I would lose our faith in him. Which was never going to happen, but he was mentally and physically deteriorating so quickly.

Nick's life seemed to get darker and more cryptic, the songs not as much a defense or remedy for his problems; but as far as we were concerned, he was drifting away and needed professional help to deal with some personal problems. After visits to psychiatrists who put him on medication that in addition to his own forms of self-medication created new problems, he would disappear for long periods of time, creating various mysteries he would vanish into.

I suppose the naïve, simplistic response of those of us working on the music at the time was that this was all part of the natural turbulence of a tortured artist, and he'd soon show up with some new music, keen to get back to work.

My solution, and Joe's as well, was for Nick to write some more songs and make another album. He was thinking of new songs; his head was full of music, even if it didn't materialize as easily as it once had. He always seemed happiest in the studio.

I suggested to Nick he use a house I had on the Spanish coast to clear his mind of disabling distractions and finish writing what was in his head. For me, moving somewhere else, somewhere outside London, was a way to beat the blues; I didn't fully appreciate that Nick's problem was more to do with what Churchill called "the black dog." Blackness was crowding Nick's consciousness, not a passing case of the blues, of being a bit down in the dumps.

The trip did help a little, if only with his music. He called John Wood at Sound Techniques and said he wanted to record some new songs. He was losing trust in people, but he still trusted John. And I had made it clear to John that if Nick ever wanted to record anything, please go ahead and get it done and we'd sort out the details later.

I don't know if it was a conscious reaction against the lushness of *Bryter Layter*, but Nick didn't want these new songs to be arranged and dressed up. He was very adamant about that—no strings, no nothing. My guess is that he didn't want anyone to come in and try to boost him up as Joe had, encouraging him that he was going to make a fantastic record that everyone would love and would sell loads. None of that had happened, and he'd decided it never would.

Nick and John worked together at Sound Techniques in the sort of isolation that was very unusual when records were made—especially at Island, where we encouraged people to wander in and out of the studio and add to the energy and vibe.

No one knew what they were up to. John found the time in his busy schedule to record Nick as quickly as he could, in case Nick changed his mind, which meant working late at night. Nick barely opened his mouth apart from when he sang. He played John the songs he'd written in the sequence he wanted in the early hours of the morning, as if the best time to start listening to them was a minute after midnight.

Inside a couple of intense, concentrated days, they recorded eleven songs that on the album would last less than half an hour—just Nick and his guitar, with a short solitary piano overdub added later on the title track, "Pink Moon."

These new Nick Drake songs were about passing into nothingness, about fading away. But even with Nick's obvious problems, no one believed he himself was as resigned and lost as the character singing the songs. His lyrics were surely just words, dark, beautiful words. We never appreciated how much courage it took him to write them and sing them.

There are many stories about what happened next. How he made a rare visit to the Island offices to deliver his album and made it no farther than reception before leaving. Or that he asked the receptionist to pass the tapes on to me, and that I, not sure what the package was, opened it only a couple of days later.

The way I remember it was that I was called down to reception because Nick Drake wanted to see me. This was out of the blue. He sat there, looking very morose and deep within himself, even less talkative than usual. He was holding a seven-inch tape, unlike the usual twelve-inch tape that albums were then recorded on, and he told me that he was there to hand in his new album. He didn't make much of a fuss of this fact, so neither did I.

I had always told him that whenever he was in the mood, he could go ahead and record in the studio, and I would cover the costs later as an advance. I asked him how much *Pink Moon* had cost. He mumbled, "Five hundred pounds." I wrote Nick a check there and then.

We chatted a bit more, or rather, I chatted, asking him how he was doing and what he was up to. He just shrugged. It was very strange, his behavior bordering on catatonia more than shyness or awkwardness. Then he left, and I never saw him again.

However it happened, it was an unusual way for the master tapes of a new album to be delivered to the label. It was Nick's way of having control over what was so important to him—there was nothing in between his having recorded it in the quiet of night, with John Wood and his carefully placed microphones, and his handing it over to the head of his record company. However ill Nick was, however incapable he was of communicating with people, he had reduced the process of making an album to a rare, unfiltered essence, something old-fashioned and artisanal.

John said the two nights of recording had taken everything out of Nick. After *Pink Moon*'s completion, he wandered off into the distance and we lost touch with him. He left us to prepare the artwork, and we sent out Keith Morris to find and photograph him.

Keith had taken the amazing photo of Nick on the back cover of *Five Leaves Left*, leaning against a brick wall as a commuter rushed past him as though he weren't there. This time, Keith took Nick to Hampstead Heath, and he found him so remote, so lost inside himself, it was truly as though he wasn't there. In those final photos, Nick looks somewhere between human and ghostly. He left behind no appearances on television, no radio interviews, and few memories of any live performances.

Island issued a heartfelt, passive-aggressive press release for *Pink Moon* written by our in-house press officer, Dave Sandison, that was almost like a short story about the strange, sad life of Nick Drake, waxing lyrical about "his weird little smile, half-mocking, half-bewildered," and bemoaning that Island had lost touch with him.

We turned the press release into a full-page ad in the music papers, more a form of anti-promotion than any coherent campaign, basically implying: "His first two albums haven't sold a shit, but if we carry on releasing them, maybe one day someone in authority will stop to listen to them properly and agree with us, and maybe a lot more people will get to hear Nick Drake's incredible songs and guitar playing. And maybe they'll buy a lot of records and fulfill our faith in Nick's promise."

In the end, this was the only way we knew how to tell Nick how much we valued him.

Remarkably, thinking about how lauded the album is now, *Pink Moon* sold the least of Nick's three albums. It's hard to fathom what people weren't getting then, apart from a select few critics who were already realizing the enchanting power of these subtly intricate songs. When I negotiated the Witchseason deal with Joe before he left for Los Angeles, he was very keen on inserting a clause in the contract that no matter how poor his sales, Nick Drake must never be deleted from the catalogue. He was convinced that it wasn't Nick who was out of step with the times but the rest of the world.

I may well have argued with Joe about this clause, as I haggled over contractual details with him even if just for the sake of it. But the truth is, I realized it was a great, farsighted idea as soon as he suggested it, and no one would have thought of it other than Joe, always dedicated to saving important music threatened by fashion and the quick turnover of pop music. He told me that he understood I would never think of deleting Nick's albums, but you never knew—I might get run over by a bus tomorrow, and so it needed to be in the contract.

The music of Nick Drake would not be allowed to disappear the way that Nick Drake himself did, dying in 1974 at twenty-six, his deep, enigmatic personal troubles finally pulling him under. Joe and John Wood had tried to start another record, but Nick couldn't muster the energy he had when he recorded *Pink Moon*, as temporary as that motivation was. The world around him, and the people in it, were becoming less relevant to him.

Throughout the 1970s, '80s, and '90s, Joe's request to not delete his albums proved an enduring way of keeping Nick alive even as he remained obscure, discovered occasionally by new fans via a compilation or boxed set. When vinyl gave way to CDs, the monthly sales of Nick's albums sometimes slipped into the single figures, well below the threshold for deletion. Like a great book that has an influence beyond its commercial value, the three albums stayed in print.

When I sold Island Records to PolyGram at the end of the 1980s, they had a characteristically nasty corporate policy where if any Island title didn't meet a minimum sales target in any one month, it was automatically culled. I negotiated my way out of that clause by demanding that I had to approve any potential Island deletions. In that, I remained faithful to Joe's original desires and our shared belief that eventually an audience would discover Nick Drake.

It took until the twenty-first century for Nick's break to come. A Boston ad agency was working on a TV spot for Volkswagen. It was originally set to feature a moody eighties song by the Church or the Cure, until one of the creative team remembered a purer, eerier song by Nick Drake that would fit perfectly under the visuals. In the ad, which first aired in 1999, an attractive, racially mixed group of young people ride under a cloudless, starry sky in a Cabrio convertible while the song "Pink Moon" plays. The kids in the car pull up at a party, which seems too rowdy, too coarse, for the purity of the night they are enjoying. With a wordless exchange of glances, they decide amongst themselves that they want more of the drive, of their moonlit togetherness, of the music. Nick Drake takes them away from their original destination and back into the unknown.

Within weeks, Nick finally made the move from obscure to popular. There was a sense of betrayal amongst some of his cult followers who felt that what was precious had been spoiled, annoyed that their personal treasure had been shared with the world, that the *Pink Moon* CD now featured a sticker that said "As Heard on the VW Commercial." But of course, such attention was what Nick had always wanted, what he thought he deserved. He was a romantic who also stubbornly believed that his songs deserved to reach as many people as possible. And it took the kind of sophisticated marketing strategy that just wasn't around in the seventies to find a way to reach an audience.

"Time Has Told Me," the opening song of Nick's first album, *Five Leaves Left*, was our original attempt to introduce Nick Drake to a wide audience; we put it on our 1969 sampler *Nice Enough to Eat,* between Traffic's "40,000 Headmen" and King Crimson's "21st Century Schizoid Man." With a wisdom beyond his years, Nick sang about how he was prepared to let time and circumstance play themselves out. "Someday," he sang, "our ocean will find its shore."

It proved an important Island mantra. We were never about quick fixes. We wanted our music to be forever.

JOE BOYD AND John Martyn didn't have the same close relationship as Joe and Nick. Joe wasn't so sure about John, as a human being or a writer, and their relationship was edgy. He also felt that John had barged into his working relationship with the singer-songwriter Beverley Kutner—later John's wife—which was very special to him. Joe felt that John was hogging the limelight from Beverley and treating her merely as a muse. When John met Beverley, *she* was the one with the more promising career.

Beverley had been recording since 1966, the first act signed to Deram, the future home of David Bowie and Cat Stevens. She had been romantically close to Davy Graham, Bert Jansch, and Paul Simon, and was on the Simon and Garfunkel *Bookends* album. Through Simon, she made an appearance at the 1967 Monterey Pop Festival, on the same bill as Otis Redding, Jimi Hendrix, and the Who.

John, still only twenty and winningly baby-faced, had met Beverley, a year older, when she supported Jackson C. Frank at his Chelsea College of Art performance. She asked John if he would play some backing guitar on an album she was making with Witchseason, by then a part of Island. They soon married, and the project evolved into a John and Beverley Martyn album. Joe initially thought that collaborating as a duo might bring out the best of each of them and imagined them as folk's golden couple.

Still, Joe already had Nick Drake, so John wasn't as interesting to him as Beverley. And whereas Nick wasn't at all competitive with musicians and colleagues, Joe and John were, and they butted heads. Beverley got caught up in that, and John took over Beverley, prying her away from Joe and, in Joe's eyes, stifling her talent and career. I think that Joe, early on, spotted something ominous about John's waywardness and nastiness: the self-destructive, unpleasant darkness that was then largely buried beneath his charming, gregarious nature.

John and Beverley, now living together with her young son, recorded four songs at Sound Techniques in London; these were successful enough for them to relocate to Woodstock in rustic Upstate New York, which seemed to be the center of the music world at that point. Dylan and the Band's *Basement Tapes* had been made nearby, along with the Band's *Music from Big Pink*, one of John's major new influences. Newly married, in a way on their honeymoon, the young couple took easily to the counterculture musical colony: Hendrix was a neighbor, Dylan lived down the road, and their new friend Levon Helm, of the Band, introduced them to an array of new influences on their music. *Stormbringer!*, their 1970 album, reflected their new sound.

John was making his move from acoustic guitar to electric, featuring his first use of the Echoplex tape-loop delay unit that would soon become a signature of his sound. There was an idiosyncratic cosmic Celtic swing to this music, a loose-limbed, countrified version of what he found so fascinating about the Incredible String Band.

Joe and John had their disagreements during *Stormbringer!*'s recording, but nothing too destructive. By the time the Martyns were making their second album, *The Road to Ruin*, back at Sound Techniques, however, John was trying Joe's patience. John thought the recording lacked spontaneity and featured too many prissy overdubs. He didn't care for Joe's fastidiousness. John liked to move quickly.

At this point, Joe withdrew from Witchseason, and John and Beverley's musical partnership dissolved, if not their marriage, which nonetheless was volatile. John was never keen on the politics of the music business, and he was not happy when Island bought Witchseason.

Despite that, I was pleased to be reunited with John. I'd loved *Stormbringer!* and felt it was everything I had hoped for. He was becoming one of those artists who always surprised me, and whom I really wanted everyone to know about. But John somehow got it in his head that Island was ignoring him. Sometimes, picking a fight was just his way of getting motivated.

Feeling undervalued, he made a solo album, 1971's *Bless the Weather*, which was him carrying on where his first two solo albums left off, back to his spontaneous way of working, but now with an electronic twist—a sound that was within reach of Weather Report and Terry Riley as much as any folk music.

Bless the Weather led to *Solid Air* in 1973, which led the same year to *Inside Out*: a trio of classic, critically revered albums where John moved through different states of music as the songs became more ambient and abstract. His voice got rougher, which he liked because he thought that his voice was too pretty when he started out.

They were all albums about how he was feeling at the time, who he was working with, where he was living, how much he was drinking, the stresses and strains of his marriage, and the guilt he felt as he toured his music and Beverley was stuck at home looking after the children. Artistically, there was a liberating irreverence about the way John merged styles. It didn't exactly make him a best-seller—he was always wilfully straying somewhere else from where musical fashion was—but it made his reputation as a spirited pioneer.

Solid Air's title track, defining this unique, experimentally sensual John Martyn sound, was about one of his best friends, Nick Drake. By 1973, Nick was spending more time with his parents; he would die the following year. They were total opposites, Nick and John. Nick became more withdrawn when he was down, whereas John wanted to smash the walls down. But they connected through playing and listening to music, and talking about it. John couldn't bear seeing Nick drift off miserably into the distance and wrote a song he hoped Nick would hear and then feel motivated by. It was both a love song and an angry song.

I still believed John could be a successful major artist. No doubt we had been a bit erratic in promoting him. But the friendly chaos of Island ensured that an artist like John Martyn could find the space to grow.

We decided to release a live album of a concert at Leeds University where John was joined by Danny Thompson on bass and John Stevens, from the Spontaneous Music Ensemble, on drums. We let John design, press, and distribute the LP himself as an official bootleg. John and Beverley sold it as a limited edition of 10,000 pressings from their home in Hastings, numbering each one, loving how money kept arriving in the post. Sometimes he stood at the front door of his house, on a cliff overlooking the English Channel, and sold a few to passersby, running a do-it-yourself indie label years before the punks.

BY THE END of 1975, as his music matured so beautifully, John's life was a mess. He was drinking heavily and with fierce purpose, sometimes falling over during performances and insulting the audience. He'd been working almost nonstop since 1967. He'd lost a couple of close friends in Nick Drake and Free's Paul Kossoff. The sparkle in his eyes gradually diminished.

Eventually John admitted to me that he wasn't feeling well. He needed help. I didn't want another tragedy after Nick and Paul. There seemed to me a natural solution to the stresses and strains John was feeling. In 1976, I suggested to him that he go to Jamaica. He could stay at Strawberry Hill, my place near Kingston, and just do nothing until he found he wanted to do *something*—even if that something was just going home to his family.

It didn't seem obvious to others, to send John out to the island, a hard-drinking, intimidating, and self-destructive Scot crammed with pent-up frustration. But I missed the early John, the poet and light-hearted knave, and I wanted him to go somewhere he could battle whatever demons he had to in order to get his music-making back on track.

Not long after John arrived in Jamaica, I introduced him to the flamboyant producer Lee "Scratch" Perry. I took him down to Scratch's house in Kingston, in the garden of which stood Black Ark Studios. I had a feeling John and Scratch would get on. They were both possessed of a certain kind of mischievous glee. I didn't necessarily think the two of them meeting up would lead to music, but I thought it might spark John, relight his fire.

After a while, working with musicians in various genres, you come to understand how one form of energy can mix and merge with another. John and Scratch got along well and were a good mix. If you think of Rastas as mystical yogis, then John got some special healing, the kind of healing Scratch only offered to those he considered special. "Anything John requested, I was okay with," he said. By contrast, Scratch had no particular love for me. He tolerated me for a time, until he didn't.

John and Lee made very different music but approached it the same way and used similar techniques and equipment. They were both into enhancing sound by using valves, transistors, and loudspeakers. They both used rhythm boxes and the Echoplex delay system. John wanted to play the guitar as soulfully as Pharoah Sanders played the saxophone, and the Echoplex allowed him to achieve liftoff. He used the gadget kind of the way old bluesmen used bottlenecks and country artists used Dobros, creating a shimmery resonance and building up layers of sound. A bit of gear and a whole lot of ingenuity. This was right up the alley of Scratch, a kindred spirit, who liked to boast that he could put water into a bottle and make it sound like a piano.

What Scratch was doing with sonic space and rhythmic momentum—his spaced-out, Echoplexed take on ska and reggae—

was called dub; what John was doing was the same sort of thing, in his way: creating music where outer and inner space met.

Putting John and Scratch together was perhaps one of the most irresponsible things I have ever done. It could easily have led to violence. John is reputed to have headbutted one of his best friends, Danny Thompson, and their drinking sessions sometimes devolved into bloody fistfights or clumsy wrestling matches. It seemed possible that if Scratch and John went too far in their friendship, they might kill each other. For a long time, the very mention of John's name in certain recording studios around Kingston was enough to rattle staff and locals who'd come face-to-face with the Scottish brawler side of him.

Yet putting John with Scratch was also one of the smartest decisions I ever made—and I wouldn't have been able to get away with it if I'd had a boss to report to.

When John returned from Jamaica, we set to work making his next album, which he called *One World*. "No passport, no borders," John said. It was one of my favorite experiences ever in terms of producing a record. For many, 1977 was the year of punk and the end of the kind of progressive, album-oriented music that had been Island's speciality. Maybe *One World* was my punk reaction to punk—my rebellion—in that, as the cities were on fire and revolution was in the air, I decided to make a reflective John Martyn album in the countryside.

Perhaps the germ of the idea for recording *One World* in the middle of nowhere was when Dave Mason of Traffic announced to me that he wanted to buy a house in the country. This was the kind of thing that the punks were rebelling against, the notion that rock musicians had become an aloof new aristocracy, separate from their listeners and fans.

The Home Counties, as the counties around London are called, were where the new rock musicians with their new money tended to find their new houses, which were also places to write and to invite friends and colleagues. Dave was looking in the Royal County of

Berkshire, so-called because it contains Windsor, where one of the Queen's castles is located.

I tagged along with Dave to look at a place he had found. This was when I had a Rolls-Royce—another aristocratic, new-rock-star trope loathed by the punks. But hear me out. In 1973, the cost of petrol shot up, and lots of Rolls-Royce owners were selling off their cars. You could get them for a pittance. So I bought a beautiful 1961 Rolls-Royce Silver Cloud. So much space, and so quiet, the seats themselves like clouds, the steering wheel thin and elegant, perfect for gliding through the countryside. The loudest noise, even as you were traveling at sixty miles an hour, was the clicking of the electric clock.

A Rolls-Royce certainly makes a statement, and I suppose I was in the mood to make that kind of statement—it was a time when it was suddenly rock-and-roll to drive a Rolls. Members of the Moody Blues and the Who had them. Johnny Cash was given one by ABC in America as a thank-you for the success of his variety show. John Lennon and Yoko Ono turned theirs into a psychedelic statement.

Dave was only too happy to have me accompany him as his chauffeur and fellow real-estate scout. The property we went up to see was an old school that had been converted into a manor. I didn't think it looked too promising because the windows were too high. I told Dave this, and he got a little upset. But you shouldn't buy an old school if the windows are too high. This was one of my roles as a label boss in the seventies, I guess. Giving property advice to musicians.

On the way back from seeing this school, we were driving along a quiet, winding country lane near Reading, and we passed a small series of lakes. It was very calm and seemed miles from anywhere. I could see a house nearby with a lovely thatched roof. There was a driveway from the main road, so I decided to zip in and have a look. You drive a Rolls-Royce, you get a little curious, and you feel you can just turn up and check things out.

Dave, still a little miffed that I didn't appreciate his converted school, wasn't keen on the detour. But there was something about the house that attracted me. I loved the location and the fact that this small, disc-shaped piece of land was surrounded by a lake, so that it was itself—appositely, given the name of my company—an island. The only thing connecting it to the outside was the driveway.

Also, even though it seemed so isolated, it was just south of Junction 12 on the M4, the main western motorway in and out of London, conveniently close to Heathrow Airport. It was in the village of Theale, which had been an ancient administrative unit since before the Domesday Survey of 1086. Close to the Bath Road, Theale had been famous for its coaching inns, and the notorious highwayman Dick Turpin was said to have hidden many times in a secret room at the Old Lamb Inn, which dates to 1487.

As though dictated by fate, I learned that the house was for sale: an old Tudor pile known as Woolwich Green Farm, with stables, barns, outbuildings, and a large garden leading right down to the lakeshore. And it came equipped with a housekeeper-caretaker from the previous regime.

I managed to buy Woolwich Green Farm in an auction and set about fixing it up as a home and a place where musicians could come for rest, recreation, and recording. We converted the dining room and one of the barns into "studios" of a kind. The housekeeper stayed on for a while and made the switch from looking after an elderly farmer to looking after young rock musicians. She was eccentric enough herself and liked a whiskey or two, and, very quickly, we had to ask her to leave.

JOHN MARTYN LOVED recording *One World* at Theale. So did I. The setup ensured that John was always on hand and never wandered off and got up to whatever he might get up to. On the rare occasion that he did go off to the local pub, he never stayed long, as he loved the vibe of the house.

He was calmer and more at peace after his time in Jamaica, if still a little on edge. He badly missed Nick and Paul, and his marriage to Beverley was on the rocks. But we had created a bucolic setting where, artistically, he could be at his best. I had Island's mobile studio brought to Theale in July 1977, and we set it up with the expert help of the ex-Island house engineer Phill Brown, who had started out as a low-level tape op and later went on to engineer sessions for Bob Marley and the Wailers, Mott the Hoople, and Led Zeppelin—a classic Island trajectory.

Phill placed the mobile between the old barn and a stable block I had converted into a studio flat. We used the studio flat as the base for John, and Phill ingeniously set up a PA system that pointed out across the lake, so that John's guitar-playing floated across the water. Phill carefully arranged the microphones to pick up this lovely, floaty guitar sound, as well as the lapping of the water and other ambient sounds.

We turned the whole area into an open-air studio. I could do some business in the morning while the equipment was being set up; then we'd start work in the middle of the afternoon, and work through the night into the early hours. It turned out to be a great way to record John. In the early hours of the morning, there would be the sounds of geese honking and the dull roar of the first flights coming into Heathrow.

It became a world within a world where John could flourish as a creator. Word got out, and our musician friends started showing up, sometimes unannounced: Steve Winwood; John's old mate Danny Thompson; Andy Newmark, the drummer from Sly and the Family Stone. And then they would add some of their own brilliance to the proceedings.

Scratch turned up too. He was in England at the time to do some work with Bob Marley. He loved where John had gone musically after his time in Jamaica and helped out on a song called "Big Muff," tickled by the title, adding a few made-up words to it, dancing so much he sometimes fell over. The album became a great example of the

My mother, Blanche Lindo, as a young woman in Jamaica in the 1930s.
ISLAND TRADING ARCHIVE

My father, Joseph Blackwell, at Kingston Racecourse, Jamaica, 1930s.
ISLAND TRADING ARCHIVE

My mother with Ian Fleming, by the sea in Jamaica, which they both loved.
ISLAND TRADING ARCHIVE

Errol Flynn showing me how to live the life. ISLAND TRADING ARCHIVE

Noël Coward at his hideaway home in Jamaica on the Firefly Estate above Port Maria, which he bought from my mother.
NOËL COWARD ARCHIVE

1950s Kingston.
LENNOX SMILLIE/CAMERA PRESS LONDON

Ernest Ranglin, the guitar godfather, mid-1950s.
ISLAND TRADING ARCHIVE

It all started here. From 1959, the first Island Records release, the first record I produced, recorded at Ken Khouri's Federal Studios in Kingston.
ISLAND TRADING ARCHIVE

One of my earliest productions, by ska pioneer Laurel Aitken, released on R&B, an early version of Island.
ISLAND TRADING ARCHIVE

A Jamaican jukebox needing new music to keep people moving in the 1950s.
WAYNE TIPPETTS

Chinese-Jamaican businessman Leslie Kong of Beverly's—part of a strong Chinese influence on Jamaican music, an early investor in Island, and the first to record Bob Marley, in 1962.

On the set of *Dr. No* with Ursula Andress and Sean Connery in Jamaica 1962.

My mother with the original and best James Bond, Sean Connery, and Noël Coward, who certainly didn't want to be Dr. No.

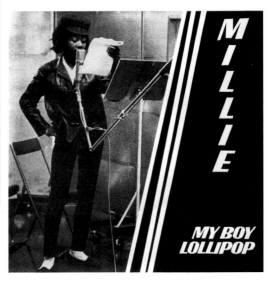

My first hit with the wonderful Millie,
released in May 1964, the record that
changed her life and mine.
ISLAND TRADING ARCHIVE

Clifton District,
Milk River P.O.,
Clarendon,
Jamaica, W.I.

12th March, 1963.

Mr. Christopher Blackwell,
c/o Island Records Ltd.,
108, Cambridge Road,
London, N.W. 6,
England.

Dear Mr. Blackwell,

I hereby give my full consent for my daughter,
Millicent Small, to go to England as a recording artist for
your Company.

Yours faithfully,

ELVY SMITH

The parental
permission I needed
at the time to make
great pop music. So
important to me I
ended up keeping
the letter and even
pinning it on my
bedroom wall.
ISLAND TRADING
ARCHIVE

The great Guy Stevens (mod-era) of The Scene, Sue, and Island, surrounded by the most important things in his life. GERED MANKOWITZ

At work in the studio, central London, May 1966.

EXPRESS/HULTON ARCHIVE VIA GETTY IMAGES

The first pink Island label design with eyeball, launched in 1967 for John Martyn's *London Conversation* album. ISLAND RECORDS

Island Studios, Basing Street, Notting Hill, London, mid 1970s, with the Island mobile recording studio parked outside. ADRIAN BOOT/ WWW.URBANIMAGE.TV

Chris Blackwell

Dressed up for a press photo, mid-1970s.
ISLAND RECORDS

One of Island's greatest debut albums, released, quietly, on July 3, 1969.
ISLAND RECORDS

The second Cat Stevens album for Island, released November 23, 1970, making him a pop star all over again.
ISLAND RECORDS

Free's third album, released June 26, 1970, featuring "All Right Now" with one of rock's greatest riffs.
ISLAND RECORDS

When albums were albums: Tony Wright's original six-sided 2D artwork for Traffic's fifth album released in November 1971, turning an album sleeve into a three-dimensional room.
ISLAND RECORDS

The first Roxy Music album, released on June 16, 1972—once I'd seen and loved the cover. ISLAND RECORDS

I was a producer of Jamaica's first ever feature-length film. It put reggae on the international map in 1972, as something more than music. ISLAND TRADING ARCHIVE

Lee "Scratch" Perry at the center of the universe, Ark Studios in Kingston, mid-1970s. He passed the Wailers sound onto me. ADRIAN BOOT/WWW.URBANIMAGE.TV

In 1990 with *The Harder They Come* director Perry Henzell, Toots Hibbert, and the film's star, Jimmy Cliff. ISLAND TRADING ARCHIVE

John Martyn's fourth Island album, released in February 1973, with the beautiful title track circling the beautiful spirit of Nick Drake. ISLAND RECORDS

JOHN MARTYN solid air

The original sleeve for the Wailers first Island album, released April 13, 1973, worked like a Zippo lighter, opening at the side to reveal the record. ISLAND RECORDS

Reggae was the funkiest, so we made sure "Funky" went before Kingston for the title of this collection of early Maytals singles, released in March 1975. ISLAND RECORDS

Toots & the Maytals — Funky Kingston

It was almost bought by Bob Marley, but I ended up owning and loving, to this day, Ian Fleming's Goldeneye. ISLAND TRADING ARCHIVE

Being inspired in the 1970s by Ahmet Ertegun, the Record Man, cofounder of Atlantic Records, and one of my heroes. ISLAND TRADING ARCHIVE

A favorite of many: Compass Point Studios, founded in 1977, ten miles west of Nassau capital of the Bahamas. ADRIAN BOOT/WWW.URBANIMAGE.TV

Compass Point—part state-of-the-art recording facility, part artist retreat, part island paradise. COOKIE KINKEAD/ISLAND OUTPOST IMAGES

At the Compass Point Studio 1 desk in 1981 with engineer Steven Stanley (right). ADRIAN BOOT/WWW. URBANIMAGE.TV

The mighty Black Uhuru, ready for action. Featuring Sly and Robbie on, naturally, drums and bass—the timeless rhythm of Compass Point. ADRIAN BOOT/WWW. URBANIMAGE.TV

A rare picture of me with Bob Marley, along with Junior Marvin of the Wailers and Jacob Miller of Inner Circle. NATHALIE DELON

At Bob Marley's last London show at the Crystal Palace Bowl, June 7, 1980, the day I first met U2. MURPHY/HERSHMAN/FIFTY-SIX HOPE ROAD MUSIC LTD.

The mysteriously graceful essence of the Compass Point Studios sound was captured on the second Grace Jones album we made there, released April 29, 1981. ISLAND RECORDS

Tom Tom Club's debut album, released October 1981—the rhythm section as artists, coming to play at Compass Point. ISLAND RECORDS

The first worldwide release for King Sunny Ade in 1982, when he seemed destined to win western hearts as the next Third World superstar after Bob Marley. ISLAND RECORDS

Tom Waits's magical first Island album, released in August 1983. It had become our job to release albums like this when it seemed no one else was going to. ISLAND RECORDS

The first U2 album to reach number one in America, three weeks after it was released on March 9, 1987. ISLAND RECORDS

Promoting go-go, the "lost hip-hop," in 1985. Sometimes we were right even when it all went wrong. ISLAND RECORDS

Me in the moment with Bono at the London launch party for U2's *Achtung Baby* in 1991. ISLAND TRADING ARCHIVE

Baaba Maal's third solo album, where the third world meets the first world, released on Island's Mango subsidiary in 1992. ISLAND RECORDS

In Miami in the early 1990s, planning a new hotel. COOKIE KINKEAD/ISLAND OUTPOST IMAGES

Before: South Beach Miami in a state of decline in the late 1980s.
ISLAND TRADING ARCHIVE

After: South Beach Miami, once I had helped return the great art deco hotels like the Marlin and Tides to their former glory. COOKIE KINKEAD/ISLAND OUTPOST IMAGES

My wife, Mary Vinson (middle), gathering material and ideas in West Africa in the early 1990s. ADRIAN BOOT/ WWW.URBANIMAGE.TV

At home in March 2021 with two of my favorite things; my own rum and a backgammon set. DAVID YELLEN

The island rhythm of GoldenEye.
ADRIAN BOOT/WWW.URBANIMAGE.TV

essential spirit of Island Records, how far the label had come since Millie, since Traffic, since the Jamaican years.

I suppose that, after his time in Jamaica, I was producing John as if he were a Jamaican artist. He had always professed to me that he was "a funky, not a folkie." And these songs wouldn't have happened without him getting up to whatever he'd gotten up to in Jamaica with Scratch.

Released at the end of 1977, in a suitably symbolic, impressionist sea-blue sleeve by Island's house designer, Tony Wright, *One World* was about as far away from punk as you could get, and from any other musical phenomenon of that year, such as David Bowie's albums *Low* and *"Heroes"* and Donna Summer's futuristic Giorgio Moroder–produced single "I Feel Love." But it was, in its way, every bit as contemporary and influential.

For one wonderful week, *One World* entered the top one hundred. But just one week. It was an Island album. It would take its time finding its audience.

JOHN BEING JOHN, our bliss was not to last. He reverted to his belligerent ways and, a little later, departed Island for Warner. In 1984, unhappy with that move, he returned to Island, and we tried to recapture some of our old magic at my Compass Point Studios in the Bahamas. Alas, the cheap rum and readily available cocaine, and the fact his terrible twin Scratch was often around as well, laid waste to that plan.

The drugs took him over. John got even harder and angrier than he'd been before. I always harbored hope that he would sober up and clean up. But he didn't. His life got rougher still. There were money problems, domestic-violence problems, and health problems. His right leg was amputated below the knee, and at one point he filled out to nearly three hundred pounds.

It's a measure of how gifted and respected he was that he was embraced near the end of his life as an elder statesman of British music. John was always the musician's musician, more for what he did during the 1970s than in the '80s and '90s. In his later years, he was like an aging jazz musician who was not as innovative as he once had been but, in his own wounded way, was at ease with how his life had turned out.

I never saw John again after the 1980s. Eventually, like Nick Drake and Paul Kossoff, he faded away. John died in 2009 at the age of sixty, not long after receiving an OBE. The John Martyn I choose to remember is the one I sat with in the quiet, bewitching, windless early hours at Theale, surrounded by all sorts of life and sound.

There's the beginning of a hint that the sun is starting to rise and bring some soft misty light to the proceedings. Phill is playing and recording endless takes of John playing his guitar that become something even more exquisite because of the way they bounce off the lake. There's a conga player over by the barn who seems to be juggling. The geese start honking.

I would joke how it was like a circus. We had run off to join the circus. It was where we had both wanted to be all along. We looked at each other, and I think we both had the realization in a state where we were quite capable of reading each other's minds that this was one of those times when life was as good as it was ever going to get. This was what we were meant to do. This was where we were meant to be. Yesterday had done its thing and tomorrow would be what it would be. We both burst out laughing.

In one way, that was truly the last time I ever saw him. Some things are meant to be, and some things are not meant to be.

CHAPTER SIX

MEETING CAT STEVENS

I originally went out of my way to avoid meeting Steven Demetre Georgiou. Son of a Greek Cypriot and his Swedish wife, he was a fan of Nina Simone, Bob Dylan, jazz, blues, and musical theater. He'd grown up in a flat above his family's café, the Moulin Rouge, in the center of the theater district in London's West End; his bedroom overlooked the stage door of the Prince's Theatre, eventually known as the Shaftesbury Theatre.

It was an area that had become the heart of the pop music business—by the mid-sixties, the café's neighbors included Dick James's Northern Songs, Andrew Loog Oldham's Immediate Records, and a great record shop specializing in folk, blues, and jazz. Music was everywhere around his home, and in his bedroom soaking it all in, watching the actors arrive to appear in musicals like *Hair* and *West Side Story*, he started to write his own songs.

In 1966, aged eighteen, having already written "The First Cut Is the Deepest"—a big hit a year or so later for P. P. Arnold—Steve caught the attention of the manager and producer Mike Hurst; he told Hurst that his name was Cat Stevens (a girlfriend at the art school where he studied had told him he had eyes like a cat).

I didn't like his music at all. His first single on Decca's trendy new Deram label in 1966 was about a dog, filled with a strange, jerky timpani-and-viola arrangement; the second jingly-jangly one was about a tailor, with another awkward, heavily orchestrated arrangement; and the third one, released in 1967, was about a gun and came with promotional photos of him carrying a revolver.

Inspired by Gershwin and Bernstein, he fancied writing musicals, and was working on one about Billy the Kid. He announced in the press that his hero was Sammy Davis Jr. His singles were all hits, but by the time of "I'm Gonna Get Me a Gun," Cat Stevens was on *Top of the Pops* dressed in Buddhist robes; there were photos of him in the music papers grinning inanely and wearing a holster with a gun in it, and I just thought he was a little mad.

After his second album, 1967's *New Masters*, at just twenty, depleted by a grueling, fast pop-star life and too much drinking and smoking, he had been struck down by tuberculosis and suffered a collapsed lung. He spent three months in the hospital, then a further nine months in bed convalescing. Which gave him plenty of thinking time.

Cat had also badly fallen out with his producer Mike Hurst over the ornate, hit-single-chasing arrangements. They were sounding increasingly desperate, and he was growing up quickly and finding the charts world less and less congenial. Listening to Tim Hardin, Joni Mitchell, and Van Morrison, he began performing regularly with just a guitar at Les Cousins amongst the more adventurous singers and guitarists finding their own folk music, and he wanted to strip away all the elaborate pop orchestras and anonymous session players Decca and Hurst had piled into his music.

Seeking to make records that sounded like him, he kept asking if he could play guitar on his own records, which didn't seem much to ask for. The clash between Cat's deeper feelings and Hurst and Deram's unsubtle approach was becoming extremely tense. He still dreamt of writing musicals, and wanted to build one around the Romanovs, called *Revolussia*.

My old friend William Pigott-Brown and his sidekick Mim Scala had formed Confederates Agency with Cat's new manager, the film and theater agent Barry Krost. It was another of Pigott-Brown's attempts to become something in the music industry—the agency's Rolls was lined with paisley silk, but they did have some good connections. Krost had put together the *Italian Job* film with Michael Caine and would eventually work closely with Sidney Poitier; with his background in theater, he encouraged Stevens's interest in musicals.

Mim started calling me all the time during 1969 to say that Cat was frustrated with Decca. His yearlong retreat as he recovered had made him much more thoughtful as a songwriter, and he couldn't face making more of those lightweight pop songs where he had no control over the production.

Mim said Stevens would love to move to Island, now that we were starting to work with the kinds of adventurous and independent English folk acts Cat had begun to identify with. I couldn't have been less interested. I could not get the image of those robes out of my head—I thought he had lost it. They kept calling even though I kept saying I wasn't interested. They told me he wanted to do musicals, but serious ones. I said, "I am not in the musical business, I'm in the record business." Eventually they just wore me down, and I reluctantly agreed to see him, just so I could get rid of him once and for all.

I had a small office at the top of this rather grand house my then-wife Josephine owned, which could give off quite an intimidating atmosphere to visitors. It was out of bounds to Josephine and the kids—whom I called "the livestock." I liked to keep myself to myself in there, and if they needed anything, they had to knock.

I suppose as a hybrid of white Jamaica and elusive English public school, I presented an unusual image to many in the business, and I came across unlike most other managers and record company bosses, whether the old-school type or the new breed looking after the Stones, the Who, and the Kinks. The music press didn't know what to make of me—my accent would be likened to that of a polite

BBC announcer and my manners described as immaculate, as if that was disturbing. Even my suede jacket and open-necked shirt caused comment—as in Jamaica, I was an insider who was still on the outside, working in my own way at my own pace.

My home office wasn't as deliberately informal as my Island offices, which were intended to put artists a little at ease, but then I was only meeting Cat so that Mim would stop calling me. I didn't for a moment consider it would go anywhere, so I met him there and not at Island.

Cat very carefully took his guitar out of its case and intently played me his first song. It was fine. A little intense. He was shy and innocent-sounding, but not Nick Drake shy and innocent, and he performed the song with more urgency and self-confidence than Nick ever showed.

I said something noncommittal because I still had zero interest. Still thinking of his press photos and those early hits, I just wanted to get it over with. There was a second song, and that was genuinely nice too. But nice wasn't enough for me.

Okay, I said, thinking of a way to tell him they weren't really what I was looking for. Maybe he could become a musical composer, like Leonard Bernstein. He played something else. He said the third song was from the Russian musical he was writing, and it was called "Father and Son." As soon as he sang the opening line, "It's not time to make a change," everything did change.

Perfectly simple, and perfectly lovely, it caught me by surprise. It might have been from his crazy dream of a musical, but it was clearly influenced by that lyrical and introspective singer-songwriter world that had inspired him to want to escape the heavy-handed Deram production.

He played it through in such a way that time seemed to stand still, and I started to notice his powerful dark eyes and something compellingly melancholy in his voice, which I suppose had been prematurely aged by his dreadful illness. The pop-star shenanigans began to fall away. When he finished, I immediately told him that I had absolutely no interest in a musical, but because of that one song I would like to sign him.

He was still signed to Decca, but he said he was very uncomfortable with the way they handled him and the sound of his music, especially now that the gaudy productions weren't even leading to chart hits. When he told me what the Decca deal was—of course it was bargain-basement—I said, "Well, I can match that and do a little better." He really wanted to come to Island, but he didn't know how get out of his Decca deal. I had an idea.

His A&R man was Dick Rowe, the executive who had famously passed on the Beatles—having been told about two bands by one of his scouts at Decca, the Beatles and Brian Poole and the Tremeloes, and wanting to sign only one of them, he plumped for the Tremeloes because they were based in London. (Still feeling raw, Rowe did get to sign the Rolling Stones, but even that never wiped out letting the Beatles slip through his fingers. But then I passed on Pink Floyd, because they seemed too boring, and Madonna, because I couldn't work out what on earth I could do for her as she seemed such a confident one-woman business. I had also missed seeing Dire Straits when they were looking for a deal because I was too busy talking at a club with friends upstairs while they played for me down below, not knowing I wasn't watching. They were not amused.)

I told Cat to tell Dick Rowe that he had come up with an idea for his next album that he really wanted to make: "It's going to be your masterpiece. You've set your heart on the concept. If you don't make this album, you will never make any more music. You'll quit the business. Tell Rowe that it absolutely requires an orchestra and a choir. The London Philharmonic would be your preferred choice, your only choice. It will need a large recording budget, but it is the only way to make your dream record."

Rowe and Decca thought it was an absurd idea and that Cat must have lost it, like I had when I saw him in robes on *Top of the Pops* singing about a gun. They let him go in a minute, and I did a deal with Barry Krost and signed him, giving him a contract with enough artistic freedom to satisfy his new desires.

I put him with Paul Samwell-Smith as the producer. Paul was the unsung if often aggressive bassist in the Yardbirds while the obvious guitar stars Eric Clapton and Jeff Beck passed through—Jimmy Page joined after he left, and the group morphed into Led Zeppelin—but his contribution to the sound and structure of their music was paramount. The Beck–Samwell-Smith five-piece Yardbirds that did "Shapes of Things" was definitely the most creative lineup.

Paul was always heading towards production—he was a coproducer and arranger of the last Yardbirds album he played on, taking very quickly to new studio possibilities, helping more than anyone else in the group to push their original blues-rock into something more psychedelic, even avant-garde. It made him think about recording more than playing bass, and fancying production more than constant touring.

He'd produced the first Renaissance album in 1969 for Island, which was the non–Led Zeppelin side of the Yardbirds, the folkier, trippier part, formed by founding members Keith Relf and Jim McCarty with Relf's younger sister Jane. It was beautiful, extremely ambitious, and anomalous, a lost Island Records masterpiece. There were all sorts of things going on, classical, jazz, prog, but without the music getting lost in itself—it was exquisite, authentic baroque in the way that the clumsy Cat Stevens Decca pop wasn't, and I thought it would be great to hear what Paul Samwell-Smith would do with Cat. That was one of my great rolls of the dice, although of course I had a hunch the odds were in my favor.

The two jelled as though they had been waiting for each other—coming from completely different directions but meeting at just the right place. That place was pretty much defined by the perfect first track, "Lady D'Arbanville," on the first Cat Stevens Island album, *Mona Bone Jakon*—with a Steve painting of a tearful dustbin on the cover, a hangover from when the record was called *The Dustbin Cried the Day the Dustman Died,* which luckily was too long to fit on the sleeve, and certainly didn't fit the nuanced, spacious album sound. "Lady D'Arbanville," elaborate, lush, but fantastically spare and emotionally serious, was at an almost exact opposite point to the overdone Cat Stevens of *Matthew and Son.* It was a top ten hit at the same time as "All Right Now" by Free, in June of 1970.

Paul's first great decision as producer was to hire the poetic fingerstyle guitarist Alun Davies, who had been in a group produced by Shel Talmy in the early 1960s and spent some time as a session musician for Fontana. His elegant, eloquent playing enhanced Cat's new style as much as Paul's sophisticated but unforced production did. It all meant that Cat had discovered his own version of folk rock that he had been looking for.

Cat could be troubled, tentative, gloomy, bitter, anguished, self-conscious; he could tell stories about death and loss like they were from imaginary musicals, and seem weary way beyond his twenty-one years. He was writing and singing as the changed survivor of a serious illness. But the sound and the arrangements were dreamy and delicate; the lavishness was extremely subtle and always supported what he was singing, never got in the way like before. Cat and Paul, and Cat and Alun, had found this great balance between confessional angst and elegantly presented, very accessible melody.

It didn't sell that well (the Island pattern), but Cat finally moved out of his parents' Shaftesbury Avenue home, and we put Cat and Paul—and Alun—together again for the next album, *Tea for the Tillerman.* Again, I just left them to it—sometimes I would get involved in the studio with an act, and sometimes my involvement would be just to put artist and producer together and then wait until they were finished.

With writers like Cat, whose work was always a matter of spiritual searching, knowing when to leave them alone can be as much a creative act as getting intimately involved. Before the album was finished, we gave Jimmy Cliff one of the songs, "Wild World," with Cat producing and playing piano, which gave Jimmy a top ten hit—and another helpful sign that a Jamaican singer could have a hit record without it seeming a novelty or connected to some craze or treated as from "the rest of the world."

A few months later, Paul and Cat brought the tapes for *Tillerman* to Basing Street for me to hear. They played the songs without the running order yet decided. They played the first song—it was great. Second song—great. The next three—great, great, great. Really great. I was thinking, *Well, they have played the highlights first, and now we are going to get the also-rans. Those first five are already enough for a great album.* The sixth song turned out to be what would be my favorite Cat Stevens song, "Where Do the Children Play," which became the opening song. All the songs were so good, and at the time I thought it was the best album Island had released.

A lot of other people thought so too. Cat Stevens went from supporting Traffic in the US, playing his American debut show in November 1970 at the Fillmore East in New York, to selling over three million copies there through his new American deal with A&M. Along the way, Joni Mitchell was coming to watch him perform, and Carly Simon supported him through five shows at the Troubadour in Los Angeles. Paul Samwell-Smith succeeded Eddie Kramer as Carly's producer. (Kramer had handled her debut and her second album, *Anticipation*, whose hit title track was about her nervously waiting to meet Cat, late for their first date; by the time he arrived, she'd gotten the beginning of a song. Cat would end up on the list of people "You're So Vain" might have been about, alongside David Cassidy and David Bowie.)

In America, they had no idea of pre-Island, Decca pop Cat Stevens. They came to him as though he were a brand-new act, and he fit into the world of James Taylor's *Sweet Baby James* and Neil Young's *After the Gold Rush* on those college campuses where sensitive souls were obsessing over other sensitive souls. There was an added unknown English exoticism and otherworldly melancholia to the comforting singer-songwriter style that really worked. He became big business, playing in vast arenas, and he got tangled up in an even bigger machinery than when he was having his Decca pop hits.

The albums that followed, *Teaser and the Firecat* and *Catch Bull at Four*, were not far behind, and with songs like "Moonshadow" and "Morning Has Broken" you could feel him trying to break away as a songwriter from the cynicism of the business, as though childlike innocence might be the answer. When Cat felt he was in a rut with Paul after four albums in two years, his signature sound becoming too predictable, I suggested he go to Jamaica and work on some ideas at Dynamic Studios in Kingston.

He produced *Foreigner* himself, musically moving into a foreign land, into rhythm and blues, with the first side taken up with the title track—and he was now living in Brazil as a tax exile. He'd gotten out of a rut, but ended up nowhere as fresh as he'd hoped, so for *Buddha and the Chocolate Box* he went back with Paul. The real problem wasn't the regular musical collaborators or his distinctive sound; it was the fact that he was no longer a pop star but a rock star—a massive, out-of-control business—playing cavernous venues, feeling adrift from himself. Steve Georgiou became anxious about the complicated impact Cat Stevens was having on his life.

He was getting restless. The issues and concerns about personal worth, spiritual meaning, creative complacency, and the fragility of love that always influenced his songs, together with an increasingly despairing discomfort with the role of superstar and the life of a rootless hotel-living tax exile, meant that within a few years he shed Cat Stevens.

We didn't know it at the time, but his last concert in the UK would be on December 20, 1975, at the Hammersmith Odeon. By June 1976, losing interest in the idea of Cat Stevens and being in any kind of spotlight, he finished touring altogether. He started reading the Qur'an after being given a copy as a gift by his brother David on his twenty-eighth birthday that July. It quickly started to occupy his thinking, giving him a new way of viewing the universe.

At the end of 1977 he formally embraced Islam, and on July 4, 1978, he officially changed his name to Yusuf Islam. He was now neither Steve nor Cat. He owed us one more album, and he made the final album he was contracted to deliver to Island, *Back to Earth*, with Samwell-Smith after some time apart. Alun Davies was still with him even at what turned out to be the end.

It was released as being by Cat Stevens, but Cat Stevens did not exist anymore, there was no one to promote the record, and it was clearly a muted and melancholy farewell. As he said at the time, he'd come down from the stars. Songwriting was replaced by Islam, and he thought about nothing else in much the same way that as a songwriter he had only thought about his music.

He disappeared from pop music completely, into another busy, serious life, which is maybe what a lot of his songs had always predicted. It was a brave move, and I think some in the business thought it was a passing phase, some eccentric, wealthy rock star indulgence, and that he would soon be back on stage and record. It would lead to an inevitable big-time comeback. Those people underestimated his sincerity.

To be honest, his embracing Islam was never a surprise to me, as definitive and unrepentant as it was. There were lots of rumors, but the truth was that faith had been his way of saving himself. Even though Cat Stevens died young, Yusuf Islam was strong in mind and body.

In 2006, almost thirty years after *Back to Earth*, he broke his public silence and recorded a new album, *An Other Cup*, and it was a lovely, warm, inspiring continuation of where he had been in the 1970s, full of faith and feeling but not obviously a religious or campaigning record. In person, he was as engaging, enthusiastic, and sure of himself as he had ever been. Why wouldn't he be? His voice, of course, remained the same, enriched by age and his newfound sense of inner peace, as it did three years later on his second mainstream album as Yusuf, *Roadslinger*.

I often thought during these years we could do something together again. When I asked him what name he wanted his music to be credited to if we did so, he said Yusuf Islam. I told him there was absolutely no chance of selling any records under that name. He asked me what name I thought he should use, and I said it had to be Cat Stevens.

His real name was Steven Georgiou, and Cat Stevens had always been his stage name, I pointed out. (In fact, I never called him Cat, those close to him always called him Steve.) He'd changed from his previous real name to a new real name—so for performance, why not keep his stage name? He didn't go for it. He reckoned it would be turning his back on Islam, although I didn't agree. He was always an overthinker. It was why he was such a great songwriter, and why he outgrew being one. Yusuf will occasionally sing Cat Stevens songs on TV, and what you still see and hear after all these years is young Steve using songs to work out what he believes in and why, and who he is and what he might do. The songs weren't an answer, but they helped him on his way.

CHAPTER SEVEN

MEETING BOB MARLEY

Bob Marley had been in Sweden for a few months in 1971 to write some music for an obscure film romance, *Vill Så Gärna Tro* ("Want So Much to Believe"), that the singer Johnny Nash was starring in. It was a decent way to make some cash, but when Bob was finished, he only had enough to get himself from Stockholm to London. The other two Wailers, Pete and Bunny, had helped him out on the project. For a time the three men had drifted apart, each pursuing his own direction. But by the end of 1972, they were all together again in London, looking to make some money, if only to get home to Kingston.

Bunny had heard talk of a man named Blackwell who distributed some of their records in the UK. Coxsone Dodd had mentioned to him that this Blackwell man had released their pre-reggae hits "Simmer Down" and "It Hurts to Be Alone" in the sixties. The truth is that I frequently took on dozens of Jamaican records as part of a deal, often just to get the one that I really wanted, and it wasn't like I was specifically, knowingly distributing those Wailers tracks; in any event, I don't think they sold particularly well. But Bunny had it in his head that I owed them some money. Maybe it was a Coxsone distraction: point the finger somewhere else.

Bunny's suspicion of the business was not unwarranted. For Jamaican musicians it was always a case of chasing royalties. There were constant financial disputes. It was said in Jamaica—you make a record, you get $20. If it sells a million, you still get $20. I remember that Millie, before we worked together, spent ages defiantly pursuing some royalties she felt were due to her. She traveled ten times the fourteen-hour, one-a-day bus journey from where she lived in St. Catherine Parish to producer Coxsone's place in Kingston looking for what was due to her. In the end when she tracked him down, they gave her ten shillings and sent her on her way.

I knew of the Wailers, but I wasn't fluent in their recorded work. Certainly, they were one of Jamaica's best vocal groups, always a step ahead of their peers, adapting their sound from ska as it slowed down into rocksteady. More recently, they had worked with the eccentric producer Lee "Scratch" Perry, who had tapped into something harder and more adventurous, adding a dark edge to the Wailers' smoothness. The work they did together in 1970 and '71 with Perry's Upsetters house band, including the brothers Carlton and Aston "Family Man" Barrett, was wonderful. Lee had done something very smart, stripping away their American influences to get to their Jamaican heart.

But the Jamaican radio stations were not playing their music. The principled Wailers didn't play the game; not for them the glad-handing of DJs and the greasing of people's palms. They were similarly ignored in America, where Black radio was booming with soul and funk but not reggae.

Yet here they were in my office one day in 1972, acting on Bunny's belief that I owed them, waiting to see what I could offer them. They showed up unannounced, plonking themselves down in my modest accommodations on the second floor at Basing Street, where there was a couch for people to sit on and a record player for me to listen to music.

They were immediately something else, these three—*strong* characters. They did not walk in like losers, like they were defeated by being flat broke. To the contrary, they exuded power and self-possession. Bob especially had a certain something; he was small and slight but exceptionally good-looking and charismatic. Bunny and Pete had a cool, laid-back nonchalance. I couldn't help but think of the serene, grounded Rastas who had brought me back to life in that little hut near Hellshire Beach.

As I took the measure of them, I thought, *Fuck, this is the real thing.* And their timing was good. Jimmy Cliff had just walked out on me a week earlier.

In 1965, at my suggestion, Jimmy had moved to England, where I thought I could broaden his appeal. With a band we put together called Shakedown Sound (featuring future members of Mott the Hoople), he played as an opening act for Jimi Hendrix and the Who, mixing ska and soul with some funky James Brown moves.

Jimmy was never completely sold on England. He found London cold, lonely, and much more racist than he'd imagined. When he first flew over from Jamaica to promote his records, I arranged for him to stay in some digs in the relatively pleasant, if somewhat down-at-heel neighborhood of Earl's Court. He had some trouble getting through customs at Heathrow Airport and eventually arrived at his destination late at night. When he woke up the next morning, his landlady was angry at the sight of him and told him in no uncertain terms that she didn't allow "coloreds" at her place, ordering him to get out within twenty-four hours. The following day, she spotted him on TV, in a television show audience as Nina Simone performed. Recognizing that Jimmy was a Somebody, she allowed him to stay.

But I was convinced that it was only a matter of time before he broke through. He was the only Jamaican artist signed directly to Island Records. I had cut back on hunting for Jamaican records to release on Island or its subsidiaries. We put out some of Jimmy's records through our Trojan label, because that seemed to be an easy way to connect him with an appreciative audience, but I was always looking for ways to make Jimmy work within the context of rock-era

Island. I even got him to sing a song by our Nirvana, "Waterfall," which became an unlikely hit in Brazil, if nowhere else.

Cat Stevens produced a Jimmy-sung version of his own "Wild World" that made the UK top ten in 1970, bolstering my belief in a commercial blend of pink-label Island and red-label Island, of rock and reggae.

But in 1971, I got carried away. Sensing I was so close to breaking Jimmy through, I sent him out to the famous Muscle Shoals studio in Alabama to record an album with the house band there, the Swampers. The resulting album, *Another Cycle*, sounded good to my ears, mixing his pure voice with expertly played country soul, but it appealed neither to Muscle Shoals aficionados nor to Jimmy Cliff fans. Instead of rating as a brilliant new hybrid, the record was considered a failed experiment.

I somehow persuaded Jimmy to stick with Island even though he had a good offer from RCA Victor, which had designs on turning him into a pop star. It was something like $50,000, which obviously turned his head, but I promised Jimmy that we would figure it out, that we'd sell records without having to compromise him artistically. "Give me two years," I told him, "and we will definitely break you."

My plan seemed to pick up speed when I got a call from a friend in Jamaica, the filmmaker Perry Henzell, who was making a scripted but vérité movie about the cutthroat Jamaican music business called *The Harder They Come.* Perry thought that Jimmy's look was exactly right for the main character in his film, Ivanhoe Martin, a charismatic ghetto singer. The script paralleled some of Jimmy's own life—the poor boy coming to Kingston from the countryside and doing his best to keep his integrity and his wits about him while dealing with gangsters, hangers-on, and the chaos and corruption of the music industry.

I told Jimmy he really should do this movie—it would represent a cultural breakthrough, an authentic picture of the Jamaican underworld that had never before been captured on film. Jimmy readily agreed, and was also commissioned to write songs for the film. We both felt great about where his career was going. But then things stopped moving quickly.

Perry, a perfectionist, kept on shooting, editing, and reshooting, and the production of *The Harder They Come* ended up taking two years. It wouldn't be widely released in the US until 1975. This was a lot longer than any of us had anticipated. Jimmy was running out of money and felt I had betrayed him by promising that the movie would change things for him. While *The Harder They Come* has turned out to be a cinematic classic and the foremost showcase of Jimmy's manifold talents—one of those rare music movies that works—at the time it had no impact on Jimmy's finances. His career as a performer, he complained to me, was stuck on hold.

I couldn't deny that he was right. I tried to persuade Jimmy not to leave Island, but he was adamant. He needed to make money. He had his own dreams. I couldn't fight that. He signed with Reprise Records in the US and EMI in Europe. It was a real blow. *The Harder They Come* was going to be great. We all knew it. I believed that I had unlocked the secret of how to break reggae into the mainstream. But then it seemed like Jimmy had left with the key.

SO THERE SAT the Wailers in my office. Maybe it was kismet, I thought—just when Jimmy stormed out, Bob, Pete, and Bunny strolled in.

I knew I could do something with them—move them away from where they were and make their music attractive to college kids who were otherwise ignorant of or indifferent to Black music. I asked the Wailers what they wanted to happen with their music. Bunny said they deserved radio play in America, Bob and Peter nodding in convinced agreement.

They were shocked when I said that there was no way their music as it currently sounded would get played on US radio. This pissed them off, as if I were criticizing their music rather than noting the realities of the marketplace. It was just a fact. In that era, there were radio stations that played only rock music and R&B stations that played only Black music. And neither category of station played reggae.

I told them they needed to come over like a Black rock act. There were no precedents for this kind of thing in Jamaica, and barely anywhere else, except maybe in the US, which had Sly and the Family Stone. Being a "rock act," I told them, did not have to mean selling out or surrendering their identity. Pete and Bunny were skeptical, but Bob was immediately intrigued. Black Jamaican music was always evolving, from ska to rocksteady to reggae, and reggae was poised to evolve further.

I had never seen the Wailers perform. I asked them if they were any good live, and Bob immediately replied, "We're great." The way he said it, I believed him. I offered then and there to give them some money, asking them how much it would take to make an album, which was still rare in singles-driven Jamaica. They asked for much more than they actually needed to make an album, but it still wasn't that much, £4,000. I said yes. I didn't ask them to sign anything, which was a risk, but it seemed right in this instance. They had been so fucked over and had so many scores to settle that it seemed correct to do it this way.

Some of my Island colleagues thought I was crazy, and that I would never again see the Wailers or my money. I was told that they were known to be impossible to work with, big troublemakers. But I figured that what these guys were really doing was standing up for themselves. In my experience, when people are described as difficult, it usually just means that they know what they want.

Their working relationship with Lee "Scratch" Perry had not ended well. They thought the proceeds of the terrific work they were doing with him in the early seventies was going to be split fifty-fifty, but when it came down to it, Lee offered them only 10 percent. I did not want to be another part of the music business that kept tripping them up and letting them down. I said I'd be over to Jamaica soon to hear what they had come up with.

A couple of months later, I walked into the tiny record shop on King Street in Kingston where I had been instructed to go. The Wailers had their own label, Tuff Gong, and were putting out their own records from the shop, which was more a hole-in-the-wall with no name than a store. There was a woman standing behind the counter who turned out to be Rita, Bob's wife, who herself had a hell of a voice as part of the Soulettes and later the I Three.

"I am looking for Bob," I said.

"Are you Chris?" she asked. "They've been waiting for you."

I made some small talk, asking Rita whether they had been recording anything. I was a bit cagey because I was prepared for the possibility that they had gotten nothing done. But she cheerfully replied, "Oh yes! I think you will like it, Chris."

I was chuffed. I went back to my hotel. Later on, the Wailers collected me there and took me to their studio, Harry J's. What they played me was what became *Catch a Fire,* their first Island album. It sounded great and they sounded like a group—it was a tremendous progression from other Jamaican music.

The first song they played me was "Slave Driver." Before feeling anything else, I felt excitement and relief that they had recorded anything at all. Very encouraging! In hindsight, that first track was a masterful piece of songwriting and playing, setting the tone for what was to come over the next few years—light and dark, heavy and easy, pleasure and pain, love and resistance, an angry, deeply spiritual song sneaking up on you, the fury of it all lying in wait.

The degradation of Kingston's slums, the description of post-colonial fallout are so brilliantly spelled out in "Slave Driver," and the music makes you a close witness without overwhelming you. It has the perfect blend of their three voices, a rhythm that totally frames the message, the crack of the whip, blood running cold, this really adventurous bass line acting like it's going to break the chains, because it stands for freedom. Then in the second line of the song there are the words "catch a fire," and it immediately occurred to me that if the rest of the record was any good, that would make a fantastic album title.

They next played me a ballad, which I said was nice (though not nice enough for me to remember its title now), but what I was really looking for was rebel music—I wanted to continue the work of *The Harder They Come*. Sure enough, they had plenty more combative songs, and we were in business.

I took the tracks back to London to mix with Bob—Pete and Bunny were not so keen on coming. We used the Island studios at Basing Street, which could get a much better sound than anything in Jamaica, where the mixes sounded rudimentary compared to what we could do in a state-of-the-art, sixteen-track studio.

The biggest change I made to their original sound was symbolized by the guitar on "Concrete Jungle," which was one of the most complex reggae songs I had ever heard, the perfect statement to begin the album. If you wanted to know where they came from, this immediately told you. They sang about their own history, about themselves, and, as Bob said, about things they didn't teach you in school. They had recorded it before, as something ghostly and desperate, and it was great, but I had to think of how listeners would hear it as though the group were new. For most people, they *were* a new group, with a brave new kind of groove. I didn't want to sacrifice the groove; I just wanted to see if we could take it out of Jamaica without actually taking the Jamaica out of it.

Having a different kind of guitar—a rock guitar with a lean, southern-blues flavor—changed everything. How this guitar ended up on "Concrete Jungle" was a happy accident, more or less. A white American guitarist named Wayne Perkins happened to be working in the Island studios. He was part of the crack session team at the Muscle Shoals studio in Alabama that had backed Jimmy Cliff while I had been there. He had also played behind such legends as Wilson Pickett, the Staples Singers, and Aretha Franklin. So impressed was

I by the Muscle Shoals guys that I plucked three of them, Wayne and the brothers Steve and Tim Smith, and turned them into a soft-rock trio called Smith Perkins Smith. Steve Smith also produced two albums for me that I consider overlooked Island classics, Robert Palmer's first two solo albums, *Sneakin' Sally Through the Alley* and *Pressure Drop*.

I bumped into Wayne on the spiral staircase in our offices as I was going upstairs and he was coming down. The studios were their own little scene, and you could make these sorts of connections inside the building. I suggested that perhaps he could play something on this new Wailers track. He was the kind of musician who offered a quick "Of course!" when you asked.

Wayne had no experience playing reggae and had barely heard any. He was more a Duane Allman type, virtuosic and chivalrous. He nearly joined Lynyrd Skynyrd and, a little later, was on the shortlist to replace Mick Taylor in the Rolling Stones, losing out to Ronnie Wood, mainly because he was not English.

I told Wayne not to let the word *reggae* get in the way, to just play what he felt. He met Bob briefly, there was a lot of smoke wafting through the studio, and when he started playing on "Concrete Jungle," he was starting from nowhere really, literally and figuratively in a kind of fog.

When the track began, you could tell he didn't know where he was in the music. He was lost. He said it sounded to him like the music was playing backwards—it seemed simple and spare but had so much nuance and complexity, so much dynamism in what seemed to be empty space. He was distracted by the bass, which sounded like it was playing lead. I told him to ignore it. To help, I got the engineer to turn it down.

Wayne started messing about, then eventually locked into something, the way the keyboards and rhythm guitar grooved together all the way through the song. He held on tight and brought in that rootsy, dirty, swampy Muscle Shoals. The fog cleared.

Bob, who had been listening intently, was thrilled. He was so excited he jumped all over Wayne, patting him on the back, stuffing a huge joint into his mouth. Wayne got pretty damned high that night—he had become a white Wailer. As for Bob, he immediately knew something important had happened: a launch in a new direction, a mysterious melding of time and place, the American South and Jamaican swagger, that somehow made sense.

"Concrete Jungle" became the first track on the record, so that guitar—which for ages people assumed was by Peter Tosh rather than a white guy from Alabama, which was probably just as well—was how this new sound, these new Wailers, were introduced to the world. And it was the sound of someone learning about the music he was inside of at the exact moment he understood it that made it so compelling. Later, Wayne added some lovely hazy *wah-wah* to "Stir It Up" and a sultry slide part to "Baby We've Got a Date."

I love the way such connections are made, little nudges from the universe—I came across Wayne in a small town in Alabama because I was there chasing a certain sound for some of my artists, brought him over to England, bumped into him in the Island studios in Notting Hill Gate because he happened to be recording on that day we were mixing. The second Smith Perkins Smith album, Wayne's reason for being there in the first place, never got finished in the end. Doors open and close all the time. Sometimes you go through a door and just happen to find yourself in the right place at the right time.

As well as the guitar, I needed some keyboards, including the kind of cool new synths that Stevie Wonder was already beginning to use on his records like "Superstition," especially the *wah-wah*-ing clavinet. I got John "Rabbit" Bundrick involved because Bob knew him through Johnny Nash and taught him how to play the reggae rhythms on organ and clavinet. Bob explained directly to Rabbit the sound he was after, and Rabbit thereby set the standard for all future reggae keyboards.

Rabbit added something to the Wailers' sound that was a little more . . . *sophisticated* isn't really the word, but it needed more technological brightness at that point, some few familiar points of reference for both the rock fans and those listening to the slicker new soul music that was coming out. Lee Perry had produced the best Wailers records to date, but we weren't going to compete with them. We were going to produce a different kind of Wailers record.

Catch a Fire is the most polished of Bob Marley's records for Island, deliberately. It was an introduction for those not used to reggae. The albums started to roughen up a little once we had an audience—even by their second Island album, *Burnin'*—but the way to get an audience first was to give it a more refined production, to produce the Wailers as you would a guitar band. In a way, I was treating them as a Black guitar band.

It didn't seem a weakening or a pasteurization to market the Wailers as you would a rock act. There was no sellout. It seemed more compromising and condescending to continue to market reggae as niche music or some kind of exotica. So I took what I had learned working in rock and applied it to reggae, just as I had taken what I'd learned from producing and selling Jamaican music and applied it to running a rock label. It was coming full circle, really.

Catch a Fire didn't immediately sell a huge number of copies, about 14,000 in the first year. I approached the release with confidence, but there was still a hesitancy at the label. In its first few months, it sold only 6,000 or so copies. I was extremely disappointed, but the prevailing attitude was: "That's good for a reggae record." My retort: "Don't think of it as a reggae record. It's a rock record. It's a record that has the chance to be something important if we get behind it."

We eventually put a lot of money and promotional muscle behind the album. In Britain, the Wailers played in large venues, opening for Traffic and other Island acts. Across the Atlantic, the Wailers opened for a highly touted new CBS act named Bruce Springsteen at some introductory shows at Max's Kansas City in New York.

We gave the album a standout sleeve, the sort of packaging, promotion, and marketing that was traditionally given to a rock act. The key was not to use the stereotypical images and colors of reggae that had become predictable verging on corny. The sleeve idea came from the art directors Rod Dyer and Bob Weiner at Capitol Records in America, with whom I had just made a deal. They came up with the idea of the Zippo lighter, a playful way of representing the title, which was actually saying "burn in hell." The sleeve had a hinge and you flipped open the top of the lighter to get to the record in its inner sleeve in the bottom half. It was obvious what it was referring to, and this was at a time when if you were caught with even just a single joint you would do jail time.

It was clever and as special as I wanted, but not particularly smart or practical from an economic standpoint. It turned out to be a damn nuisance, in fact, and there were only 20,000 copies issued with the Zippo sleeve. If you have one of these—I wish I did—you are very lucky.

The replacement cover featured a different kind of catch a fire, an Esther Anderson photograph of a serious but romantic-looking Bob smoking a gloriously sized spliff under a tree outside the Island offices at 56 Hope Road in Kingston. Bob loved to sit and think under an old mango tree in the yard. He never liked to meet me anywhere there was a desk involved. He'd say, "A man sitting behind a desk can con you in every kind of way." I didn't disagree. So when I was in Kingston, we would have our meetings under that mango tree.

It may not have sold a huge amount, but *Catch a Fire* got great reviews, especially for a music that still wasn't taken seriously by most of the rock press. The Zippo sleeve did its job getting people talking, and the album was definitely changing minds and setting things up for the future. And over time, *Catch a Fire* carried on selling. As was the case with a lot of great Island records, it didn't open big but it sold forever.

And it led to the next Wailers album on Island, *Burnin'*. I enjoyed playing records I liked to Bob, sometimes simply to share my enthusiasm, and at other times to see if these songs inspired him. I was a big fan of Norman Whitfield, who was making bold, uncompromising records for Marvin Gaye, Edwin Starr, and especially the Temptations. One day I played Bob the last group's "Papa Was a Rolling Stone," a Whitfield cowrite, and I could see from his face that it had switched something on in his brain. When you played him something he liked, he would have a very visceral response to it, and process his own response very quickly. "Papa" was transformed through Bob's mind into "Get Up, Stand Up," the powerful political lead-off track of *Burnin'*. Listen closely and you'll hear the influence; it's right in the bass. *Burnin'* was swiftly followed by *Natty Dread*, whose single "No Woman, No Cry" began to take Bob's music to an international audience.

FROM THE MOMENT that Bob and I set to work remixing *Catch a Fire* in London, Peter Tosh and Bunny Wailer felt threatened. To them, it seemed it was now me and Bob. They were so protective of the three of them, which was understandable. It had always been their thing. They had fought hard to keep their band going when so much conspired against them, and then here, all of a sudden, was this white guy deciding for them that they needed to move in a different direction.

Even Bob didn't initially understand my line of thinking until I took him to a show in America, an Island tour with Traffic, Free, and John Martyn. It was sold out, even though none of these artists had actual hits. They represented the new album market: white college kids into Led Zeppelin and Cream who thought pop was too superficial and throwaway. Their fans were believers in something more substantial and permanent. Appealing to this audience wasn't a betrayal of your integrity.

Bunny, a fundamentalist Rasta, started getting anxious about the kinds of venues we wanted the Wailers to play, the rock clubs and colleges. He was unsure about the types of people who went to those clubs, their diversity. To him they were full of freaks, which freaked him out. He also never got used to the cold in Britain and the difficulty getting the vegetarian ital food. Whereas Bob took to exploring possibilities outside Jamaica with relish, sensing exciting ways he could maintain his Rasta beliefs while expanding his horizons, Peter and Bunny were uncomfortable.

Soon enough, the Wailers became known as Bob Marley and the Wailers, not least because, although Tosh and Bunny were formidable talents and had great rebel presence, Bob had by far the most charisma and the most songs. He was clearly the leader—and, in a wider sense, transcending music, *a* leader. He was always hungry for experience and loved traveling and seeing other parts of the world.

Peter Tosh didn't like me. He suggested I favored Bob because Bob was half-white, with an English-born father. Behind my back, he referred to me as "Whitewell" and "Whiteworst." All I can say is that his suspicions were misguided, as were those who accused me of exploiting Bob to make money. I never paid a Jamaican act a penny less in royalties than an English act. I was helpless without the artists. I wasn't a singer or a writer; it made no sense to rip them off. I put my all into getting Bob's music, and Jamaica's music, into the mainstream.

The last Wailers single to feature the original Bob-Peter-Bunny lineup was "I Shot the Sheriff," taken from *Burnin'*. Released in February 1973, it wasn't a hit, reaching only number sixty-seven in the UK charts. But a smooth 1974 cover by Eric Clapton ended up being Clapton's only number-one single in America and helped open more ears to Bob's music.

By 1975, I felt it was time for a Bob Marley and the Wailers live album. We used the Rolling Stones' mobile recording studio to capture the band at the Lyceum in London in the summer of 1975. They had just completed a long American tour promoting *Natty Dread* and added four British dates in what was fast becoming a home audience.

They were battle-hardened and at one with the music, which made the timing ideal for a bid to make them bigger still. For many listeners, Bob Marley and the Wailers were still a new act, and the departures of Tosh and Wailer weren't a factor. The band still had its original rhythm section, drummer Carlton Barrett and bassist Aston "Family Man" Barrett, and they were now joined by Al Anderson on guitar, Tyrone Downie on keyboards, and Cuban percussionist Alvin "Seeco" Patterson, a father figure or big brother to Bob who had been in the first iteration of the Wailers in 1964. The harmonies formerly supplied by Peter and Bunny had been replaced by those of the I-Three trio: Bob's wife, Rita, and Marcia Griffiths and Judy Mowatt.

The atmosphere at the Lyceum was electric, and I saw—and heard—the reaction of the audience to "No Woman, No Cry," and how they started chanting the chorus over the organ intro and the I-Three even before Bob had started singing. This was quite a moment—the group hadn't had a hit yet, but the white post-hippie college crowd was out in force and already knew the Wailers' songs inside out. At the same time, the venue accommodated a large contingent of blissed-out local Black fans, which created a then extremely rare mixed audience. This was a time, remember, when dreadlocks still needed to be described in the mainstream press as "waxy plaits."

The resulting album, simply called *Live!*, includes what have come to be thought of as the definitive versions of certain Bob Marley songs, "No Woman, No Cry" especially. I kept telling my engineers, "Give me more audience!" I wanted the home listener to hear the ecstatic roar and unison singing of that mixed Lyceum crowd as Bob urged them on. The live "No Woman, No Cry" became Bob's first hit outside Jamaica, reaching number twenty-two in the UK charts. Thinking of Bob's transcendent popularity now, that seems relatively low-key, but at the time it was a mind-blowing milestone. For all the lovely, infectious melodies of Bob's songs, they were still about tyranny and anger—as rapper Chuck D has put it, "battle cries for survival."

*   *   *

ALMOST A YEAR to the day after Island released *Live!* in December 1975, there occurred a horrifying event that signaled how quickly life was moving for Bob, and how consequential his position as a Jamaican spiritual and cultural leader was.

A Jamaican election was due to take place on December 16. Two days before Bob was to headline the free, optimistically titled Smile Jamaica concert in Kingston on December 5, arranged to help lift spirits and ease the palpable tensions between the country's warring political parties, he was shot and wounded along with Rita and his manager, Don Taylor, at his Hope Road home.

A couple of years earlier, Bob had moved to what had previously been called Island House, the sprawling office compound/apartment block I had set up as Island Records' Jamaican base in an uptown residential area of Kingston. Basically, it was a converted mansion, and I had passed it on to Bob as a place to live and work. Now that it was his home, he was two doors down from the governor's house and surrounded by politicians' homes and embassies, all of them very well protected from what were, in those fraught times, siege conditions.

Kingston had become a violent city, totally at odds with the idea people might have had of Jamaica as a laid-back paradise. Its beauty was being smashed up. There were bombings, beatings, power cuts, and curfews; supermarkets were running short of food, and the island seemed full of guns and gangs. Bob believed that his Rastafari lifestyle and message offered a way to unite people, but unfortunately, nearly fifteen years after the bright promise of independence, the island was slipping backwards as a society.

Bob kept his home as open as possible, and the basic iron gate at the front didn't exactly suggest his premises were impregnable. It was where he lived but also where he could play soccer with his friends and blast music outside all day long, plus his center of operations. The complex also housed his Tuff Gong Studios, part of Tuff Gong International, which Marley had formed in 1970 and had evolved into a collective of people, businesses, and musical activities.

Marley had become known as Tuff Gong partly for the way he dealt with being treated as a white boy on the rough, unforgiving Trench Town streets because his father was a white Englishman. *Gong* was a reference to Leonard P. Howell, widely regarded as the original Rasta—an honorific shortened from Howell's chosen religious name, Gangunguru (teacher of famed wisdom) Maragh (king). When the term was passed over to Marley, Tuff was added, indicating his resilience in dealing with the bullying.

Now that he was such a public figure, everyone knew where Bob Marley's base was. He didn't want to cut himself off from the people, from the outside world. Perhaps he thought no one would ever make him a target. But with its poor security apparatus, his house was easily stormed by gunmen, although it is still not clear who they were and why they were shooting. One suggestion is that the shooters were gangsters working on behalf of Edward Seaga's Jamaica Labour Party, possibly proxies of the CIA, attacking Bob and his entourage because of his apparent ties with Prime Minister Michael Manley of the more socialist People's National Party. Others have suggested that there was a drugs link. Amazingly, and much to my relief, there were no fatalities.

I was due to arrive at Bob's to watch him rehearse for the Smile Jamaica concert, right at what turned out to be at the time of the attack. Beforehand, I had gone to visit Lee Perry at his Black Ark Studios, where he was recording a track called "Dreadlocks in Moonlight," which he had written for Bob to sing. Lee sang it for me in his tiny studio's tiny control room, made even smaller by its wall coverings of red, green, and black fake fur. Hearing anything by Lee at the time was like suddenly dropping through a trapdoor into woozy outer space. His voice was so tender and frail, I couldn't imagine even Bob improving upon Lee's performance. Watching the wired, wiry Lee at work in his cap and shorts was a privilege in itself, like watching Picasso bring a painting to life.

Instead of driving over to Hope Road for the rehearsal, I hung around late while Lee finished up; surely Bob wouldn't mind. This change of plan may have saved my life, as I was still at Black Ark when the shooting started—according to one person, right as the band began rehearsing "I Shot the Sheriff." Bob had gotten bored and wandered off to somewhere other than where the gunmen thought he would be. He still got struck.

I went with Perry Henzell to see Bob in the hospital. There was blood on his shirt and shock on his face. A bullet meant for his heart had grazed his chest and lodged in his upper arm, where it would stay for the rest of his life. I quickly had Bob moved to my place up in the Blue Mountains outside of Kingston, Strawberry Hill.

Tensions in Kingston were raised after the shooting, which even by recent standards was brutal. To Bob's disgust, he found that the election date had been brought forward to coincide with the Smile Jamaica show, making it seem like a pro-government rally. Bob's attempts to remain neutral and apolitical were being tested. He still performed in front of eighty thousand people because, as he said, "The people who are trying to make the world worse aren't taking a day off, so how can I?" He was scheduled to sing just one song in front of the huge crowd, but ended up playing for ninety minutes with the bullet freshly lodged in his arm and his wounds clearly visible.

Within days of the concert, Bob was back in England. He needed to get out of Jamaica and enter a kind of exile, at a time when, luckily enough, London supplied all that he needed musically, spiritually, and creatively. The city had become a much more fertile and welcoming place for Jamaican music, with the emergence of new British reggae bands such as Aswad and Steel Pulse. Signing them to Island, with its reputation as the home of reggae, was proof that British Jamaican reggae was authentic. And although we didn't appear to sign punk bands, with Steel Pulse, in a way we did, but one with rhythm and a new kind of Britishness. At the same time, at Island, after Bob's success, we started regularly releasing Jamaican reggae again, signing up Burning Spear, Max Romeo, Toots and the Maytals, and Junior Murvin.

It was a dismal time in Britain—"No future for you," as Johnny Rotten sang—but despite that—because of that—there was some compelling music. The punks had an affinity for the Jamaicans, and the Clash brilliantly covered Murvin's "Police and Thieves" on their debut album.

Bob loved this cross-pollinating mix of energies and genres. He acknowledged what was happening by recording with Lee Perry a new composition called "Punky Reggae Party" that name-checked the Clash, the Jam, and the Damned (along with the Maytals and his own Wailers) and included the chant "No boring old farts."

I think this exile period marked the first time that Bob felt important—not in a conceited way, but in the knowledge that he was on the right track, influencing music and politics. Combined with the development of his songwriting and the evolution of his band, he had a creative momentum I had never before witnessed.

Bob was madly prolific, handing me his new songs as they happened—he recorded them, I mixed them, and then we worked on the running order. We soon realized that we had two albums' worth of new material. I separated this material into two sets, with the loose idea that one set represented the revolutionary Bob and the other the romantic Bob, with both sets of songs conveying the whirlwind of emotions he experienced after being forced out of his homeland: frustration, anger, happiness, liberation.

The songs became two albums: *Exodus*, a direct, militant response to the assassination attempt, and *Kaya*, an album of love and dance where he consciously cooled off some of the tension. I decided to release revolutionary Bob first, even though romantic Bob was more commercial, because *Exodus* seemed to capture the mood of the moment and express how he was maintaining his righteousness after his near-death experience. It didn't seem right to bring out the love songs first. Majestic rebel music first, and then the calm, the peaceful and harmonious, the inspiring of a new world without being so overtly political. Bob obviously had in many of his songs what was seen quite rightly as political, but he was also very aware that, as he said, "'Tis music. It can't be political all of the while."

When it came to these sorts of decisions, it was very easy to make them with Bob, who often seemed to be thinking the same thing as me anyway. Probably before me, bending me to his will even if I seemed to be coming up with some of the ideas. The two albums seemed to fall into shape very easily—"Is This Love," for instance, didn't belong on *Exodus,* and it did lead some critics to suggest there was some kind of sellout singing these so-called softer songs, but Bob was very committed to the idea that they demanded a better, fairer, safer world as much as his more explicit protest songs. And there were some darks clouds on *Kaya* as well, and the chilled, stoned quality of the record had its own defiance, a response to Bob being arrested and charged with possession of cannabis and fined £50 while he was staying in London. It wasn't going to stop him smoking what he wanted to, not least because it was a sacramental part of his religion, a holy rite for a holy person.

Many of the *Exodus* tracks blew me away as soon as I heard them: the artful, not-quite-reggae of "The Heathen"; the feel of "Natural Mystic"; the fantastic energy of "Exodus"; the beauty of "Waiting in Vain," confirming that he seemed have an endless supply of rapturous melodies. I felt that there were several killer songs that had political or sociological relevance, so I decided to lead the first album with them. Side one had "Natural Mystic," "So Much Things to Say," "Guiltiness," and "The Heathen." And then after "Exodus" itself, the heart of the album, you would flip the disc over to side two and start dancing and mellowing out with "Jamming"—Bob's feel-good way of saying no bullet was going to stop him—"Waiting in Vain," "Turn Your Lights Down Low," "Three Little Birds" (the song people think is called "Don't Worry About a Thing"), and "One Love," an old Wailers song from 1965. I suggested to Bob that he revive "One

Love" and bring its sound up-to-date. He was always very happy to rework old songs, because he felt he understood them more after living with them for a few years. Songs evolve, and, as with "One Love," he would move from what he called raw inspiration to comprehension. But because the song bears more than a passing resemblance to Curtis Mayfield's "People Get Ready," I also suggested that, to be safe, he split the royalties with Mayfield. This version of "One Love" has gone on to become a global anthem, and the Jamaican tourist board has used it as their theme song.

I thought *Exodus* would break it wide open for Bob Marley. This was 1977: mainstream rock had become a bit stale and punk had changed a lot of things, instantly making a lot of pre-punk musicians seem irrelevant. Bob was something very, very different from punk, but he also shared a lot of its rebel attitude. When *Exodus* appeared, to my mind it was like Jimi Hendrix coming out with *Electric Ladyland*.

Time magazine has rated *Exodus* as the album of the twentieth century, ahead of Miles Davis's *Kind of Blue* and Jimi's *Are You Experienced*. Does it stand out for me as Bob's best? Probably, but it's close. *Catch a Fire* is fantastic, an experiment in blending different kinds of music that just about came off perfectly. *Survival*, a couple of years after *Exodus*, is fantastic too, explicitly acknowledging its African influences and reinforcing Bob's militancy after the softer *Kaya*.

But *Exodus* is the one that is the most dead-center. It's pure Bob Marley, cycling through his experience of exile and his return to righteousness via love, ganja, music, and dancing.

BOB AND I didn't talk much in the studio—or, I should say, we mostly talked about the music, acknowledging our personal lives and interests very rarely. There was an open flow of ideas between us; Bob sometimes stood his ground but was warmly receptive to suggestions that he saw had potential, and he never once protested that he was being told what to do by the guy running the record company.

A great example of the way we worked together was "Redemption Song" from *Uprising*, the final album released in his lifetime. That's one of Bob's songs that I can say I really produced, rather than just being responsible for the mix.

He was terribly ill with cancer at the time of its recording and not sleeping much, cognizant that his time was coming to an end. His writing and thinking were taking on an intensely contemplative tone.

He had been working on "Redemption Song" for months, trying it out in various styles, touching on all the varieties of Jamaican music he had been part of, from upbeat, post-sound-system ska to hypnotic reggae. He'd taken some of the song's lyrics from a speech delivered in 1934 by one of the major influences on the Rastafari movement, the Afro-Jamaican Pan-Africanist Marcus Garvey: "We are going to emancipate ourselves from mental slavery because whilst others might free the body, none but ourselves can free the mind."

Bob really wanted to get the song right. When he played the various versions for me, I liked them but didn't really love them. Something was missing. Then it hit me. Because the lyrics were so obviously important and deep, the song would work best presented as simply as possible, with just Bob and an acoustic guitar. Bob took some persuading to try it this way, but he listened patiently to my reasoning and then agreed to record an acoustic take.

Eyes shut, lost in the words, he sang a spare version to me as an audience of one. It sounded hymnal and hypnotic. The understatement of his performance made the song seem so much more dramatic. I thought it would be amazing if everyone heard "Redemption Song" the same way, as if it were sung directly to them, just you and Bob in the room.

It was me as the first listener taking the responsibility on behalf of his fans to decide how the song should sound. It so clearly didn't need anything else. In its simplicity, it transcended genre, so that it wasn't reggae, folk, pop, or rock. It was Bob Marley.

Bob loved how it turned out too. But he was concerned over how it would fit in with the rest of the album, whose songs featured his full band. So we decided to make it the final track, after an empty space in the groove: an epilogue, part of the album but also slightly removed.

I didn't dare think of "Redemption Song" at the time as the end of the road, his final statement. There was part of me though that realized this could be the last song he would write, and the last one we worked on together. Both of us in our own ways wanted to get it absolutely right, and the emotions we mostly kept to ourselves helped give the song its soul-stirring intensity. It worked beautifully as the last track on what would turn out to be his last album: a summary of everything he stood for and a showcase for how gentle and persuasive he could be even as he was singing something with great power and moral weight. If his work had to finish this way, long before any of us would have wanted, then there was no better way of bringing it to a close.

IN BOB'S LAST few years, after the shooting, there was a lot of pressure on him. He was ruffling some feathers because people in positions of authority feared the power he wielded over his audience. During this period, I was summoned to the office of the US ambassador in Jamaica, a strange request but one I was not about to ignore. The ambassador warned me that the intelligence community had its eye on me. I asked him why on earth they would waste their time on a guy in the record business. He replied that I had drawn their attention because I was working with someone who was capable of destabilizing politics and inciting young people. He meant Bob Marley.

Really, they had their eye on Bob more than me. They saw him as dangerous and subversive, enough for the CIA to keep a file on him, as though he were some sort of malign influence. (In his song "Rat Race," Bob defiantly sang, "Rasta don't work for no CIA.") And it wasn't just the Americans. Even in his native land, the powers that be cast a wary eye upon Bob, uncomfortable with the world's embrace of him and the fact that he, a song-singing, ganja-smoking Rastafarian with dreadlocks, had become the face of Jamaica.

Yet Bob, though he took his role as a leader seriously, never lost his humility. He consciously chose to drive a BMW rather than a flashier, sportier car, because he didn't want to come off as showy and arrogant. (Though it didn't hurt that "BMW" stood for Bob Marley and the Wailers.) And he never locked his car. He once told me that if you did that, you were creating a barrier between yourself and everyone else. After that, I never locked my car.

Bob, a gifted athlete and soccer fanatic, badly injured his toe while playing a pickup match in May 1977. He carried on with his mesmerizing live shows undaunted, seemingly none the worse for wear. But he sought no treatment for the toe, which deteriorated. Even after he was diagnosed with a malignant melanoma under the toenail, he disregarded the seriousness of his condition. He rejected a doctor's advice to have the toe amputated, to prevent the cancer from spreading. The thought of compromising his ability to play soccer troubled him, and his Rasta beliefs suggested that perhaps he could overcome his illness by faith alone.

By the time he was touring the *Uprising* album in 1980, he was doing an admirable job of staying stoic and keeping to himself how much pain he was in. But there was clearly a change in his appearance: already slim, he was getting even thinner. Bob was by nature a quiet, contemplative man, especially when he was writing; but even by his standards, he seemed uncommonly preoccupied and deep within himself.

As famous and beloved as Bob was, he was not the superstar he became posthumously. In September of 1980, he played two consecutive nights at Madison Square Garden, but not as the headliner. Rather, he was the opening act for the Commodores. After the second show, Bob nearly passed out. The following day, he went for a run in Central Park to sort out his head. As he was running, he collapsed, suffering some sort of seizure. He was rushed to a hospital, where the doctors found that the cancer had spread to other parts of his body. The prognosis was that he had weeks to live.

When I heard this, I was totally shaken. It couldn't be real. When Bob had injured his toe in 1977, the doctor attending to him said he should have a checkup every three months to make sure there were no lingering complications. But nobody—including me, I'm sorry to say—pressed Bob enough on the matter, ensuring that he was following through on the doctor's recommendation.

As soon as I heard how ill Bob was, I realized I should have insisted that he have the checkups. I did to an extent, but there are only so many times you can say it without its becoming a kind of nagging. I thought he must be doing what he had to in order to deal with it. It was a situation where everyone around him thought that someone else was looking after the problem. In the end, we didn't talk about it amongst ourselves. Cancer was something very much in the shadows in those days. Not like now, when there's a more open acceptance of it, and more general information. We weren't as experienced as people would be forty years in facing up to it. A ridiculous awkwardness got in the way.

Bob soldiered on to play one more show, in Pittsburgh at the Stanley Theatre on September 23, 1980. Terminally ill, on the verge of collapsing at any moment, he played "Redemption Song" accompanied by percussionists playing congas and double-timed bass drum, as if he were being backed by the ghosts of the Maroon drummers in the Jamaican hills who had influenced the rhythms of the music that the Rastas played. The show ended with "Get Up, Stand Up," the band chanting the chorus as Bob left the stage before the music stopped. The rest of Bob's dates were canceled.

We located a specialist in West Germany named Dr. Josef Issels who had devised a potentially lifesaving, or at least life-extending, treatment for advanced melanoma. Bob managed to get over to the doctor's clinic and seemed to improve for a few weeks—but it didn't last. Dr. Issels conceded defeat, and Bob chose to return to Jamaica to spend his final days. But while he was flying back home via Miami, he fell ill, and died in a hospital in Florida. It was May 11, 1981. He was only thirty-six.

I saw Bob one last time before he passed, at the clinic in Germany, in a quiet little town near the Austrian border. He had virtually no hair because of the chemotherapy he had reluctantly consented to receive. Only a few straggly bits remained of his mighty dreadlocks. He must have weighed less than a hundred pounds. His life was coming to an end and he knew it. But there was something still there—the something I had noticed when he, Peter, and Bunny first walked into my office in 1972. His charisma. His spark. His pride.

He offered a barely audible "Hi, Chris." We talked for a few minutes about the sort of stuff you instantly forget, neither of us really finding meaningful words to say. Then we fell into silence, simply keeping each other company, one last time. Bob was so frail, but he had a resolve about him. There was still work to be done—but now it was up to his songs. They had always been his weapons.

CHAPTER EIGHT

VOICES, VISIONARIES, AND VIDEOS

Island specialized early on in what was called blues rock, an English transformation of an American style that satisfied both my and Guy Stevens's needs at the time. The music was within sight of blues and R&B, and the musicians could really play. It was that period between John Mayall, Alexis Korner, and Graham Bond and the upcoming Yardbirds and Led Zeppelin, as guitar-heavy British blues coming from deprived working-class regions was getting harder, tougher, and louder on the way to heavy metal.

In the first year or two, even as we were moving into folk, Traffic was getting psychedelic, and King Crimson was extending rock as far as it could go before it became classical, it was like this was our house style. We had Blodwyn Pig coming to us through our deal with Chrysalis, who also had Jethro Tull; we had Spooky Tooth, Tramline, and Free. I produced the first Tramline album and Guy produced the second one. (Mine was sensibly titled *Somewhere Down the Line*; Guy's was the more danceable *Moves of Vegetable Centuries*. Guy produced the first Free album, *Tons of Sobs*, and then I took over.)

Both Free and Tramline were very serious white teenagers straining for some authentic blues feeling. Free always seemed to be in turmoil, which helped with the yearning authenticity, but Tramline didn't last long enough to suffer for their music as much as Free did.

Free came to me on the recommendation of the great blues campaigner Alexis Korner, at the center of a series of musicians and apprentices in the sixties that included Eric Burdon, Long John Baldry, Dick Heckstall-Smith, Jack Bruce, Mick Jagger, Graham Bond, Ginger Baker, Robert Plant, and Zoot Money. When he told you about some new band he liked, you listened—and you didn't need a demo tape.

Many times I would make a decision about signing an act more on meeting them than on hearing a demo, especially if they came with persuasive references. Alexis had guided and mentored Free, and then passed them on to me—I sent him over a bottle of champagne for the introduction. I did see them live, supporting Albert King at the Marquee. They knew the blues, but also had a unique form of timing, and weren't afraid to let some calm appear in their music.

I had them come to the Island offices the next day. There was a lot of hair, and they looked like a group, like they belonged together, and in their scrappy way had a certain charisma. I'd asked ex–Spencer Davis roadie John Glover at Island to take a look, and he wasn't so sure. They were a little fiery for him, but for me that energy was what made them so compelling. John eventually loved them, and managed Free as long as they were together.

They'd decided to smoke cigars to look a little older, which I didn't pay any attention to, not least because all it did was make them cough and splutter and seem even younger than they were. Because of Millie Small and Steve Winwood, it didn't concern me that they were so young—their bass player, Andy Fraser, had just turned sixteen. He'd been playing for a few months with John Mayall before he was fifteen, so you knew he must have something, however young he was, for John to use him.

The son of a Barbadian-Guyanese father and an English mother, Andy had played in West Indian social clubs in the East End and Harlesden and had a style that was both ornate and funky. He knew how to make the most discriminating soul listeners sway to his bass, and his was the kind of playing that could easily fit into the Jamaican music that had slowed down from ska and rocksteady into the gluier, slyer reggae.

Singer Paul Rodgers, guitarist Paul Kossoff, and drummer Simon Kirke were seventeen, eighteen. They were very sure of themselves, with that no-nonsense teenage mix of solemnity, cockiness, and defensiveness. Fraser and the shy Kossoff—hiding behind his massive mane so he didn't have to make eye contact—were especially serious students of music. They reminded me of Steve Winwood, who at sixteen had that attitude of *no one can tell me anything; just let me get on with it.*

Guy Stevens was still around at this time and wanted to call the group the Heavy Metal Kids, a name he had applied before only to a made-up band. He told the foursome that they were to agree to this name or no deal. But young Andy Fraser, the sharpest of the four, effortlessly assumed leadership duties and told us very forcibly that it was Free or no deal. They liked their more abstract name at a time when group names were beginning to get a little flowery. They wanted to be Free, Andy said, backed by his nodding bandmates, and eventually, after they had left and a few hours' thinking about it, Guy and I backed down. I called Andy and told him the news. It sounded like he'd been expecting my call.

Their first album, *Tons of Sobs*—another Guy title—was done in four days for a basic Island starter budget of £800. Guy as gently as he could encouraged the inexperienced group, feeling awkward in a studio environment, to just be themselves and play the music in the same unfussy but gutsy and fearless way they played live.

As great a debut as it turned out to be, *Tons of Sobs* was barely noticed. We quickly put them back in the studio for a second album, but the group was already falling apart. The talented but acutely sensitive Kossoff felt rejected by the group's center of creativity and pissed off when he was bossed about by the sixteen-year-old Andy. He thought of himself as an artist, and his guitar playing was all about feel. He discreetly auditioned for Jethro Tull when they were looking for a new guitarist. Like Wayne Perkins, he even had a flutter on replacing Brian Jones as the new Rolling Stones guitarist, the role taken by Mick Taylor. I had a quiet word with Paul about staying, and even though Guy seemed resigned to their splitting after their wonderful debut, I persuaded Free to keep going.

I put them on the grueling Blind Faith tour of the US, and they were invited to play the Woodstock festival but somehow it didn't work out. So back home they came, slogging up and down England's primitive new motorway system in an uncomfortable small white transit van. They were so hardworking, and of all the groups we promoted at Island, they were the only ones who carefully balanced their books, looking after the business end surprisingly well.

But a gig somewhere in the north of England on a grim, rainy night in March 1970 seemed to mark the end of the road for Free. Rodgers was from the area and expected more enthusiasm, but instead he encountered stultifying audience apathy. They played their hearts out as they always did, to about fifty stoned students in a venue that could easily hold a thousand.

Back in their scruffy dressing room, the group held a meeting in which they acknowledged that their loping, mostly medium-paced white blues songs weren't cutting it. A faster, more immediate song was needed, an upbeat rouser that might wake up an audience taking for granted their honest, no-nonsense way of playing.

It's not quite clear if the idea for their signature song started with Andy Fraser trying to cheer up the group by madly chanting "It's all right now" or with singer Paul Rodgers arguing that what they needed to connect with the audience was a hook as basic as "It's all right now." Both claim credit. Whatever happened, in just a few minutes backstage that night in the gloomy north they wrote a self-consciously up-tempo rocker called "All Right Now."

The song turned out to be a sort of dramatic trailer for what it was that made them special as a group—the prowling, brooding Paul Rodgers on the hunt for sensation; the timing and balance of Andy's bass; the intense, yearning raw power of Kossoff; Simon Kirke's banging drums like his life depended on it. They knocked the song into shape at sound checks at the next few shows, started opening with it, and then realized it should close the show.

Free honestly viewed their new song as something of a throwaway, a three-chord sop to teenagers. It was the last song recorded for their third album, *Fire and Water*, which they were producing themselves at Basing Street, albeit with me keeping a watchful eye.

I was in my apartment above the studio, and this was one of the reasons I liked being so close—I got the call about midnight to come downstairs and hear this new track they'd been working on. There were a few people with me, and we wandered into the studio. I liked sometimes having some friends hang out in the studio, just to get a sense of how they reacted to a song, and of how the musicians in the studio reacted to hearing their new work being played.

When I heard "All Right Now," I didn't need to check what others thought. It wasn't simply a nice new album track. I knew immediately that with some attention in the mix and an edit for the radio, it would be a hit. I had the same feeling I'd had when I heard the Millie version of "My Boy Lollipop."

The group couldn't believe I was making such a fuss over the song and were outright alarmed when I told them I wanted to make it shorter. It wasn't going to work on the radio at five and a half minutes, but they argued that its length prevented it from being a cheap pop song. To Paul Kossoff, it was as if I had suggested cutting off one of his limbs.

I explained to them that we could put the original longer version on the album, and if we made an edit for radio, more people would hear it. They muttered amongst themselves, and then shop steward Andy reluctantly agreed to the terms. I didn't win many arguments with the group—at least, not that they knew about—but this one was worth winning. I think Andy could definitely see I wasn't budging. For once he treated me as the guy they usually joked I was—their boss.

I suggested where the cut should be and left engineer Roger Beale to perform the tricky operation—back then you had to use a razor blade to cut the two-inch tape—while I dragged the group to the pub. A couple of pints might dull the pain and stop them sulking. When we returned an hour or so later, the edit was perfect, although they all winced upon hearing the playback.

"All Right Now" was soon thereafter released as Free's new single. There was some last-minute panic when the BBC thought that the lyric went "Let's move before they raise the fucking rate" instead of "Let's move before they raise the parking rate"—some dirty-minded vetter perceived the song to be about Paul picking up a prostitute. We had to supply an isolated vocal track for whatever committee of prurient officials decided such things.

Once that was smoothed over, "All Right Now" did so well in the charts that Free's worst nightmares came true. When the single suddenly jumped twenty-six places to number four, they were invited onto—perish the thought—*Top of the Pops*. Whether they liked it or not, the blues-rock purists Free had written a pop classic.

In their eyes, serious groups didn't go on *Top of the Pops*. Led Zeppelin wasn't going to be on the program. You played along to a backing track as if you couldn't play your instruments or sing in tune. To them, it was a kids' show. Of course, they actually *were* kids. When they made their appearance on the show, trousers as tight as Simon's drumming, they did their best to mime with some dignity and hide their shame when the edit hit. Andy had grown a flimsy mustache to add some years to his baby face.

They weren't now traveling only from town to town. As the song moved from the British charts through the European charts, a classic summer hit, they were flying from country to country. Before it was a hit, we'd booked them onto the Isle of Wight Festival at the end of August, pretty low down on a bill that included Jimi Hendrix, Joni Mitchell, the Doors, the Who, Miles Davis, Sly and the Family Stone, Procol Harum, and Joan Baez.

We flew in on a helicopter to the festival site, sailing over the heads of hundreds of thousands of people. Much better than an uncomfortable transit van. Free was due on in early evening, when it was light, but our slot got later and later. Sly and the Family Stone ran over; Emerson, Lake & Palmer ran over. It was all a bit chaotic. It got darker. I grew annoyed that Free was still hanging around after ten, drinking, smoking weed, trying to deal with their nerves, not in any fit state to perform.

I arranged that they would play early Sunday, which turned out to be a good idea. Free hit the stage around midday as the audience was just waking up. The sun was shining. The group was refreshed and in the mood, and when Free was on form, they played like they were the greatest rock band in the world. And now they had a big, rousing hit to underline that. They could already see the difference—a crowd was now singing along with one of their songs. Watching them in their element, it did seem they were now in control of their own destiny, which was what they had always wanted.

The hit didn't initially knock the group off balance, and they did a couple of tours with renewed vigor. It all started to go wrong when I began looking for a follow-up single and another album. Maybe as "the boss" I was asking them for too much, and they needed a break from the constant combination of touring and recording. The hit single was welcome, but they were reluctant to follow it up and become known as a singles group.

They wanted a slow, steamy song called "The Stealer" to be their next single. They saw it as a truer representation of their sensitive, grown-up music. I warned them it was too world-weary to be a hit, and it duly stalled outside the top forty. "All Right Now" proved that sex sells. "The Stealer" proved that musicians often don't know as much about why people like them as they think.

From inside the band, the pressure of fame was increasing, turning what was once an escape from expectation into its opposite. Instead of kick-starting a new period of energy, their big hit proved to be the beginning of the end. A certain laid-back, almost resigned tone to their next album, *Highway*, seemed to acknowledge that Free was more confused by their sudden success than liberated by it. Even the pale, unfocused sleeve suggested that the group wanted to withdraw from the dangers of pop fame, and maybe that was behind the thinking—which was mine—not to even have the group's name on the cover.

I lost whatever control I'd had over the group, and the group lost control of each other. They were so wrapped up in their music that it was difficult for them to get any distance from it. They had made it their world, especially Kossoff, who seemed to use his guitar to ward off personal demons. His guitar-playing didn't come from nowhere, and it seemed every time he came up with a fantastic new riff or a torturous, transcendent solo, he sacrificed a little bit of himself.

The sensitive souls who find the music deep inside themselves are inevitably rocked when things turn sour. When Free broke up, Kossoff was really hurt, and so began a downward spiral where playing music was increasingly replaced by chasing the next fix and numbing the pain.

He was devastated by the death of Jimi Hendrix a few weeks after his final appearance at the Isle of Wight Festival. Paul had been infatuated with him ever since he heard Jimi try out a guitar in an instrument shop he'd once worked in, and mourned him as if he were a close friend, even a brother. After Hendrix's death, Paul started listening to his music more than playing his own.

Free split in 1971, then re-formed in 1972 to try to rescue Kossoff from the chaos and misery of his life. They had a few hits the second time around—great songs like "Little Bit of Love," "My Brother Jake," and "Wishing Well"—but the original magic had gone and they weren't the same group.

Rodgers and Kirke found an escape by forming Bad Company with Mick Ralphs of Mott the Hoople, a second chance with a new group that had much to recommend it but never became as great or as loved as Free. Fraser formed Sharks with the great session guitarist Chris Spedding—I had Chris's Pontiac modified with shark teeth and a fin for a publicity shot—but never found a setting as close to the perfection of Free for his kind of bass-playing. Music is so beautiful when it works and so frustrating when it doesn't. The end of Free seemed to take Paul Kossoff's life force away. He was dead by the age of twenty-five, a rock-star casualty like his hero, Hendrix.

It is amazing how something that begins with such innocence and hope, as it did when the four of them sat squashed together on a sofa in my office, ends up truly as a matter of life and death. I would come across it many times as Island grew: close, creative relationships quickly turning one way or another into something less wonderful and sustaining.

In 2020, as publisher of "All Right Now," I worked hard trying to stop Donald Trump using it as he left the stage at the end of some of his speeches, crudely hijacking its history. His kind of "All Right Now" has nothing to do with the sentiment that Free was offering. There was something revolting about the cynical co-opting of this inspiring bolt of youthful energy.

BOTH MUFF WINWOOD and I were pretty indifferent to Roxy Music when they were first played to us in 1972 by a very keen Tim Clark, the group coming through E. G. Management, who had brought King Crimson to us. At first I didn't know what to make of Roxy's music. I listened to it in a meeting, wearing a Russian fur hat (probably to keep out the cold, or to hide from Tim's hopeful face), and just stared into space, not sure what to say about it. Muff, of the 1960s, thought it sounded like the Tremeloes, which both annoyed and amused Tim and David Enthoven, who was the "E" in E.G. What

I didn't know was that Tim had already offered their manager—and Tim's future business partner—David a deal, assuming it was obvious Muff and I would give it the green light.

I changed my mind when I saw some fabulous Roxy Music artwork in the Island office a couple of days later. Enthoven was bringing it in to show Tim, oblivious to the fact that the deal hadn't yet been approved. It was nine in the morning, and for some reason I happened to be around. I am quite a night owl, so I might have been up all night in a session or had an idea the meeting was about to happen and wanted to unnerve Tim a little.

Whatever the reason, I happened to pass by at the exact moment Enthoven was showing Tim the artwork. It was the oddly flirtatious sleeve for the first Roxy record, very bright and appealing but slightly sinister, the group represented by someone I didn't recognize, but she was posed like an icon. It was unlike anything else around at the time, which always gets my interest.

The photos of the group in the center of the gatefold seemed simultaneously old-fashioned and futuristic, so there was something of the rockabilly and something of the robotic, and kitsch clashed with something classier. It all made off-kilter sense, and it dawned on me that the fact there was no chorus in their song "Virginia Plain" and it sounded like the sound of classic Stax soul gone wrong was part of the song's intended beauty, not a fault. I casually asked a very relieved Tim Clark if we had managed to get them signed. I was always happy to have my mind changed. Well, sometimes I wasn't.

I often responded to the visual style of an act as much as to the music, because increasingly music fashion and original, intelligent, even subversive imagery were as important as the sound. Roxy Music had their very own independent and uncompromising approach to sound and design, which flourished because of Island's overall sense of independence. I'd be very attracted by a group that had an attention to detail that seemed very Island, which I made sure from the start had intriguing artwork, consistent with my roots in the beautifully presented jazz record sleeves of Blue Note and Verve. Island's relationship with Roxy Music over five albums became one of our best-known; in terms of my own contribution, that was because in the beginning I loved how they looked and how, at their best, they sounded like they looked. Sometimes the most creative moment for me was the moment I made my mind up to do something, however capricious the reason. After that, one thing would lead to another, sometimes for quite a while, sometimes for a short while—and sometimes, as with Fairport Convention, one group containing almost too much talent in one place would split into wonderful new variations.

Out of Roxy Music came a fantastic series of adventurous solo records for Island by Brian Eno after he left the group and for a while sang some songs. Albums like *Here Come the Warm Jets* and *Another Green World* came about because Eno and all his smartly chosen collaborators from prog rock and various experimental genres were allowed to come up with whatever they wanted in the studio without anyone wondering about chart positions or even what music was happening at the time.

Roxy Music's way of playing with pop sound and image would seem to have set the stage for the arrival of the wonderfully screwy American pop artists Sparks, but I was still a tough nut to crack. When Dave Betteridge and Muff first played me Sparks, I more or less just shrugged. For some it would seem obvious that Sparks was well-suited to Island, but my first impression was that they were more pop than usual for us. It was the look and the humor, and ultimately the intelligence, of the Mael brothers that made me realize there was more going on under the surface. Intelligence was another great factor in what I encouraged Island to sign, artists who had an approach to their music and performance that I had never thought of, nor anyone else for that matter.

*   *   *

I ALWAYS FELL hard for a great voice. The artists I tended to believe in the most had singing voices I found irresistible. It all goes back to Jackie Edwards and Steve Winwood. I had been a big fan of an English band called the Alan Bown Set, an earthy, early mix of rock, soul, Hammond organ, and horns. Bown was not the singer but a trumpet player and bandleader who hired various front men.

There was a chance in 1970 for me to sign the Alan Bown Set. I wasn't too interested in them by then, to be honest, as their time seemed to have passed. But when I went to see them in some packed, grungy club, I was taken by a glamorous couple who swept confidently into the venue, looking completely out of place. Everyone else present looked like poor, scruffy students, but this couple could have been on their way to St. Tropez.

It turned out the male half of this spiffy pair was Robert Palmer, the new singer for the Alan Bown Set, arriving with his wife, Sue. Already dazzled by his looks and the fact that his clothes had no creases in them, I was even more dazzled by his voice. Over time, I would also be endlessly dazzled by his knowledge of music, which seemed to take in everything from obscure jazz to the most cutting-edge soul and funk. Robert was also the first person I ever heard talk about African music; he turned me on to King Sunny Adé.

After we became friends, Robert explained to me that he had lived in Malta when he was younger and was able to pick up African music stations on his radio. He was incredibly well-informed about music from all over the world, and throughout his life continued introducing me to artists I knew nothing about. He wasn't a musical virtuoso in terms of playing an instrument—his bass-playing was competent but nowhere near as graceful as Andy Fraser's—but as a listener, he was virtuosic. I think he knew more about records than anyone I ever met besides Guy Stevens.

I had to bide my time to sign Robert as a solo artist, waiting for him to get through his Alan Bown Set phase and then a stint in a band we signed to Island and called Vinegar Joe, another Guy Stevens coinage. In the end, I had to bribe Robert to leave that band—I made him a gift of a house in the Bahamas, where I was building my new Compass Point Studios near Nassau. A pad in the Bahamas was something the suave, high-living Robert couldn't resist. My mum was in the bungalow next door, and he was right by the sea.

Robert made himself at home in the Bahamas, a picture of elegance, his hair and clothes always immaculate. He still managed to get hold of the obscure music he wanted, sending out carefully compiled lists of his latest favorites, and he still made sure the most up-to-date equipment he needed to write his songs was flown in to order. Every so often he made an album and set off for some travel around the world. It was a lifestyle that suited him before he decided drugs needed to be a part of his life.

I once had some visitors pay me a call at Compass Point who didn't know what I looked like. They eventually found Robert working in one of the studios, in crisp luxury linen and a pair of immaculate espadrilles. He was so tanned and cool looking, with such luxuriant hair, that they naturally assumed he was the boss, me, the owner of the whole complex. Moments earlier, they had walked right past me, a seeming vagrant in crumpled shorts and old flip-flops, hair in need of a comb.

Given his stylishness, it was entirely appropriate that we gave Robert a bespoke band suited to his needs for the first album. It ended up being a dream-scenario collective that included the New Orleans masters of funk the Meters, the legendary piano man Allen Toussaint, the great New York rhythm and blues musicians Cornell Dupree on guitar and Bernard Purdie on drums, the Barry White collaborator and string maestro Gene Page, and the superb guitarist and leader of Little Feat, Lowell George. It was the kind of band you could see backing Elvis Presley.

Steve Winwood turned up as well, on the last, twelve-minute track, "Through It All There's You," which is ideal if your dream of the perfect groove is to imagine Traffic jamming with Louisiana's finest in Allen Toussaint's Sea-Saint Studios in New Orleans.

It was a short-term supergroup, and everyone rose to the occasion, Robert not at all intimidated by working with such a class collection of musicians. The Black musicians quickly noted that Robert was no white English flake. He wasn't what they thought he was when they first saw him, a dilettante in oddly conservative clothes with some record company money behind him.

He had the kind of confidence that persuaded them to give their all because he felt this kind of company was where he belonged; the first three tracks were written by Lowell George, Robert Palmer, and Allen Toussaint, and they flow together beautifully. He'd been taking his time for more than ten years, never following an easy route, and now he was ready.

Commercially, *Sneakin' Sally Through the Alley* was a noble failure; but as a representation of Robert Palmer, it was perfect. I'm not sure how you would label the music—which would always be a problem with the genre-fluid Robert—and the sleeve didn't offer many clues, except that he lived an exciting life leaping from adventure to adventure, usually with a model wearing very little or, on the next Steve Smith–produced album, *Pressure Drop*, nothing at all apart from a pair of stilettos. Robert liked to have a good time all the time, even when he was having his photograph taken.

Pressure Drop didn't sell as well as I had hoped, either. Robert seemed to be in a zone with David Bowie's and Bryan Ferry's English takes on American soul, but he wasn't seen to be as specific, even as sincere, which was peculiar considering how arch and conceptual Bowie and Ferry were being. There was something about the fact that there was an authenticity about what Robert was doing that strangely appeared inauthentic.

Nonetheless, Robert cruised through his next few records the way he appeared to cruise through life, as though he were showing off his eclectic knowledge, his constantly updated musical smartness as he skipped from rock and roll to disco to heavy metal, from romantic crooning to big-band swing to electro-pop. Always, as part of his unorthodox mixing and matching, his albums featured sophisticated white funk with the perfect groove he was as great as anyone at perfecting. There were the occasional hits, including a very cool upbeat song written by Andy Fraser, "Every Kinda People," which we gave a Caribbean swing, and a breakthrough American hit, "Bad Case of Loving You," which gave just the right sense of the hedonistic high life he was surely living.

Robert existed in a strange stratum somewhere above cult figure and below major pop star. But his relaxed, charming sense of style, those international-playboy record sleeves, a pure, unflustered love for just singing, and his quick-witted reaction to new pop styles meant he could charge into the slick, well-dressed 1980s without looking like a trend-chaser.

In 1984, as if he were on an all-expenses-paid holiday, he took on the role of lead singer in the dance-pop supergroup Power Station, formed with the guitarist and the bassist of Duran Duran and the drummer from Chic, Tony Thompson. This temporary alliance prepared the way for a brief energized run of chart-topping hits that deftly mixed the energies of rock and disco, produced by Chic bassist Bernard Edwards with glistening simplicity. The big hits came ten years after those fantastic first two albums, but Robert finally became the star I was always convinced he would become, with traces of every style, pose, and dream musical combination he'd tried as he'd been sailing along. Robert represented what I believed Island stood for, getting behind artists who were looking not for quick, short-lived success but a lifetime of making music.

In 1985, when I heard a new song Robert had written called "Addicted to Love," which suggested an undercurrent of further addictions to sex and drugs, I thought: *That's a hit.* But it was six minutes long and needed an "All Right Now" edit to be more radio- and TV-friendly.

These were the MTV years, so we needed a video that was as direct and stylish as the song. A great video would complete the song. Videos were adverts for singles, and I wanted to break outside the usual pop-video clichés and create something that projected Robert's world.

Aware that Robert always seemed to look better when photographed with a woman, I thought of Terence Donovan, the London photographer whose sensual, tousle-haired portraits of a mysteriously moody Julie Christie helped launch the Swinging Sixties.

Terence had a knowing sense of irony similar to Robert's, a playfulness when it came to creating imagery. I called him and asked if he'd do a video. He wasn't so sure—it wasn't something he usually did. I said I would send over the song. He called me back and said he liked the song and that he had an idea for it: a band made up of some models he had spotted on auditions and liked the look of. Robert would sing the song in front of them.

To me, this sounded dreadfully corny, almost a non-idea. Even so, I had a lot of confidence in Terence. He was an artist, and not the usual kind of video director from whom you would want a detailed proposal. With an artist, you look to get something that can't simply be put into an outline. You want their imagination.

Robert came back to the Bahamas straight after filming the video, and I asked him how it went; he thought it went really well. "The girls looked great," he said, which was the first thing on his mind. It didn't look corny? No, no, not at all, said Robert, looking a little shifty. I wasn't convinced I believed him.

The finished video was sent over to me a couple of weeks later, and we sat down to watch it. It wasn't what I expected: the five models were in severe makeup, all flaming-red lips and accentuated cheekbones, their hair slicked back from their pale skin. They held their instruments like they weren't even going to pretend they knew how to play them, and they twitched robotically, out of sync with the music. Which, of course, was what made the video so fantastic and, eventually, iconic.

Robert was dazzling but no-nonsense in his dress shirt and expensive tie, pretty much his daily outfit, with jacket off to show he meant business and was feeling a little loose. He had filmed his part separately, so he didn't really know what the girls were doing behind him. He stood out front in his own state of limbo and sang it perfectly straight, and with a straight face, and behind him at a video distance was this glorious indifference, five girls in their own world creating their own rhythms. We sat there a little open mouthed and then both at the same time said, it's unbelievable. And really funny and sexy. I checked in with Island Records and told them to press all the switches they could to make sure it was a hit. Terence had found a distinct way to create a spectacle perfect for the cavalier swagger of the song. "Addicted to Love" ended up as one of the defining videos of the 1980s, and the "band"—Terence Donovan and the girls, with Robert confirming in surreal videoland that this was the life he really led—stayed together for a couple more singles, playing deadpan in the promo clips for "Simply Irresistible" and "I Didn't Mean to Turn You On."

"Addicted to Love" and those off-kilter robotic girls elevated Robert to something beyond the versatile, adventurous white-soul singer I had first met. The song was number one in the US and Australia, number five in the UK, and Robert won a Grammy for Best Male Rock Performance in 1987—the same year Steve Winwood won a Grammy for "Higher Love" with Chaka Khan, who was originally set to sing "Addicted to Love" with Robert as a duet until her record company stopped her doing it. Another great diva, Tina Turner, made the song a spectacular staple of her live show, which thrilled and flattered Robert as a huge fan of Tina, especially from the Sue days.

One consequence of "Addicted to Love" was that other labels started to get interested in Robert and offered the kind of money that Island never could. EMI massively outbid me for his services, and not even my nice recording-and-living complex in Nassau could keep him around. His Island years came to an end. I lost touch with him, which happens even with artists you have become friendly with. People you've been close to wander off on another path from you, and you both have plenty to occupy your time.

I missed him, especially when I visited the Bahamas where we had enjoyed such good times together. There was a moment in 2003 when I was going to call him, see what he was up to, but something came up and I never got around to it. A few days later, I heard the news that he had died while he was doing some promotion in Paris.

He was only fifty-three, but that life that he lived so well—sometimes a little too well—had caught up with him. Terence Donovan died too early as well, tragically committing suicide at sixty. They both knew how to have a decent amount of fun and not take themselves seriously, though their commitment to louche decadence evidently took a toll. Still, I am glad I brought them together to create such a shared memorable pop culture event.

CHAPTER NINE

THE SEVENTIES: ST. PETER'S SQUARE, HAMMERSMITH

We moved Island's head offices out of the Island Studios in Basing Street in 1973, not least because lots of labels were reluctant to use the studios when the head of a rival record company was sitting nearby. We renamed it Basing Street Studios, with a staff of nineteen run by Muff Winwood, and moved the record company offices out into Hammersmith, west London, to an elegant large garden square filled with grand white villas built in the classical style. There were plenty of well-known inhabitants of the square, including Sir Alec Guinness, Vanessa Redgrave, the theatrical producer Sir Trevor Nunn, and the artist John Piper. Island moved west, which happened to be towards Heathrow Airport, making it more convenient for me, years before other record companies followed suit and left their traditional homes in Soho. It was an unlikely setting for a record label, but somehow perfect for Island.

The Island offices were three linked houses that had been for a time the Royal Chiswick Laundry Western Dying and Cleaning Works and then a film editing suite, with the address 22 St. Peter's Square. It would be the home of the label throughout the 1970s, '80s, and '90s.

Still believing there needed to be a close connection between the label and the recording of its acts, we built a small basement studio in the rear of the building called the Fallout Shelter. It made clear what the central point of the building was—making music—and meant there would be music happening on the premises twenty-four hours a day. I could walk in on a session, make a comment, suggest a change, and then move on to wherever I was needed or decided to go next.

It was dark and intimate, with a great bunker mentality, and acts like Stevie Winwood would come in at a moment's notice to craft new songs. Bob Marley would work there on *Exodus* and *Kaya*, and as with Basing Street, some great engineers began working there, including King Tubby devotee Paul "Groucho" Smykle, who would do some great dub mixes for Black Uhuru, the ace rhythm duo Sly and Robbie, and Grace Jones, starting as a second engineer and soon starting to play around with tape.

It was a great place to use when Island started to release more Jamaican music again, and British-based Jamaican music—a series of little scenes would revolve around the Fallout Shelter, whether it was Bob using the place literally as a shelter as he recovered from the shooting in 1977, or the poet and activist Linton Kwesi Johnson and his innovative producer, Dennis Bovell of the reggae band Matumbi, coming in and out as they worked on his records, a fantastic combination of word and rhythm.

One-time British Black Panther Linton had been very angry with me and suspicious of my motives for what he saw as my commercial exploitation of Bob Marley. We came to an understanding that treating Bob like a rock star and bringing in the white audience didn't mean he had no effect on Black British youth or compromise his power. Marley's success encouraged British reggae music and brought attention to artists like Linton.

We did a couple of gloriously word- and bass-heavy albums with Linton and Dennis, *Forces of Victory* and *Bass Culture*, at the end of the 1970s—and a dub version of Linton's music, which dropped the words to somehow celebrate the spirit and timing of the poetry. Linton's fiercely articulate politicized commentaries formed an important link between the toasting of Big Youth and U-Roy and rap. The records definitively proved that British Jamaican music was in no way inferior to the very best and most adventurous Jamaican reggae.

I wanted to keep the relationship with Linton going. I think he thought I wanted to go rock star on him, lighten the load and soften the blows, so to speak, and I did think he had the charisma and force to be a more public figure than he was. He turned me down and went his own way. Dennis Bovell, meanwhile, helped me out with the Slits, whom I loved because they believed in themselves so much, but I didn't know what to do with them. Dennis did, producing their Island debut *Cut* as if they were a female post-punk London reggae band and that was the most natural thing in the world, a rare and wonderful case of a man getting inside the heads of four determined women; this somehow led to his invention while producing Janet Kay of a whole new romantic British twist on reggae, lovers rock.

A link developed between the Fallout Shelter and Jamaica. Groucho knew that dub and jazz were not far from each other and was the first producer to use dub techniques on African music with King Sunny Adé. There was a sort of circle-of-life vibe to how all this worked. Groucho started out as a tea boy and assistant engineer for producers like Alex Sadkin and Steve Lillywhite; then when he started doing his own sessions, he would be assisted by Stephen Street, who, given the chance to use the mixing desk, quickly picked it up and went on to produce the Smiths, Blur, and the Cranberries.

Bob Marley once said that a record label was a machine to make money, but we made sure at Island that it was also a place where people had ideas and remixed the ideas of others. It was the perfect unorthodox office building to be both—a center of business operations, but also a mazy series of rooms and areas with a large "war room" at the center where talented specialists whose main love was music worked on bringing in and then selling the best artists we could find who suited the basic Island principles.

I viewed each person who worked at Island as being as important as every other, all working on the same project; whatever their main role, the key was allowing them to be fluid and work across all areas. Groucho, for instance, did artwork as well as working in the Fallout Shelter. The intention was to make things happen in what amongst us we decided was the Island way. At the meetings we had, everyone pitched in.

The central team by the mid-1970s had settled down nicely. There was Tim Clark, who had been with me since the beginning, as managing director, and Dave Domleo, who had a sure marketing temperament. Tom Hayes, who'd been sales manager between 1965 and 1967 and then ran the international department, was now Island's in-house lawyer. My chief assistant and liaison officer, Denise Mills, performed a multitude of tasks including looking after Bob when he came to London after the shooting.

Musicians are rarely happy with their record companies, and we tended to sign the sorts of acts who by the very nature of their sensibilities were particularly suspicious of labels and their motives, but you won't find any musician who had dealings with Denise who had a bad word to say about her. Musicians will moan about the lawyers and even what they call the spies who work for record labels, but Denise was one of those who made Island different as a label.

She became very close to Bob in those last years. She was the one who took him to see the doctors in London who recommended the amputation of his wounded toe. To use a word like "assistant" when talking about Denise is, of course, an insult, and it's why I never liked giving people job titles. She was so good at what she did there was no job title in existence to properly represent it.

I've never known what job title to give Suzette Newman, but she's another essential influence on the soul and personality of Island, the sort of character who's given the description "chief fixer" and gets the reputation for being a disrupter on my behalf, making sure things tick over while I am already impatiently moving on to the next thing. Like all the best people I work with, she's always got an opinion about everything, and it's an opinion always worth listening to. Most of the time.

If I did give her any kind of title, she'd bite my head off. She started working at Island Studios in 1970 straight out of school, and she instantly demonstrated Island credentials by thinking outside her given tasks and showing interest in how the studios worked, and what was going on inside them.

She survived all the changes in Island personnel, and all the changes to my relationship with Island, and we still speak regularly and spark off each other—and spar with each other—fifty years after we first met. Maybe she's still with me one way or another to make sure I never land her with a job title.

Designer Tony Wright, who I'd found through his *Bumpers* prints, had become part of this St. Peter's Square team. He'd worked on the Traffic albums and produced Marley's great *Natty Dread* cover. The very fine and thoughtful *Melody Maker* writer Rob Partridge was putting together a fantastic press department with Neil Storey and Regine Moylett, who would go on to be U2's permanent head of publicity. Press relations isn't just a key connection between the label and journalists; it's also the area where your acts tend to socialize most with the company. The department is a kind of radar system for what's happening in music, dealing with the writers who often discover a great new act first, and often discovering new acts first themselves. Having the intelligent, insightful Rob lead the department was crucial, as he had earned the trust of both music-paper editors and writers and the musicians we signed.

By 1979, Nick Stewart started to work in A&R; his first two signings were U2—with the considerable input of Rob—and Killing Joke. He says he wanted to sign the Thompson Twins, but I hated their name and rumor has it I tore the contract up. I might not have been taken by the Thompson Twins, or their name, but I'm not sure I was as worked up about them as all that.

Nick joined Island the very week that we had our first number one—finally, which did prove that we really hadn't been a singles label. We had never deliberately chased a number one, but it was good to have one at last. There was a momentum that had been picking up since the sixties, and here we were, based in a grand building on a lovely London garden square, the pieces all falling into place with a song that as far as Island was concerned seemed to come from left field. But then, that was very Island.

Our unlikely first number one was the nicely put together techno-pop song "Video Killed the Radio Star" by the Buggles, featuring Trevor Horn and Geoff Downes, with a name meant to echo the Beatles.

I loved the track as soon as I heard the demo, even if no one else at the label seemed too excited. I thought the title was very clever, and it had a new kind of sound I couldn't quite put my finger on, largely due to Trevor, up to then a thirty-year-old jobbing musician who turned out to be taking record production into a new era. It was the first-ever music video played on MTV when it launched on August 1, 1981, perfectly setting up a new world by seeming sad about losing the old.

Trevor seemed to have his finger on a new kind of high-tech pulse, and the pop music he was making seemed on the surface quite normal, even slick, but had an obsessive edge. His productions were very pristine and precise, but they had a lot of energy. He followed up the Buggles by producing hits for a middle-of-the-road boy-girl duo called Dollar as though they were another version of the Buggles.

On the other hand, Trevor made music with animated Sex Pistols manager Malcolm McLaren that was seriously out there, raiding the rhythms of South Africa and documenting the early hip-hop sounds of New York and producing a really contagious dance music that sounded as Black as anything. He intrigued me, and I loved that his wife, Jill Sinclair, who was managing him, had bluntly told him—after he'd made a couple of albums with the Buggles, never followed up "Video Killed the Radio Star," and joined the progressive supergroup Yes for a while—that his future was not as a performer but as a producer.

Jill had started a studio with her brother John in the early 1970s in the East End of London and had a lot of experience running it before she met Trevor. I had a meeting with them, and I said that if they started a record label within Island, in return they could take over Basing Street. It seemed the best way of shifting Basing Street, and the idea of how Island worked there as a record company and a studio, into the 1980s, and letting someone else who knew what they were doing bring it up to date.

The first material Trevor played me was some stuff where he had been messing about with his regular engineer and collaborators on some bits and pieces they had brought back from New York and South Africa while working with McLaren. It was a half hour of largely instrumental music, very abstract, lots of new forms of samples and rhythms stuck together, with some beautiful melodies that turned out to be played by a young classically trained musician named Anne Dudley, who had started to do Trevor's string arrangements for Sheffield pop dreamers ABC. She was so straight and proper, so unlike anyone I had ever met in a group, that I got excited as much by her involvement as by the sound. She was so very English; the sound was otherworldly.

Trevor had hired the then-notorious *NME* journalist Paul Morley to come up with an identity for the label, and it was Paul who organized Trevor's freelance unit of engineers, computer programmers, and musicians into a group called Art of Noise. Trevor told me that Paul wanted to call the label Zang Tuum Tumb (after an early-twentieth-century sound poem by Italian futurist Filippo Marinetti), and it was one of those occasions when I thought, *Well, if that's what he wants to do, let him, and see what happens.* It was either a good idea or silly. I'd worked with Guy Stevens. He'd come up with the name Mott the Hoople. Ideas have a way of making sense, or not. You get used to them, or you don't.

It was the record Art of Noise made called *Into Battle* that got me excited that the label would work as a label, more so even than when within a year they had number-one records with epic productions of Frankie Goes to Hollywood. These were extraordinary state-of-the-art productions, up there with what Quincy Jones was doing at the time with Michael Jackson, and exactly the sort of thing I had hoped Trevor would use the Basing Street Studios for. But it was the idea that Art of Noise was the label's house band that made it a label, and the way they romanticized the technology they were using as they used it. The best-sounding records were still coming out of Basing Street even though the music world had changed beyond recognition in fifteen years, and its history continued when Bob Geldof and Midge Ure used the studio to record their Live Aid "Do They Know It's Christmas" song at the end of 1984.

The music on the Buggles record in 1979 was all played—there wasn't a sequencer on it to quickly create the sounds and effects; there were no computers—but Trevor and Geoff and collaborators like the now-famous film composer Hans Zimmer performed it like it was sequenced. Hours of painstaking work that by 1983's *Into Battle*, when it was all computers and sequencing, would take a matter of minutes. Things moved that fast. What was possible was incredible. Trevor had predicted the future, and Art of Noise was the perfect example of the rapid changes there had been in recording in just a few years.

BY THE EARLY eighties, Island had a staff of over a hundred, and from the outside we looked like a big label, the biggest independent perhaps; but in many ways, in spirit, we hadn't moved on from where we were in the mid-sixties. Cash flow was always a problem, and we were never entirely secure. It didn't bother me completely, except when it caused me problems that seemed insurmountable, but it certainly troubled those looking after the money.

I knew the tenacious and ambitious Dave Robinson, who, fresh off the boat from Ireland, had tour-managed Jimi Hendrix and then Graham Parker and Ian Dury before forming the defiantly independent and irreverent Stiff Records with Nick Lowe manager Jake Riviera. It started almost as a hobby, and then it turned out they had some good ideas and loved the idea of poking fun at the slow, uninspiring major labels.

Stiff was very much an "anti-major" record label, seeing the big players as nothing more than manufacturers and distributors in the business of selling plastic, with music as a marketing aid. Any creative element, the finding and nurturing of the artists, came from the independents, they believed; the majors had their own A&R departments only to compensate for the unreliability of the indies—they'd rather not deal with all of that, but sometimes they had to find their own acts to keep the plates spinning.

Stiff made itself a brand, which Virgin had done around the same time; we helped both labels get off the ground with distribution. Stiff was the first to release a punk single in the UK, starting to have fresh, exciting hits with Nick Lowe, Elvis Costello, and Madness, and was pro-musician in a way the majors never could be. Dave was very good at coming up with new, often provocative ways of promoting and marketing, and I thought he might be a good addition to Island and help us have more aggression as a label. We couldn't carry on with our ad hoc sixties mentality. I figured we might need his battling temperament.

I said I would buy half of Stiff, and he could run both Island and Stiff from St. Peter's Square. I persuaded him it would be the perfect partnership, although I might have exaggerated some of the details in terms of how financially buoyant we were as a company.

Even when he knew the reality, I think he liked the challenge, and in front of him was the possibility of working with U2, who were recording their fourth album; the Trevor Horn label, which was making these sensational pop records that clearly whetted Dave's appetite for big hits; and the definitive Bob Marley greatest-hits albums we wanted to put out.

We made the deal, each of us keeping a wary eye on the other but deciding it would be an advantage for us both, and in 1983 Dave charged into Island like a rhino. The first Frankie Goes to Hollywood single, "Relax," for all its explosive sound started selling slowly; but within a few months, at the beginning of 1984, it was number one through a combination of Dave's wiles, a lively ZTT ad campaign, and the fact that the song was banned by the BBC.

There were also some pounding twelve-inch remixes Trevor did, which became a Frankie thing (including a last-minute one done in New York after I took him to the Danceteria and he heard the most modern electronic music played through the most advanced speakers)—not to mention what Trevor described as "the pissing video," a hard-core video for the song commissioned by Paul Morley and directed by Bernard Rose (who later made the first *Candyman* film). Trevor was definitely dipping into the Guy Stevens/Andrew Loog Oldham playbook. Dave remade the video as a more lightweight pop version because he wasn't after the niche, expert pop fans; he was interested in going for the jugular. In the long run this meant spending a lot of marketing money, but the immediate results were impressive. The follow-up to "Relax," the hard-driving "Two Tribes," which left me breathless when I first heard it, was number one for nine weeks, not least because Trevor in his element generated half a dozen twelve-inch remixes that created a constant demand for the same song. Robinson made sure the Frankie album *Welcome to the Pleasuredome* shipped a million copies, for the sake of some sort of record.

It was all hype and mirrors, and it wasn't how Island had worked before; but in 1984, with ZTT, we had a single in the top thirty every single week of the year. It was fun while it lasted—and of course it was the kind of fun that can only happen because it won't last long.

Dave also shrewdly and actively chased a wider audience for Bob Marley, even though we thought we had already reached a wider audience. He wanted to get to an audience that maybe bought only one or two albums a year, who weren't interested in fashion or the latest hip sound.

Robinson was surprised when he saw how few albums Marley sold—in the UK, his best-selling album, *Exodus*, had sold fewer than 200,000, and in the US about 650,000. We thought they were decent sales, but Dave didn't. Bob's profile was massive, especially after his death, and the sales didn't reflect that. He was reggae's biggest star, but he wasn't a best-seller.

When we planned to put together a "best of" compilation after Bob had died, I spoke with Dave about how I saw the record. I talked about how Marley stood up for the dispossessed of the world, saying that I didn't want to lose the intense, militant edge to how we presented him.

Dave shook his head. This was ultimately what contributed to the indifferent sales, he said—the way Island had packaged Bob as a drug-taking, politically motivated, heavily religious iconoclast targeted in an assassination attempt limited his audience. Dave had his own plan—not something that could have been done if Bob were still alive.

He decided very pragmatically to go heavily for the white audience, which meant stripping back obvious references to his beliefs. We thought we had made Marley's records more accessible to a white audience, but not in the way Dave envisaged. He wasn't emotionally as close to Bob as we were at Island, and he started to do some market research both with white suburban record buyers and the faithful followers, just to make sure he didn't go too far. The market research group asked three different age cohorts for their thoughts.

The danger with market research is that you do get to hear what you want to hear. The casual record buyer liked the idea of Bob Marley, liked many of his songs, certainly the hookier, more hummable ones, but didn't like his image and didn't really get reggae as a genre.

Trevor Wyatt at Island, who was responsible for the reggae catalogue, gave Dave a list of potential songs for a best-of, and Dave tinkered for months based on his market research feedback. He wasn't after a definitive collection, just the perfect, accessible introduction. This meant there would be no songs from *Survival*. The title *Legend* came about because even those people in the focus group who owned no Bob Marley records would use the word *legend* as part of how they described their impressions of him.

Dave then put together artwork and a marketing campaign that presented Bob as a striking but inoffensive entertainer, getting Paul McCartney to appear in a video for "One Love" to emphasize Bob's comforting presence in the rock canon.

There was no mention of the word *reggae* in the marketing; Dave bought expensive ad space on radio and TV as though he were selling an easy-listening record. When various sleeve ideas were presented by the market research group to their sample consumers, it was clear most people were not too happy about his dreadlocks. The eventual album cover focused more on his reflective face than his hair.

At Island, the cover vote was for a great Annie Leibovitz shot with his locks almost possessing a life of their own that had made the cover of *Rolling Stone* in 1976. For Dave, that was too challenging, as was any photo of Bob where he wasn't wearing socks. Bob Marley had written "Money is not my richness / my richness is to walk barefoot on the earth," but Robinson wanted to sell him, not sanctify him. He was very curt and dismissive when faced with how Island treated working on Bob Marley as a labor of love. I think he thought we were being totally unrealistic, expecting Marley to seriously represent the powerless.

He would always grumble about why we wanted to be so militaristic. In his view, you couldn't sell a Black rebel. You could sell a fantastic set of already well-loved songs by a major cultural figure who was well on his way to being world-famous.

Island's art director, Bruno Tilley, raided a market stall on the Portobello Road in Notting Hill for all their bootleg Marley paraphernalia and souvenirs and made a collage in the centerfold, which showcased how much of an icon he already was, and the front cover was moody but not at all menacing.

The results in Britain for nonmilitant, neutral Bob were instant. *Legend* became the one Bob Marley album you had to own. It could have gone badly wrong and been completely bland and empty, a cynical cash-in by the label that had always been faithful to his character, but the power and the brilliance of the songs still came through even if the spikier, more revolutionary ones were missing. It wasn't put together with love, but it was put together with a great deal of care.

Legend took a little longer to catch on in America, but slowly it became one of those important records that just keeps selling, up to the streaming era, at a rate of around 250,000 copies a year. It was not only a successful compilation of his best feel-good moments for the suburban whites, possibly their one reggae album, but also an introduction to Marley for the younger, more urban audience who did get to know him as a prophet, mystic, herbsman, and shaman who knew that words have a mystical power. Some went on to discover the artist who used fighting words to get his messages across.

As I write, it has sold over 12 million copies in the US, over 3.3 million in the UK, which makes it the seventeenth-best-selling album of all time. It's sold over 27 million copies worldwide. It spent a total of 609 nonconsecutive weeks on the Billboard 200 album chart, second only to Pink Floyd's *Dark Side of the Moon*. It was ranked in the top fifty of the greatest albums of all time in *Rolling Stone*, a testament to the way Dave compiled it—as a complete, self-contained album, not a thrown-together list of songs.

You couldn't deny that *Legend* contributed to the developing iconic presence of Bob Marley, and to the fact that his music and message increased in universal significance. And you couldn't deny that Dave Robinson's combative mass-market tactics produced results.

Oddly, in his own way, he was quite militant. Dave put a rocket up Island; we had our best couple of years commercially, but in the end, it wasn't really Island. He clashed with our long-established rhythms. His stormy methods didn't change our DNA. However big we got, we still functioned like a small label, suspicious of structures, of making too many plans.

Within a couple of years, Dave Robinson left, taking what was left of Stiff back with him; he ended up partnering with Jill Sinclair and Trevor Horn, who had decided they and ZTT were too big for Island and deserved a better deal. It was the eighties. Everyone wanted a bigger, better deal, a bigger slice of the action, and everything was moving faster. I came from another time and another place, which sometimes put me ahead and sometimes left me a little adrift.

There was also a part of me that thought *Legend* was wonderful, and that Robinson had skillfully managed the difficult task of selling a complex revolutionary figure to the masses. You would get to hear Bob Marley singing in places that weren't exactly Black-friendly.

There was a part of me that was uncomfortable with how *Legend* simplified the image of Marley and edged him away from the religion and the revolution. It had to be done, but I wished there were a world where you didn't have to do it, where people hummed the chorus of "Zimbabwe" as much as they did "Could You Be Loved." It also turned Bob Marley into an industry, which had its own problems in terms of rights, ownership, claimants, and aggrieved musicians demanding royalties they felt were due to them. That never got any easier the more it sold. Bob never made a will, so the conflicts and lawsuits became their own endless jungle, Jamaican music-business shenanigans a million times over.

My own direct response to what Dave had done came a couple of years after *Legend* was released. I put together my own alternative compilation, thinking of the more enigmatic, fearless, and trenchant ghetto philosopher Bob railing against the patterns and systems of injustice, who wrote urgent songs of freedom as much as he wrote songs of love to dance to.

I called it *Rebel Music*, because Bob was easily called a legend but he was also a rebel. That shouldn't be forgotten. *Legend* was the mellow Bob, and *Rebel Music* was the angry Bob. One couldn't exist without the other. It was perhaps the "best-of" that might have been put together if Bob were alive.

Despite *Legend*, I remained of the persuasion that his music keeps getting rediscovered by new generations because it's still kind of underground. It's still not in-your-face. Bob keeps his secrets, and there is still a sense of discovery to the songs. That was where *Rebel Music* came from, and it came from the Island that followed our own instincts rather than asking questions of a random sample of consumers and letting them make decisions for us.

Bruno Tilley worked with Adrian Boot, who had photographed Bob many times, to choose an image of Bob at his most soulful and questioning, without worrying if the dreadlocks were going to upset anyone. He also created a revolutionary logo, Marley's fist in the air holding a Rasta flag with the lion of Judah in the center. This was more how Island did business, for better or worse.

Rebel Music didn't sell the way that *Legend* did, but it supplied a corrective, because what made Bob more than just a musician were those qualities and causes that would inevitably alienate the sensibilities of those potential customers being used in market research, those who just wanted a quiet life.

Legend helped Marley's music travel from Trench Town to every corner of the world, reaching totally different cultures and languages. It helped him become posthumously the only third-world global music superstar—but what made that mean something was how seriously he took his work as an uplifting freedom fighter and political rebel. He worked hard to get his music heard because he knew it was important. It was why he was being monitored by the CIA.

The last time I spoke to Bob was over the phone from the Island offices in Hammersmith, where people were doing what they had to do to prepare for the inevitable. It was a strange time. I had flown back after seeing him in the depressing German hospital. We needed to get him on a Concorde flight back to America on his way to Jamaica, so he could get home, where some of his friends and family thought there might still be hope.

He joked that he wanted me to make sure I didn't get him "one of those propeller things" for the journey to America. There was no time to lose, and he didn't want me to try to cut costs. After all, I was the record company boss, and everyone knows they always try to rip off their artists.

CHAPTER TEN

THE EIGHTIES: COMPASS POINT, THE BAHAMAS

I think, honestly, after Bob passed away on May 11, 1981, and it was becoming increasingly obvious that Yusuf Islam had formally and completely retired from making music even as a Muslim educator, I lost a lot of interest in the day-to-day schedule of music that I once had. There was something so exciting about Bob Marley because you knew it wasn't just about the charts. It was literally about changing the world. To see him grow and grow and be conquering the world was the high point, really. It wasn't just the regular record business; it was something bigger. I don't even know how to describe it. It was special for a certain time, and it felt important. But it wasn't the same after. It was hard to carry on as before, because of the loss both of the performer and, mostly, of the man.

Island had gotten too big for me, I suppose. There was a point where it had been something that I could hold inside my head and feel I was running all elements of it. It was incredibly exciting to play a part in Bob Marley and see that happening, and to help guide it. But after Bob, things sort of shifted for me. I'm always at my most comfortable when I am starting from scratch and searching for what to do next.

*   *   *

I'D ALWAYS REGRETTED that because of how much I was concentrating on Bob Marley around 1975 and 1976, I didn't feel I could focus on a New York band that I would really have loved to sign, Talking Heads. I would go and see them play at CBGB in the East Village with Andy Warhol and Robert Palmer when there was hardly anyone there. They were just a three-piece band then, David Byrne, Tina Weymouth, and Chris Frantz, and we all found different parts of them we really liked. Andy thought they looked cute, saw a bit of himself in David, and knew they were more interesting than most musicians, while Robert liked the rhythm section, which had found a nice, nervy, soulful groove in the middle of all the New York punk rock at the time.

Although as part of a great new New York scene, the Talking Heads were being lumped in with punk groups like the Ramones and played with off-the-wall art rockers like Television, for me they were the one group from that time that seemed to be playing a new form of funk, and there was even some weird disco and African rhythms in there as well.

Seymour Stein of Sire was also a fan, chasing them all around the New York clubs they were playing before they outgrew them, and signed them to his label, as he had the Ramones and would with Madonna. It took him about a year to pin them down, because I'm not sure they even thought of themselves as just a band, but he finally got them in late 1977. Seymour was the boy genius of the modern music business even before he started Sire. In the sixties, he was quick to spot the English rock phenomenon that broke out of the British blues scene, and then he was quickly onto the New York community that happened in the mid-seventies. He is one of the funniest human beings on the planet. He came up with the term *new wave* to describe Talking Heads, because they were being described as punk rock. They obviously weren't—but being called punk meant that radio stations wouldn't play them, because they didn't play punk. Radio was always very funny about things being fixed—Chic was a fluid kind of band but had to be labeled disco before they got played; Prince found it difficult to attract radio play at first because he looked like one thing and sounded like a lot of other things. Talking Heads had covered Al Green's "Take Me to the River" and it was funk more than punk but wouldn't get played because they were seen as punks. Well, Seymour told the radio people, thinking of the late 1950s French *nouvelle vague* art film movement, they're actually new wave. Radio was fine with that. New wave sounded unthreatening, even if it was done in the spirit of iconoclasm.

Late 1970s New York was an amazing place musically as groups in small, dark venues took punk as an opportunity to experiment with their look and sound. Boundaries were being blurred all over the place: groups seemed to be punk but love disco or free jazz and think of themselves as Warhol-attached (because it all began with the Velvet Underground, whom Warhol praised and promoted as a form of manager for a time).

The mix of styles was very Island, and very hard to pin down, and I really wanted to get involved. One of the greatest labels we ever associated with was ZE, named for the initials of the label's two founders and because New York was "ze place to be." The label just popped up out of nowhere, formed by Parisian book and record shop owner Michel Esteban, who had been living the quintessential New York life hanging out with Patti Smith and Richard Hell, and the mild-mannered, secretly wild Michael Zilkha, an Oxford-educated music fanatic from a rich family working as a theater critic for the *Village Voice*.

They'd been introduced at a party by the Velvet's John Cale, and their talk was soon of Talking Heads and Television. Michel was dating a friend of mine, Anna Wintour of *Vogue*, and I got to know both men; they were in one way very naïve, but in terms of their love of music and pop culture, incredibly knowledgeable—and they were right on the spot where things were happening in New York when it was exhilarating, seedy, and dangerous.

You could see how fast things were moving in the city because if there was now new wave, very quickly there was a reaction against it, as though it was already the establishment. This response was called *no wave*. Because I had missed the new wave—Talking Heads, but also Blondie, the Ramones, Television, and Patti Smith—I gave some money to supreme collaborator Brian Eno, who was keen on working with this new generation of Lower East Side bands that quickly followed, and he got together DNA, Mars, and Teenage Jesus and the Jerks, which included James Chance and Lydia Lunch. Eno was in town working with Talking Heads, so he seemed at the center of the action, and I thought something might come out of it.

To many of these artists, Eno was larger than life, with a sparkling creative résumé, recently including his own pioneering ambient records and new work with an experimental-sounding David Bowie on *Low*. The fact that he wanted to work with these groups perhaps prematurely shined a light on the scene and created a coherent sound amongst a disparate set of conceptual musicians.

The music he recorded in New York was all a bit intense and insular for me and leaning more towards noise than rhythm. It was the experimental Eno, whose Obscure label of ten records featuring avant-garde composers inspired by John Cage had been released by Island. Obscure music needed to be recorded, and it was the same with Eno's no wave. I put out the album because I liked the idea that the scene was documented before it burnt itself out, even if it wasn't going to sell many copies—which it certainly didn't—but it didn't encourage me to take any of it further or sign any of the groups.

ZE did know what to do with some of the musicians who were close by, or part of, this no wave, so Island was still in touch. I could happily leave them to it. They made sense of where the downtown freakish experimental edge of no wave connected with the uptown dance freaks, and developed their own brand of sleazy listening.

Because they were from the Danceteria, Paradise Garage, and Studio 54 as much as the darker Lower East Side aesthetic—so part punk, part dance—there was more pop (however deviant) and there was rhythm (however twisted). It was more John Cale than John Cage, and it was more the Eno of Roxy Music playing with pop music than the Obscure Eno.

ZE was the definitive Island splinter group really, an untamed, lovable, sometimes creepy stepchild who liked to hang out and have fun but on the side was up to no good. They operated in the creatively flexible Island spirit, putting contrasting music and personalities together to see what happened, making a few gambles. They had a great house producer, Bob Blank, who'd worked with Chic and Sun Ra and made sure even the craziest ZE projects sounded fantastic and featured the best local session musicians. Their glamorous, provocative artwork reflected their playfulness and their belief that whatever they did, however far-out or noisy, was still pop music.

Their roster was impressive. They asked Bill Laswell of Material to make disco as strange as he could imagine. Was (Not Was) was itself a splinter of ZE that developed its own massive cultural influence. The label's first signing, Cristina—Zilkha's future wife, who was an art critic at the *Village Voice*—could have been as big a star as Debbie Harry, and it was a shame the attempt we made to have her produced by Robert Palmer at Compass Point never happened.

Another lost star, James Chance, was free-jazz disco, while ZE's great mascot and another of their house producers was the seriously underrated August Darnell, who as show-business shaman Kid Creole with his Coconuts made a significant and deranged charge into the mainstream charts. ZE got Ric Ocasek of the Cars to produce New York electro-duo Suicide's second album, a hopeful clash of sensibilities, and the way ZE freely mixed an experimental energy with high production values got me thinking.

Their way of looking at what was around them to make something of their own and imagining what the sound of the eighties was going to be was on my mind as I started to think about my new studio.

WHEN TALKING HEADS started making records and New York was a tangle of punk, post-punk, dance, electronic, early rap, performance art, and art rock, I had just opened Compass Point on the island of New Providence in the Bahamas, ten miles west of the capital city, Nassau, near the airport.

I'd wanted to build a studio in the Caribbean, because I had learned that the best records were made when the artists were in some kind of isolated location where they could create music in a relaxed setting. I'd seen it with Traffic in their Berkshire cottage, John Martyn at my house in Theale. There was nothing around for miles, so the focus was on making music, on devising the right kind of circumstances to create, compose, and perform, and then outside the studios there was tranquility and a sense of being apart from business and other distractions.

I envisaged Compass Point as a sort of artists' community for musicians, and along with the most technologically up-to-date studio facilities I could imagine, I created a resort setting where the musicians could stay. It was the beginning of my interest in the hospitality business, the creation of a sanctuary that was filled with some mysterious energy. There was the studio with the best equipment you could get at the time, and outside its walls was a paradisiacal setting. There was also the fact that, other than the sunshine and the bright-blue ocean, the place was a little dull. You had to find things to do. If you were a musician, you could fill your time after you grew bored with the sun and the sea by making music.

In an ideal world, I would have built it in Jamaica. I had passed over to Bob Marley the Hope Road Island base with its little studio, which became his Tuff Gong; but in the mid-1970s the political climate in Kingston was very volatile and Jamaica itself under all sorts of political pressure. Violence was becoming common. International airlines were canceling flights to the island.

It was a dangerous place to be, and plenty of guns were coming into the country. Kids would have guns, and some said they got them from the CIA, which, guided by Secretary of State Henry Kissinger, was trying to destabilize the democratic socialist Michael Manley government because of his ties with Fidel Castro and his criticism of American foreign policy. The fear was as much that empowered Black people on the island might spread through the Caribbean as it was of any identification with communism and Russia. Jamaica's influence was always disproportionate to its size, and America was worried it would become a powerful English-speaking force in the area.

It was hard to imagine building a secluded high-tech studio there that would create the right mix of relaxation and creativity. Such a studio would draw too much attention to itself, especially being used by the kinds of bands I hoped would use it. I wanted a place in the region where artists would come and work.

The local studios worked in the context of Jamaican music, but they were always in the center of the city, surrounded by chaos and distraction. What I wanted was a studio set in the middle of nowhere, with just enough access to some basic luxuries and, a few miles away, a town or city, if you needed a little more action. The Bahamas supplied all of that—and was closer to America and still in the Caribbean.

Gary Kurfirst, who'd opened what became Bill Graham's Fillmore East in New York, was managing the Talking Heads. I'd known him since he'd managed Mountain in the late 1960s and promoted an outdoor rock festival outside New York that inspired Woodstock; we had a very similar sensibility and would become business partners on a few projects. Like me, he was a fan of keeping things low-key, and he had a motto he would tell his acts if they became successful: don't smile in photos, it looks like you're making too much money. It was advice I would use myself.

He'd helped me with Bob Marley in America in 1975, which led to him managing Peter Tosh, and I offered Talking Heads a really good deal to come out and record their second album at Compass Point, which became *More Songs About Buildings and Food*. I thought having a group like Talking Heads in the studio would be a good advert for it, because they were so hip at the time, and they were also going to record it with Brian Eno—he'd seen them in London with John Cale and won a race between the two of them, both excited as always at finding kindred spirits, about who would get to produce them.

They started recording in the spring of 1978, and you could say unofficially opened the studio for business—the wiring wasn't quite finished, so they were doing a bit of road-testing as well.

They weren't an Island band, but having them in the studio re-created that feeling I had in the early days, where we'd have bands recording on Island and the best of non-Island recording in our studios at the same time, creating a vibe that would help our acts. On *More Songs About Buildings and Food* you could hear the "studio-as-instrument" approach that was part of Eno's aesthetic, the desk and room perfect for what Eno and his engineer wanted to do. But the environment has an influence too—in this case, especially on the way the group subverted dance music. It started to make me wonder what sort of fusion music a Compass Point house band would specialize in.

The Rolling Stones came to the studios not long after, as usual needing the kind of stimulating haven the studio provided, an international recording base for an international band. They were also a great draw for the studios. If the Stones wanted to record at Compass Point—and they were always on the hunt for the best places, with the best energy, someplace like nowhere else they had been before—then others would follow. The Rolling Stones had become the leading experts at discovering hidden gems where you could find the energy to work when it seemed you'd already been to all the finest facilities and made your best music.

Emotional Rescue was not one of their greatest records, although it might have been one of their best-sounding. The title track, melting between disco and rock, New York and the Caribbean, and the genre-crunching "Dance" groove, clicking between Keith's riffs and funk, added to my musings about what a Compass Point signature sound would be. Music coming into the studio from all around the world, from other countries and their different influences.

That late-night Stones thing worked well at Compass Point—in the heat, there was no need to start work until later in the day, so the day was for clearing the head and relaxing, and taking care of various bits of business, and the night was when the work and a different sort of play started.

Soon we were getting enough bookings to need a Studio A and a Studio B, which I had previously liked at Basing Street, so that there was different music happening at the same time, encouraging a discreet, or even more explicit, positive interaction between the two rooms. One session can infect another; musicians can slip between the two worlds and another world materializes. Studio B was smaller, but the sound was as good. It was also good to have two studios so there would always be time for my own projects.

There was a sense we were slipping between the 1970s and the 1980s, and there were going to be some big changes. It would be the decade of cocaine and AIDS, Reagan and Thatcher, MTV, and records being replaced by compact discs. Because of the advances made in recording studios and electronics and the arrival of drum machines, music was starting to sound different.

Dire Straits was one of the first groups whose albums would be released on CD. They were in Compass Point at the end of December 1978 recording an album that would be released, as they were then, on vinyl and cassette; but by the mid-1980s their *Brothers in Arms* album was the first to be recorded entirely digitally, and the first to sell a million on the new compact disc format. Initially, the CD was just an addition to vinyl and cassette; by the end of the eighties it would be the dominant format, and labels started to release their back catalogues again and again. Vinyl had a heyday of about thirty-five years, and then CDs about the same.

That early eighties period was both the end of an era and the beginning of something new, and those unstable periods of transition always made it into the sounds of pop and rock records. It would happen at Compass Point, musicians reacting first to changes in the air—and the well-played, anti-punk, jazz-blues-soaked, laid-back sound of Dire Straits on the *Communique* album they recorded in the Bahamas, in the middle of disco and new wave out in the world, also supplied hints of a distinctive studio sound. You needed to be plugged into how disco, techno-pop, and new wave were developing, but also have great players, as Muscle Shoals did with their Rhythm Section, Spector had with the Wrecking Crew collective, Motown in their Studio A, and Stax with Booker T. and the M.G.'s.

Because his promiscuous love of funk and soul and electronic music also seemed to point towards a new studio sound, I had asked Robert Palmer to move there. This was important in establishing the place as a community, because he relished the setting and the studio, and symbolized how it would work as an artists' retreat. It wouldn't just be about sun and sea—you'd be feeling good about your life and you'd want to turn that into music.

Acts would arrive at the studio, and Robert was living in one of the condominium apartments I'd built nearby, making it clear this was a safe place for musicians to get themselves together. Recording is a mysterious process, but one thing I had learned was that it always works best when the artists, and the producers and engineers, feel at home even when they aren't. Robert was like part of the welcoming committee. Even if you didn't necessarily see him, you knew he was there, experimenting in his apartment on all sorts of musical ideas that he'd taken from around the world.

I took a new signing to Island out to Compass Point to produce their first album. I'd wanted the B-52's after I heard the single that they released themselves, "Rock Lobster," which made me laugh but also made me take them seriously, because it was out of its skull but fantastically played.

They brilliantly mixed irony and intensity, amateurism and professionalism, like a ZE band, and I had seen them play at Max's Kansas City, where they were supported by Lydia Lunch's Teenage Jesus and the Jerks. One of my favorite writers and thinkers, the stylish visionary Glenn O'Brien, had written about them in Andy Warhol's *Interview* magazine, so they were very much in the moment. ZE wanted them, which would have been fine, because that still meant Island; but I really wanted to produce them, so I took them directly to Island. The B-52's were where Island demonstrated its own ZE style.

The rhythms of "Rock Lobster" were madcap but superbly tight, right out of mid-seventies downtown New York, where bands like Talking Heads weren't afraid to jerk their sound to create their kinky version of early funk. It seemed instantly like a classic pop song, and they played it like it was no big deal and tomorrow something would replace it, but also with irresistible energy.

The B-52's knew their pop music, and their pop culture, and turned it all inside out and this way and that. I'd never heard anything like it, but it also reminded me of pop records made in the fifties and sixties that fought limited primitive equipment to get a new kind of modern sound. They reminded me a little of early Roxy Music, novelty pop music made with a deadpan avant-garde sensibility. It was pop art, but also it was underground.

I had an idea how to produce them, which was to re-create the circumstances of recording on more basic equipment to capture their sound as it was when they played live. I was thinking of ska, all that manic energy and wired wordplay, party music made with intent.

I didn't want to polish them up, as I thought that would lose their haywire freshness. It was like how Guy Stevens had produced the first Free album—if this was the only record they ever made, then you'd know exactly what they sounded like at the time. And in a way how the B-52's had ingeniously arranged their songs was itself a form of production, and I didn't want the studio to crush them.

I was being a bit perverse, maybe, recording like it was 1960 when recording techniques had moved on so much, but it was also a conscious decision not to smooth away their idiosyncrasies. It was recording them very bare and unadorned, but it was also recording them on modern equipment, so it didn't sound exactly like it was 1960. It was 1960 turned upside down into 1980. It took new technology to capture cleanly and with contemporary power and a lot of detail that low-tech retro sound.

The group were a bit underwhelmed and nervous that I didn't pump them up and decorate them, as they thought I was being halfhearted with them. I don't know how they thought a producer was meant to behave, but they were nonplussed when I would put my feet on the desk, light up a spliff, and tell them to play the next song. They thought they were doing all the work.

They were, initially, and I didn't want to get in their way. They didn't exactly lack ideas. It was one of the reasons I signed them. Some artists are musicians, and that's what they do: play music. Then you have artists like the B-52's, who have enough ideas to build their own reality, which they then inhabit. And in that reality, they were great playing live, totally in control of all the chaos. There are few groups as exhilarating in full flow. Once getting them down on tape was done, there was other work to do, where it all comes alive as a record—the mix. I'd hired the best engineers I could find for Compass Point, the kind who could take a good idea and make it so much better. Their rough mixes sounded like finished mixes, which was how I loved to work, so that you could hear something that sounded finished very quickly. Or you knew what you needed to change.

It was the B-52's' first album, it was in a brand-new studio, it was the first time out of the country for some of them, and they were expecting some big transformation. When nothing fancy seemed to be going on and it was all done in three weeks and sounded like they sounded playing live, they looked disappointed. I think over time they got used to it.

I asked Tony Wright, Island's art director, to do the sleeve. There was a black-and-white picture the band really liked that the New York photographer George DuBose had taken to go with Glenn O'Brien's *Interview* piece. Tony hand-colored it, giving it more of a bright, cartoonish look to go with their music, and it was perfect. Tony didn't like their music and credited himself as Sue Absurd.

Forty years later, the album still sounds fresh; if we had tried to make it sound like other things at the time, it would now sound dated. The cover hasn't dated either, because the band managed to choose poses and looks from the past and the future. The album somehow updates itself every time pop is rebooted, because it's about the future as much as the past.

It made me realize that Compass Point was succeeding as a great place to work spontaneously and create studio magic. That debut B-52's album sounded magical, not simply achieved, which it had to do if it was to belong with the kind of music it was inspired by. It was of its time, of other times, and of no time at all, and this was the sound of Compass Point. When we released it in the middle of 1979, it sold well and was reviewed with a lot of enthusiasm, and there were a couple of hits; but it would be another ten years before their monster hit "Love Shack." They had to wait for the world to catch up.

John Lennon heard a lot of Yoko Ono on the B-52's' first album, and it's said he was inspired to come out of retirement by a kind of energy he could identify with. Kurt Cobain as a kid marveled at the energy Lennon also savored and later would be impressed that something so eccentric had been released on a major label, although I would have argued with him about the "major" part. It was the kind of record I wanted to come out of Compass Point, at a time when all kinds of genres were flying around and meeting in some sort of floating middle. I wanted to make strange and unexpected records that would go on to sell over a million copies and get even more interesting over time.

At the same time, an album recorded at Compass Point during April and May of 1980 during a series of tropical storms, AC/DC's *Back in Black*, would go on to sell over 50 million copies and become the second-biggest-selling album of all time. That brought some other energy to the place, adding to what energy was originally there. Their new singer, Brian Johnson, replacing Bon Scott, who had recently died, was not immediately taken with the low-key, communal downtown vibe of the studio. He thought the accommodation was a little limited, and he kept some six-foot fishing spears by the door while he slept in case the place was invaded by Haitian thieves, who he'd heard were on the prowl. As he said, it was a long way from his hometown in England, Newcastle. During one session, recording had to stop while a crab scuttled across the studio floor.

I STARTED BUILDING my dream ensemble—inviting to the studio a set of musicians I'd worked with or knew of who I hoped would generate that mixture of disco, new wave, and electronic without losing sight of jazz, blues, and, of course, reggae. Around this time, Talking Heads were about to tour their fourth album, *Remain in Light*, a masterpiece part-recorded at Compass Point, and were pausing while they worked out what to do next. There was a little turbulence in the group.

David Byrne and Jerry Harrison were going to make albums of their own through Sire, and Seymour Stein told the other element of the group, husband and wife Chris and Tina, that he couldn't afford three solo projects. They were the rhythm section, and there was a sense that a rhythm section is in the background—that's the point—so how could they be the main performers?

The band's manager, Gary Kurfirst, mentioned to me that Tina and Chris wanted to make a record of their own. They didn't want to make two separate solo albums but come up with some sort of new ensemble, something that didn't sound at all associated with Talking Heads. They were one of my favorite parts of the band, and their feel had been just as important to the sound as David's voice and Jerry's keyboards, sometimes more so. I don't think "Psycho Killer," "Burning Down the House," or "Once in a Lifetime" would be what they are without Chris and Tina giving a nervy art-rock tension to Motown and Memphis sources.

Rhythm to me was always king, and in reggae it is at the front of everything. Rhythm sections were always at the heart of great Jamaican albums—often they were the lead instruments.

I said to Gary, "Why don't Chris and Tina come down to Nassau and record a single?" There was nothing to lose. I was sure they would have some good ideas and would be great to have around, and I said if I liked the single, they could make an album.

The first idea was that they work with Lee Perry, who had a bit of downtown New York himself. They loved how he pulled songs apart and found different ways to put them back together. I arranged a meeting for them with Scratch at the Holiday Inn in Manhattan, and it all seemed to go well. We booked the dates in Nassau when he said he was available—but he never turned up. He'd never let on, but it appeared he was outraged by my behavior when we opened the studios and I performed a Jamaican custom meant to bless the property when you lay the foundations of a new home or move in.

I'd taken a bucket of chicken blood and, dipping some chicken feathers into it, sprinkled it around the perimeter of the premises. The idea was that this was how you kept evil spirits away and warded off duppies, the local ghosts intending to make the new place their home. Lee was there when I performed the ceremony, and his version was that I drank the chicken blood from a rum glass and spat it everywhere, then offered him the glass to do the same. He saw it as a blood sacrifice. Voodoo. For Scratch, that was the outer limits.

Our relationship was rocky anyway because I had not put out one or two of the records he recorded for Island in the mid-seventies, and he thought I owed him money for the work he had done with Bob Marley and the Wailers before they signed to Island. He called me an "energy pirate," and when I gave him a check so that he could get his studio back in shape after he had wrecked it, he spent the money on an antique silver serving set for investment purposes.

He was so angry that he even turned down an offer to produce Talking Heads, because he saw them at Compass Point and assumed they were signed to Island. Scratch told his version of the chicken blood story in a song, "Judgement in a Babylon," where he called me a vampire and my assistant Denise a witch—the job title he gave her was my "high priestess." Island's head of press Rob Partridge issued a statement refuting many of the accusations in the song, which ranged from extortion to murder, and with regards to Denise stated: "She has many talents but has never yet revealed a penchant for witchcraft." We didn't take any legal action, even though I disagreed with Scratch's overall assertion that I was a vampire and that Denise was a witch. It was a great track after all, and he had perhaps saved my life by delaying my arrival at Tuff Gong when there was the shooting.

Chris and Tina hung around for a few days waiting for Scratch to appear. They gave a name to the condos where the musicians stayed, Tip Top, because they were at the top of a hill behind the studio. You didn't have street numbers in the Bahamas. They called their own apartment the Tom Tom Club, inspired by some club they went to in downtown Nassau, and it turned out the Tom Tom was the name of a club in the Cliff Richard teen idol movie *Expresso Bongo*. There was a place I owned where U2 would stay when they came over called Press On Regardless, which they nicknamed Pass Out Regardless, because as a young group beginning to travel the world, they liked to have a good time. They came out after their *Boy* tour in 1981, and they fancied the sunshine rather than being locked away in the studio, so it wasn't one of Compass Point's greatest successes.

After three weeks, with no sign of Scratch, who was off radar,

Chris and Tina asked if they could work in the empty Studio B with one of the house engineers at Compass Point, the twenty-year-old Jamaican Steven Stanley, a Kraftwerk fan who'd worked on the early takes of "Once in a Lifetime" and gave it quite a punch. They said he was like a junior Scratch but without the . . . Scratchiness.

It seemed like a good idea, and they were raring to go. They worked in a way I recognized, liking to write music as the result of creating situations and seeing what happened. As great listeners to music, and where music was at the time, they imagined smarter, wonkier disco and early hip-hop, when it was still based on graffiti, break dancing, and electric boogaloo, as though it were part of new wave, three New York scenes and some overlapping reggae wrapped together to make something new.

The first track they came up with was "Wordy Rappinghood," which was brimming with this combination of sweet and smart and sounded like a funky nursery rhyme. Tina wasn't a singer, so she was rapping. Back then, this was such a new thing; it first reminded me of Jamaican toasting over beats. It was the same when Debbie Harry rapped on "Rapture" at about the same time. You couldn't knock their flow as being inauthentic because there wasn't a right way to do it yet, and they weren't copying anything and getting it wrong. They were just not singing words, just following the rhythm. It came out of the same New York mix of the everyday and the uncanny that ZE artists did, but the sound was very Island.

I loved it immediately and decided to get it out as a single for the summer of 1981. I wanted to hear more, so I asked them to make an album. The single started to do well outside America and made the top ten in the UK, so I imported 100,000 twelve-inch singles into the US. That's when Seymour and Sire took notice—the hits started coming from the less obvious part of Talking Heads, and Sire signed Tom Tom Club.

Chris and Tina got all kinds of friends and family involved, and it was just the spirit I wanted for the studio, ideas coming out of all sorts of places and memories, lots of happy accidents, musical moments that couldn't really be planned. Visits into Nassau on nights off also led to discoveries.

They found a dynamic Bahamian guitarist playing in a hotel band in Nassau, Monte Brown, who'd been in a local disco-funk group called T-Connection that had had a couple of hits for a subsidiary of the Florida label TK Records, home of George McCrae, Betty Wright, and KC and the Sunshine Band. He was there on the doorstep, and played the perfect understated but totally infectious guitar part for "Wordy Rappinghood."

In Studio A next door to Tom Tom Club, the house band I had pieced together was working on another project, and they started to slip into Studio B, creating that link between worlds. The project in Studio A was also New York–based, but centered around a performer who had brought other countries, energies, and visions into the city, with a voice we'd purposely built the studio band around.

CHAPTER ELEVEN

TIMING: GRACE JONES
AND THE ALL STARS

IN NEW YORK I was friends with the very good writer and pioneering pop journalist Nik Cohn, who had written an article for *New York* magazine in 1976 about emergent disco that was based on sixties London mods, which turned into the film *Saturday Night Fever*. Nik mentioned to me at a lunch or drinks that there was this Jamaican girl really taking off in New York, a singer, did I know of her: Grace Jones. I hadn't heard of her, or at least her name hadn't stuck, even though it turned out she was signed to a label that Island distributed. We were distributing a lot of little labels, and I didn't necessarily listen to everything.

About five or six days later I picked up the latest edition of *New York*, and there was an incredible picture of this striking woman holding a microphone and balancing unnaturally on one leg. An extraordinary, super-real photo, and I realized that this was who Nik had been talking about.

Grace came from the fashion world, and I would not have known anything about fashion or Jamaican models. I had my music business blinkers on. Other people were telling me I just had to meet her, she was Jamaican, put on great late-night live shows that were disco but rocked the place, but I did not think it would mean anything to me.

We eventually met at the Russian Tea Room, which was adjacent to my offices in the Carnegie Hall building. The offices there were fantastic, with all these dance rehearsal rooms next door. What I wore, my flip-flops and usual wrinkled trousers, seemed to have made as much of an impact on Grace as it later would on Bono.

Grace, of course, looked as though she had just done a photo session for some hip magazine and was on her way to dancing till dawn with Andy Warhol and Bianca Jagger. What won me over and took me by surprise, because she seemed to be bohemian French-American and had spent a lot of time in Syracuse, Philadelphia, and Paris, was how Jamaican she was. She was the ultimate modern, ambitious representation in an infinitely connected world, of a Jamaica that came from everywhere, a Jamaica that had absorbed hippie, LSD, disco, punk, New York, Paris, Japan, London, you name it. She was an orgy of hybrids.

Hearing about Grace from someone I greatly respected, Nik Cohn, helped finally break through my indifference, because otherwise it's another case of "There's this model who wants to be a singer . . ." Yeah, sure. There is always a model who wants to be a singer. What's new? And then you see this sensational picture of her, where she just looks incredible, not like a model but like this amazing alien creature. My God, the art direction, which turned out to be by her French boyfriend, Jean-Paul Goude, a graphic-design genius, was fantastic. Truly out of this world.

Sy and Eileen Berlin at Beam Junction, where Grace was signed at the time, were happy to sell the contract. They weren't music-business people; they were dabblers, really, a couple who earned a living in the rag trade chancing their luck and thinking the music biz was an easy way to make some extra money. They got that wrong. They thought of Grace as a kind of Diana Ross. They got that wrong. They wouldn't have thought of Nina Simone, or Nico, or areas of borderless intrigue where rabble-rousing Grace really lurked.

Their label was one that Island was distributing, but I hadn't paid any attention to Beam Junction's records, not least because they were disco, and I didn't think there was much for me there.

Sy and Eileen were completely out of their depth making records, and completely out of their depth working with someone like Grace, who even in relative obscurity acted like a star and demanded absolute commitment. She knew what she wanted even before she was able to ask for it.

They started making the first Grace album expecting to spend at most about $10,000, which even then seemed a fortune to them. The cost ended up close to $80,000, and they were freaking out wondering how they would ever make any money from it. When they came to meet me to see if I would be interested, you could almost see the sweat on their brows. They were desperate to sell the rights to me. When we worked out a deal and I took the project on, they almost cried with relief. They recovered their investment and then some, making their extra cash after all, and it meant Grace and I could start working together.

GRACE'S DISCO WORLD was hugely different for Island, and very different for me. Island had traditionally been about folk, rock, and reggae. It was distant from the action and artifice of Studio 54, where Grace reigned like she owned the place. We'd had some dance things, but very few. We had a few disco hits, but usually on self-reliant subsidiaries like Beam Junction. And disco was being really looked down upon by the end of the 1970s, and it didn't seem to be the genre where an interesting, challenging artist would be working.

I wasn't initially sure what I was going to hear when I listened to her music—I was a bit doubtful. Sometimes when you see something so visual, you are a little let down when you hear the track; but I wasn't with the version of "La Vie en Rose" that Grace had done on her debut album, *Portfolio,* the first of three disco albums she made.

The intro went on forever, which was very unusual at the time, and there was no sign of any singer. After a couple of minutes, when Grace finally came in, it was a tremendous moment. The whole track lit up and came to life. The intro had created a kind of fabulous entrance for Grace to make, building up anticipation so that she arrived in a predatory blaze of glory. I still think it's one of the best Grace tracks.

The intro that went on forever consisted of little more than a drum machine and a gentle groove, but it was brilliantly produced to create this sense of drama. That was an early part of the movement into technology, where electronics were being used to generate very precise rhythm. Grace's disco producer, Tom Moulton, had remixed into classic status Gloria Gaynor's "Never Can Say Goodbye," and he was one of the originators of the idea of the twelve-inch mix, the repeated instrumental extension of the rhythmic parts of a track. Moulton didn't want the singers he worked with in the studio until the track was done—that was the only problem really in how he worked. It was a new way of making records, where the artist had minimal contribution to how the track was built; in fact, the singer was low down amongst the priorities of the producer, just something to add at the last minute to give the track some identity.

As he made more music for the clubs with Grace, Tom distanced her from being involved in her own music, and the tracks consequently had less and less impact. More drum machine than Grace, which is an outrage really, as Grace was no faceless session singer but a vocal artist, and a living work of art.

With Tom, there was no artist, just an image. In his Grace Jones music, there was less and less a sense of the identity of Grace herself, because she was not allowed to be a part of the creative process, even if just in terms of the music reacting to her presence and her energy.

This was the problem with disco ultimately, that it became more and more anonymous despite it being all about performance and visuals. Those early Grace Jones disco albums represented that, how an extraordinarily strong, dominant character like Grace is somehow ignored by the music and the producer. The music needed to be all about Grace, but here it was ultimately more about the producer, who used her as the face, but not the spirit. The first album was so strong, and it was a great place for Grace to start, but the next ones tended to copy that. The first record still sounds very contemporary.

From my perspective at Island, now that we were taking over from Beam Junction, it seemed we were in a bit of trouble after the third album, which was half as good as the second one, which was half as good as the first. It didn't do very well, and I thought that although Grace was incredibly powerful and cosmopolitan, the music was getting weaker—this wasn't the Grace I had met and who was in the photograph Jean-Paul Goude had built around her energy. She needed a new kind of electric modern soul music to represent her, not a faded, even derided and predictable disco sound.

Part of Grace's trip, as I saw it, was that she was really scary and intimidating. She was not a mere celebrity; she was performance art in constant action. It seemed closer to where Talking Heads and those New York new wave—and no wave—acts were, downtown music mixed with an underground art sensibility, and if there was any disco, it was dirty, it was funky. Grace was part of that Andy Warhol world of self-invention more than the seasonal fashion scene. And in the turbulent 1970s, New York was filled with weird, brilliant people, but there was no one as weird and brilliant as Grace.

There was a sharp shock when you saw her, and shock in the ways Jean-Paul was exaggerating her physique, enhancing her mystique. And after I met her—discovering, *My God, she is Jamaican*—I thought, let's give her some heavy, militant Jamaican bass and drum. Disco was international to the extent that it didn't sound like it came from anywhere. It was placeless. It came from the disco itself, if anything, but Grace was larger than life, and definitely larger than disco. I started to imagine what a group would sound like that had someone like Grace Jones as their lead singer, and those ideas started to coincide with the thoughts I was having about a Compass Point house band.

On paper, the blend I was after seemed impossible; but then, Grace was impossible—as a performer and an artist, as a human being, and certainly in those images Jean-Paul Goude was fabricating. We needed impossible music for an impossible being who was destined to sweep through our imaginations.

At that time at Island, we had the compelling and militant post-reggae collective Black Uhuru, which was the first thing freewheeling rhythm section Sly and Robbie came up with after I had signed them as a production team (since they were already signed as an act to Virgin's Front Line).

First of all, Black Uhuru's name is great, and it has bloody connotations: the Mau Mau rebels used to daub the word *uhuru*—freedom—in blood on the houses of those they murdered, and their fighting insignia is long braids smeared with blood.

The name Black Uhuru was very intimidating because of that, the *black* reinforcing the *uhuru*. Then you'd see Uhuru's singing trio—Sandra Jones, Michael Rose, and Duckie Simpson—plus Sly Dunbar and Robbie Shakespeare walk into a room, my God, you'd run for the hills. Michael and Duckie were from one of the toughest areas of Kingston and looked as though they could handle themselves whatever the circumstances. They were intensely Jamaican with a pure Rasta consciousness, but performed like a rock group, and I thought they could be as internationally known as Bob Marley. Although they never filled the space that Bob left, they won the first-ever Best Reggae Recording Grammy in 1985 for *Anthem*, which was recorded at Compass Point and Dynamic in Jamaica and made enough noise outside Jamaica, considering how provocative they were. They didn't know what to make of the Grammy, and after all that quickly fell apart, which seemed such a waste.

Black Uhuru's music sounded like their name, hard and shadowy, and I thought it would be great to get Sly and Robbie, the bass and drum at the center of so much important, groundbreaking reggae, to give their kind of deep, dark, disorienting edge to Grace. People were scared of Grace, and it was no use trying to pretend that wasn't the case by presenting her as simply a disco diva. They also seemed to like being scared by her.

There was something about Grace that was more from Sly and Robbie's world than from disco, and there was a knowledge of disco in what they did, and of its deviant relation to funk, but they bent it around a more radical idea of a steady pulse and a more fluid way of using electronics. Grace was more a member of the Uhuru tribe than the disco tribe. Above all she is an actress, and she is tremendous at playing Grace Jones, so what we needed to do was write the best script for her to perform.

Sly and Robbie had been part of Channel One's house band the Revolutionaries and appeared on Culture's apocalyptic *Two Sevens Clash* soundtrack to Kingston in crisis, but came together most successfully as a drum and bass duo mapping the groove on the Mighty Diamonds' indispensable *Right Time* album. I asked them to come to my apartment in New York in Essex House, and they were fine listening to me when I came up with an idea for them, not least because Sly for one was a big fan of "My Boy Lollipop."

I mentioned Grace and gave them her disco albums, but I don't think they ever listened to them. They seemed intrigued, just by the idea that I was trying to get some musicians together from different places; always wanting to add outside influences to their pulse and movement, they were in.

With Sly and Robbie—who had been redrawing the rhythmic map of Jamaican music ever since they came together in the mid-seventies—you would be getting an unmistakable, authoritative Jamaican sound even if you weren't exactly making reggae. Once you had a handle on the rhythm, then you could build around that.

Island had just made Marianne Faithfull's bruising, punkish comeback album, *Broken English*—one of those records, and singers, that don't appear to belong anywhere, but often found a home at Island. It featured this fierce, screaming guitar by Barry Reynolds, who had been in one of Island's blues bands, Blodwyn Pig. I thought his experienced, nervous rock playing, technically brilliant but also with a real nomadic-seeming edge, was something to get into the Compass Point mix, a solid sense of the midrange, because reggae rarely had an interesting midrange. When I rang Barry, he didn't know who Grace Jones was, but he knew who Sly and Robbie were, and said he'd love to play with them. He was quite wry about it, realizing I was asking him along to represent "the old world." We needed some of that, though.

It was still the early days of synthesizers, but I wanted to find someone who could do something in that area, to boost the midrange. Wally Badarou was recommended to me by the record producer Daniel Vangarde (the father of Daft Punk's Thomas Bangalter), whom I knew because we used to distribute one of his acts, the Gibson Brothers. Badarou had played on one of their tracks, "Cuba"; there's a lot happening on the track, it's a carnival of sound, but it seemed a good recommendation. I'd soon realize that Wally was smart and receptive enough to fit into any kind of group, from Level 42 to Foreigner, and he contributed significantly to Gregory Isaacs's graceful and classic *Night Nurse* album, doing his overdubs in Studio A on his treasured Prophet synthesizer with just an engineer and an assistant in two hours straight after a twenty-hour trip from Paris.

Wally's DNA, his Parisian/West African roots, was perfect for what I was looking for—when he was young in West Africa, he'd listened to James Brown, Ray Charles, Otis Redding, Stevie Wonder, Congolese rumba, Afro-Cuban cha-cha, pre-salsa, but also Hendrix, Herbie Hancock, and Santana, and he was influenced by twentieth-century classical music and always experimenting with electronics. He'd also played on M's worldwide number-one *Pop Muzik*, which came out of the same retro-futurist world as the Buggles. Tuned in to new sounds, he turned Sly on to Syndrums. From there, Sly and Robbie drifted from the organic to the electronic, which led to their leading part in the Jamaican dancehall era of the early eighties.

Wally was deeply passionate about the studio toys that were constantly emerging at the time, and felt he was more a studio animal than a live performer. He was a multi-instrumentalist who saw the synthesizer as a way of opening up the number of instruments he could play, back when people were still working out how to connect it with the studio. Wally was doing something interesting in the area I was looking for, and it was just what I needed in terms of creating an eclectic variation on funk for Grace.

It was new territory—there were no scripts to follow, bringing synth music into other styles—but Wally had the right pan-cultural musical instincts. He had also worked on anonymous disco records in Paris, so there was something coming from that side of Grace—a continuity, a link with those continental disco records and the Parisian element. He saw disco as "funk for the masses," but also as the death of funk. When he played on disco records, he did all he could to give them some deeper funk feel.

I gave him a call but didn't really mention Grace, which was probably a good thing as she was very disco then. I just told him how long and how much, and he was the first to arrive. He came over to Nassau thinking it would be just another session, not really sure what was happening, and ended up staying on the island for over ten years. With Steven Stanley engineering, Wally quietly made his own beautiful instrumental album there in 1984, *Echoes*, a cerebral sonic summary of Compass Point, in that it belonged simultaneously to a few genres and yet none at all, coming out of jazz funk, rare groove, Afro-Caribbean, John Martyn's Big Muff, ZTT's Art of Noise, dub, and new age while predating acid house, Balearic, and chill-out. "Mambo" made it more or less intact as a sample used on Massive Attack's "Daydreaming" seven years later, to prove his sound was really from the future.

I ALSO HAD Wally write the incidental soundtrack music for a film I produced in 1982 that was very important to me, *Countryman,* not least because of his understanding of how important music is, and what a difference it can make to a film.

The film was directed somewhere between cult movie and work of art by a close friend of mine, Dickie Jobson, who'd worked at various Island companies and for a time managed Bob Marley. The titular protagonist of the film is played by the real man he was based on, a Rastafarian-Tamil fisherman who was also a deep thinker, poet, comic, family man, and athlete. He actually went by the name Countryman.

He lived on the beach in Hellshire, which I had discovered to my horror in the 1950s was only accessible by boat. I was introduced to him by Dickie and by our mutual friends Sally and Perry Henzell, who had done *The Harder They Come* and thought he should be an actor.

Countryman escaped from his home when he was five or six and grew up on his own in the swamp in a very isolated part of Jamaica. When I met him, he was very cheerful, very bright. He had little or nothing. He lived on the beach, with a sheet of zinc for his roof. We came one time and found the zinc wasn't there; his wife wanted a radio, so he'd sold the piece of zinc in order to get her one and now they literally had no roof over their heads. But his whole energy was full of joy and positivity, not complaining about anything. He was so ageless and inspiring, a kind of enigmatic barefoot philosopher, and we were saying, "This is incredible, we should really do a film with Countryman. Because he is so articulate but is able to be the most basic native type of person." He was so down-to-earth but also such a complex thinker. Once he really chastised me because I had come to see him but then I had to leave. He said, "Where are you going?" I said, "I'm going to England. Have you ever been to England?" And he said, "No, I have everything right here." Even though he owned nothing he was happy with it. He was somehow able to say, "I have everything." That does not normally happen. People have to go through a whole process before they realize that having lots of things is not the answer to life. He was a truly exceptional person.

Countryman was opposite to the rough and urban *The Harder*

They Come, more mystical, natural, and timeless, which made Wally perfect to write the music, because he had grown to understand the spiritual relationship between Jamaica and music. Modern Jamaica was in the background, but the film was mostly about a more haunting, fundamental Jamaica. It was a box-office success in Jamaica, and Countryman became something of a household name, representing for many the essential Jamaican spirit that never changed over time however much the island's politics and rules changed.

Countryman was loosely based on the experience I had in the 1950s, when I was cared for on the beach by a group of Bible-reading Rastas. When I told Countryman my story, he claimed that he had been in the hut as a young boy and remembered it happening. It seemed improbable—but on the other hand, it was entirely possible.

Sly and Robbie suggested a couple of musicians they thought would be good for my musical company. Mikey Chung, someone who was soaked in top-drawer Jamaican musical history, gave the sound another more rhythmic guitar style different from Barry's. As part of the Now Generation studio band responsible for most of the hit sessions in Jamaica, he'd worked with Scratch, Joe Higgs, Toots, Ernest Ranglin, Peter Tosh, and Inner Circle, and inevitably with Sly and Robbie and Black Uhuru.

Reaching further back into Jamaican history, there was the venerable percussionist Uziah Thompson, who got the nickname Sticky. He'd started as an assistant to Coxsone Dodd when he was running the Downbeat sound system; worked with the Skatalites, Joe Gibbs, the Congos, and Culture; contributed to Wailers sessions for Lee Perry in the early seventies—it was Scratch who told him to take up percussion—and came along with Sly and Robbie straight out of Black Uhuru. Sticky brought the seasoning, the great tempo, in the background but always present, and a sense of seductive steadiness that came from where he'd come from, helping shape a succession of Jamaican beats.

Putting all these musicians together, there were different histories and styles—the reggae rhythm, the rock energy, and the new, relatively unexplored electronic element coming from someone with an African background yet a European touch. Later—when Wally wasn't available, once the mood had been established, Jamaican roots music as the key sound of the modern world—there was Tyrone Downie, who had played keyboards with Bob Marley and the Wailers and Burning Spear.

We were supposed to start in November 1979, but Grace had just given birth to her and Jean-Paul's son, Paulo, so we started a few weeks later. I didn't turn up for the first few days because I knew it was going to be difficult as the musicians all settled in. They didn't know each other, and they didn't necessarily all get on at first. Different worlds. They sized each other up, not really sure what they were doing there or what they were expected to play. I wouldn't have been any help, so I just let them start jamming amongst themselves, getting a feel for something even if they didn't quite know what it was.

By the time I arrived, the personalities had gotten themselves orchestrated. This is what made it work in the end—the tension between the various factions in the group that gave the music both its tightness and its edge. Robbie came from a world where he was as likely to have a hand grenade in his bass guitar case as an instrument. Not that he ever did of course, although he liked to be prepared for all eventualities. He was so prepared on one occasion, entering the country with something a little borderline in his case, I had to sort it out with the Jamaican government. He was a tough guy from a tough world.

Wally was a gentle soul, a pure music nerd, quite professorial in his manner. It took him a little time to get used to the way everyone appeared haphazardly, and I was the last to arrive, and without much ceremony. He just looked up and there I was, and I made no fuss, but expected things to be happening.

The combination of Sly's raw toughness and Wally's thoughtful, formal gentleness, of paranoia and innocence, made it into the music, once they found a way to get on, at least in the studio. Wally initially felt a bit like he had been dropped into something he knew nothing about, and was bemused by how nothing really started to happen in the studio until sunset, and there was very little small talk.

He didn't have any expectations that something special was about to happen. This probably helped something special happen, once he realized who he was playing with and that the seeming nonchalance of everything didn't mean that the aim wasn't absolute excellence. The different factions didn't have to say much to each other to bring the very best out of each other. Incredible things started to happen.

Once assembled—next to the ocean, to their initial surprise—I called them the Compass Point All Stars. They were an experiment in making up a studio house band, like the one I'd seen in action at Muscle Shoals. They were all working on various projects for me elsewhere, and I brought them together, imagining Grace as a performance artist as much as a singer, who needed a version of the best band in the world.

It was a good moment for Grace because she was experimenting with her voice and realizing that there was no point in trying to sing in the generic radio key as a conventional soul singer, the one Tom Moulton expected from her. She had made a decision not to try to be like the gospel-inspired female singers she admired. There were male singers she admired who perhaps made more sense, James Brown, Bobby Womack, and, of course, Barry White.

Once she started singing accompanied by the heavy, threatening bass of Sly and Robbie, effortlessly slipping into the driver's seat, it was an advantage that she had the low talking voice that she did. There was no place for a standard soul or funk voice in that sound. A disco diva would have dissolved inside the sound's fierce attitude. Her voice was perfect for it, a gothic gospel somewhere between half-speaking and half-singing, between expressing deep-down desires and not expressing anything at all, just existing. This voice suited her radically modified appearance in the Goude photographs, and this elevated new sound suited her voice. Once she had these musicians working with her, she really found her place, and her voice.

They played together as a group for the first time in the studio for her records, which made it incredibly unique. I hadn't told her I was putting these musicians together; I just went ahead. She had this international shape, so there was the rock and roll side, even though she was never rock. She could bring it as a character into the music. There was the French, Euro, synth part, and the deep Jamaican drum and bass, the enigmatic island rhythm, and the downtown New York grunge. It also had a little bit of the naughtiness she had. It wasn't a complete break from disco, but it was disco mating with darker, deeper music, disco evolving into a new state of mind, just as in New York it had incorporated progressive elements and become house. And whereas disco music had proved to be temporary, this Grace music sounded indestructible.

Grace had never seen the musicians play before she was actually singing with them. There was no rehearsal, or if there was, that was instantly recorded as a performance, to make sure first thoughts and spontaneous moments were captured. Grace liked to rehearse, a lot, but it was sometimes her way of delaying things, of not having to commit to the moment. I wanted to destabilize her, get her to live off her wits. She came into the studio one day to record, and the musicians were there, ready and waiting. She had no time to be surprised. This was how it was. This was her new environment. Start singing.

She was hearing the group from within, immediately a part of what they were doing. And before she arrived, I got a photograph Jean-Paul had taken when she was pregnant blown up and put on the studio wall, her arms folded, her hair shaved, her expression unreadable. Myth and reality merged. I told the musicians the music had to sound like that photo looked. She was in the room even when she wasn't in the room. The music became like a soundtrack to a movie, even though it was a still photo. The photograph had as much going on in it as a movie.

When she was on the island, she loved the environment, a place where she could work and play, which for Grace is usually the same thing. She always loves being near water—wherever she lives, London, New York, Jamaica, Italy, she is always by the sea or a river. If Grace spends a day without swimming, she starts to get miserable.

She also had plenty of visitors to play with, another of her favorite pastimes. I once invited Sean Connery over to stay in one of the apartments, and he was around at the same time as Grace. Whenever they bumped into each other, she would always whistle the James Bond theme tune. It sent him around the bend, and eventually it drove him from the island.

We recorded from scratch. It was exciting, because I had had the wisdom to get the meticulous and dedicated Alex Sadkin as the engineer for the sessions. I worked with him on the Bob Marley *Rastaman Vibration, Kaya*, and *Survival* albums, and he'd done great work on *Journey to Addis*, the Third World album on Island bravely but elegantly fusing soul and reggae that included their hit version of the O'Jays' "Now That We Found Love." The drum sound he got on the album, and his precise direction, was a precursor of the Compass Point sound. I felt that the house band I was after needed the engineer to be part of the ensemble, because the studio was an instrument as much as the synthesizer or the congas.

Early on as a tape op, Alex was in the studio when Todd Rundgren produced Grand Funk Railroad's *We're an American Band*, which was a great apprenticeship. He'd started out as a mastering engineer, which gave him a perspective about the finished sound of a record, and was beyond compare for his talent, his taste, and his ear, and for how much care he took preparing the room for the musicians, taking hours to set up Sly's kit to make sure no sound, intended or not, went missing.

Alex was the final part of the puzzle, treating this island music, which came from all points across the globe, as though it was as serious as anything, and needed the most professional attention. It needed someone fluent at mixing on the go to capture the groove as it was happening, mostly played live, to give the process a certain, constant coherence. His first mixes, assembled on the hoof, were usually near-perfect.

He was also a master at restructuring things once they had been recorded, moving sounds around, creating different angles. It disconcerted Wally at first, but then he realized that this way of layering the sound opened it up to new possibilities. The way Alex encouraged him to almost paint sound around what Grace was doing generated those eerie, unspecified noises that gave the tracks so much atmosphere. You couldn't write those sounds; they came out of that kind of probing and Alex's way of seeing sound in 3-D, so that you could move things around inside it.

The studio staff were great, because on an island where music was so important, they now worked at the sort of place that usually existed only in London or New York. Once I had gotten everything organized, I would just sit in there and sort of nudge it in the right direction. When they were rocking, which started to happen most of the time, I would start smiling, I couldn't help myself, and this made them rock even harder. I didn't have to tell them what to do—that's why I'd booked them—but I became the bandleader and musical director by default, because they needed to know in their own minds when they were hitting the spot and when it was time to try something else. A glance at my expression would be their cue. I had to be careful I didn't give anything away with a wrong look.

It became Grace's band; she had never been exposed to that kind of thing before, a live band dedicated to her music, but it suited her personality, and that in turn influenced the direction of the music. Previously she was not really involved, which was why the music had become less and less about her, in terms of how it sounded, very generic. This was music that sounded like she really was—all that international input, the different energies, the soul, funk, gospel, rock, and show tunes that had flowed into disco, but given a progressive reboot, and at the heart of it very Jamaican.

The first song that came together was a version of one Daniel Miller of Mute Records had recorded as a group called the Normal. "Warm Leatherette" was doing well in the underground gay clubs, and when we sent out the message that we wanted new, unexpected songs for Grace to sing, which resulted in hundreds of suggestions, this one made immediate sense. A couple of people had suggested it, including Chris Frantz of Tom Tom Club.

I was looking for songs that would introduce Grace to an audience that had gone beyond disco and would go to the newest clubs to find the latest dance music, the newest artists. Songs that were doing well in marginalized, enigmatic spaces, that took a bit of getting used to if you weren't familiar with those spaces.

"Warm Leatherette" was based on *Crash*, a book about sex and car crashes by J. G. Ballard, a writer who viewed reality as a stage set, and Miller had turned the atmosphere of the book into a lopsided electro-pop song with a psychopathic edge and an erotic charge. Grace had done Broadway songs on her disco albums, but as soon as this song was suggested, it seemed perfect for the kind of more deviant standards she should be singing, songs about car crashes as a sexual stimulant, where you made love because you were about to die.

None of the All Stars would usually have thought of playing such a song, not getting past the burning flesh and the hand brake penetrating your thigh in the lyrics; but on the other hand its sinister and minimal arrangement wasn't that far from some of the more apocalyptic reggae the Jamaican contingent had played on, and Barry and Wally were used to playing in sessions where the lyrics were way beyond their control. They put their heads down and got on with the job.

The All Stars slipped into instrumentally playing an electronic song like it was the most obvious thing in the world, even if Wally wondered why I'd asked him to play acoustic piano on an electro-track, and you could see their eyes light up and even a few smiles forming as soon as Alex started to finesse the sound and Grace did her version of the talk-singing on the original. They each realized what their role in the sonic outcome was, and realized I was only asking them to do what was most natural to them, and respond to each other's performances and to Grace's presence.

She sang it like it was already a classic, a kind of modern standard, Sondheim on acid. I couldn't really explain what I was after, but when it happened, that was the explanation.

It wasn't a huge hit, it was very underground, but it was much more imaginative than other songs we thought of doing, like Marley's "Concrete Jungle" and the Stones' "Brown Sugar." They might have been hits, but they were too literal. "Warm Leatherette" was a calling card for the new Grace, one that said this was where pop music was heading, here were some secrets she knew about the future.

It looked like the cover of the album—the photo that I had stuck on the studio wall—which was important, that it looked like the kind of song the person in that photograph would sing. We had found her sound, male and female, black and white, skin and metal, beauty and beast, European and Caribbean, American and alien, and in a way, we made a genre of which there was only one exponent—Grace Jones. It couldn't be copied, but you would hear echoes of it in a lot of other music.

When the All Stars recorded "Private Life," the Chrissie Hynde song, I couldn't believe it: it was so smooth and cool, ominous music played as if it were easy listening. It was like we'd shattered lots of genres to create a new one. It all worked out better than I could have hoped, and you could see that the musicians themselves knew something special was happening, which gave them more confidence and ease and allowed them to play freely. If they didn't get it at first, they began to now.

They started to play in their own worlds but as a seamless unit, not a disparate bunch of musicians uncomfortable in each other's company doing what they were told. Chrissie herself said that was how "Private Life" was meant to sound, and it was also how Grace was meant to sound, and the Compass Point All Stars. Alex was crucial in getting the drum sound, where Sly played an acoustic kit, but after it was treated and tweaked, it sounded electronic.

The sessions worked so well; we were often getting a song nailed in one take and were soon running out of material. Song ideas and lyrics were coming from all over the place, and we got all the songs for the first two Compass Point albums, *Warm Leatherette* and its sequel, *Nightclubbing*, recorded in not much more than a week. By the third Grace album I produced with Alex, *Living My Life* in 1982, the cover songs had been completely replaced by originals, and the hybrid of machine and humans, music and menace, reggae and dream had gone as far as it could—we'd completed a trilogy, the first one out of the blue, establishing terms; the second one extending the range; and the final one a kind of curtain bow. We'd said it all; there was no need to keep repeating it.

Grace never had mainstream hits, but she didn't need to—her "hits" were the notorious appearances on chat shows where she demanded attention from the host, her roles in the James Bond film *A View to a Kill* as an anti–Bond girl and the Arnold Schwarzenegger film *Conan the Destroyer*, the images manipulating her energy that Jean-Paul Goude would create in photos and car adverts. The music was just there, slowly picking up power, and in the essential Island sense, it would be interesting forever.

Grace moves at her own pace, which sometimes bears little resemblance to time as we know it, but she's got a very quick mind, and in the studio she responded to the camaraderie that was evolving. Sly and Robbie were instantly up to speed and understanding the spirit, getting their eye in, knowing how to play along with Grace, read her moods and bring out her wit and style. They helped come up with "Pull Up to the Bumper" and "Nipple to the Bottle," which was where disco would have gone if it had been an experimental art form and not a moneymaking scam for lazy record companies.

Instead of there being a lot of overdubs and a precise layering of the music, I would get the All Stars to play together live. They would start playing, and then when they were locked in the groove, I would tell Alex to turn on the tape.

We were so lucky to have Alex: he was responsible for the sound, and he got a sound that is respected to this day, in any form of music. It came out of the same balance of sound that Bob Marley had, and Alex loved to make the percussion, the congas and cowbells, take a starring role, just like Jimmy Miller did. It was in all ways a modernized Island sound.

I do not like a crowded sound—I want clarity—but this was a whole different approach. It was rooted in the dynamic minimalism of reggae, but with new electronic elements and a rock dimension. You could hear everything really clearly in the space it occupied, but it was all completely together. It was a classic sound, which you hear in all sorts of music since, from hip-hop to electronic dance music, and that was down to Alex and to the engineer who had been working with Tom Tom Club, Steven Stanley.

For a while, it seemed like the Compass Point All Stars were the best band in the world. I kept telling them this, and at first I think they just thought I was being nice. But I never waste words like that. I wasn't doing it simply to boost their egos.

They started to appear on other Compass Point projects, including Joe Cocker's *Sheffield Steel*, Mick Jagger's *She's the Boss*, Ian Dury's *Lord Upminster*, and the Gwen Guthrie album, and there was plenty of Wally all over the music Robert Palmer made while he was there, from *Secrets* to *Riptide*. There were a few sessions that didn't quite work out, not necessarily because they weren't interesting and worth trying, but because the chaos that often was at the heart of the recording didn't lead to completion. The one session that really did fail was perhaps me flying too close to the sun, and making the mistake of working with one of my heroes.

My dream was Sly and Robbie producing James Brown with Alex as the coproducer and the All Stars as the band. James Brown was the king. He should be having the best musicians backing him. I would have wanted Elvis to have worked with the Compass Point All Stars if he'd lived. James Brown flew down to Nassau and brought his people with him, including Al Sharpton, who would get his hair right before he came into the studio. It was quite a circus, and we were all looking forward to what would happen.

It didn't go well. Brown immediately started telling Sly and Robbie what to play, which was the sort of stuff he'd done twenty years before and not the invigorating Compass Point update I wanted. Robbie was humble at first—it was the Godfather after all—but then became frustrated at being told what to do. He told James Brown to play the bass himself if he wouldn't let Robbie do his own thing. He snapped at James Brown, and to the Brown entourage, who treated him as a living deity, this was sacrilege. It got a little tense. Communication ensued between Sly and Robbie and Brown's hairdresser. James Brown had not encountered musicians like Sly and Robbie before.

Brown conceded a little, even if he did think they were perpetually stoned, realizing he should maybe let Sly and Robbie show him what they had in mind. The sessions picked up some speed, and after two or three days some interesting grooves of all shapes and sizes were happening and things started to look positive. Not what we were looking for, but enough to make me think it could work.

Unfortunately, Mr. Brown considered all work done for him in the studio to be his property, and wanted 100 percent of the publishing to be his, even when the songs were being created between Sly and Robbie and Wally.

I expressed concern at this arrangement, and James Brown quit on day four. All that credit stuff was nonsense; we'd only just begun anyway, and it didn't augur well for the making of an album. I realized that my dream of James Brown and the Compass Point All Stars wasn't going to happen, and I gave him the tapes of what had been done. He was still the Godfather, the number-one soul brother, the beginning and the end, but his outlandishness wasn't much fun when you had to deal with it on the ground. Sometimes dreams are best left where they came from, your sleep.

BACK IN REALITY, where things were actually happening, the All Stars would inevitably turn up in the Tom Tom Club's studio next door as their album was being put together. Chris and Tina had gone on the road with Talking Heads, and when they came back to finish their album, they had Sly and Robbie, the best rhythm duo in the world, come in to add handclaps—creating an incomparable handclap sound, one that fascinated David Byrne—Sticky Thompson play congas, and Tyrone Downie of the Wailers contribute some keyboards.

Studio A and Studio B were a music scene in themselves, and it was exactly the vibe I wanted, a hive of information-sharing, creating a new set of sounds and rhythms for a new decade.

You could hear the Compass Point sound on both Grace and Tom Tom Club, even as they were very different—perhaps it was because as well as the drums, keyboards, synths, and guitar, there was a lot of space in the air, as if the studio were an island in outer space. Tina's talk-singing, sometimes with her sisters Laura and Lani, not a million miles away from how Grace presented her voice, revealed a different kind of female singing.

The tempos were being slowed down to generate a different kind of swing, which made sense for where the music was being recorded. Also, the engineers were more officially part of the ensemble, having a very distinct role in the group, to the extent that Tom Tom Club would include Steve Stanley amongst the songwriters. That's a generosity many sound engineers deserve but very rarely receive for their contribution to the songs they record.

Tom Tom Club's first American single was "Genius of Love," with a ridiculously hypnotic Tina Weymouth bass line that was like a lead vocal. That alone proved that a rhythm section could lead a band. It was exactly the sort of record you'd hope the drum and bass of Talking Heads would come up with, deeply hip and oddly blissful, an open love letter to their favorite soul artists from Bootsy Collins to Bob Marley, Smokey Robinson to Kurtis Blow, James Brown to Sly and Robbie—"reggae's expanding with Sly and Robbie"—with an unexpected commercial edge, because it was so damned charming. They got the idea of mentioning all these names from how DJs at the Danceteria scratched in artists' names over their live mixes.

The bass line almost immediately started to have a life of its own, getting the song played on Black radio stations at the same time it was hitting the underground dance floors of America, crossing over to the white new wave fans and beyond, being remixed and sampled into new shapes and sizes, becoming the foundation for a whole array of hip-hop songs. They were the first white act after Elton John and David Bowie to play the American TV show *Soul Train*—you couldn't get much more proof that you had soul than by being invited onto that show.

Within weeks there was a "Genius Rap" and Grandmaster Flash was beginning a trade where the rhythm got passed on down the line through to Public Enemy, 2Pac, 50 Cent, Busta Rhymes, to a Ziggy Marley album that Chris and Tina produced, and to Mariah Carey, where it became "Fantasy," which debuted on the Billboard charts at number one in 1995.

"Genius of Love" made it as a highlight into the great Talking Heads film *Stop Making Sense*, because during the tour it documented, while David Byrne changed into his famous oversized white suit, the Tom Tom Club materialized to play the song. The "sister group" had revitalized the mother ship. I think Compass Point can take a lot of credit for that, and I think of Chris and Tina being All Stars in their own right. It did so well for them that it also meant they could buy their Tip Top apartment.

It was natural to think of the house band making an album of their own. It wasn't easy to imagine how this might happen, because as the abstractly appointed musical director I was often elsewhere keeping tabs on the wider world of Island Records and making a perhaps foolhardy move into producing films. If it was in any sense a real band, rather than just an ideal band, it needed more of me than I could give at the time. Wally described this drawback as being because of my complicated business life, which was very well put. It was difficult to concentrate on producing, on working with a group of musicians, when I was trying to deal with what was beginning to get too big for me to control.

Even if I could have found the time and space, the tragic death of Alex Sadkin in 1987 took the wind out of me and took the heart out of the Compass Point All Stars. He'd returned to the studio just recently after working on other projects like Duran Duran, and I needed him there as a steadying influence because the studio was losing its way, infected by the crack cocaine that was becoming a problem on the island. Alex started to organize things and weed out some of the problems, and for a few weeks I felt positive the studio was in safe hands again.

A friend of his had come to visit, and they went out for a drive in an open-top jeep and took a corner too fast. Alex was thrown from the jeep, hit his head, and died instantly. Absolutely tragic, death once more interrupting what the opposite of death should be.

There was an inevitable loss of energy after that, for the All Stars, for the studio itself, and by the end of the decade the place was adrift. I brought in the engineer Terry Manning and his wife, Sheree, to get the studio back into shape in the early 1990s, but the Compass Point All Stars were not a factor in the studio's revival. It was as if they had never been there in the first place, only their sound left to prove they really did exist.

I never produced Grace again after those first three albums, and she left Island Records in 1986 after receiving an offer from Capitol that was a few noughts more than we were able to pay. Lots of millions. She was worth it, but we had paid her by helping her come up with her own sound.

She took the money, and I understood why she took the money, because artistically, in the unreal world, the Compass Point Grace was worth millions, but not in the real world. The same thing happened with Robert Palmer and Steve Winwood. I hate it when relationships break up, but they were looking for deals that could guarantee their financial security for life. We couldn't compete with that—and in the end, even if we could have, we didn't want to. If you pay someone that amount of money, you're playing the role of an insurance company. You're saying that it is definite that they will sell enough records to make it viable that you pay them such an advance. We could never ensure that. There's no point in making a deal if one side is going to be miserable.

In 1985, the last record Grace made for Island, as a kind of good-bye from us to her and her to us, was with Trevor Horn: *Slave to the Rhythm*, the end of the ZTT/Island era combined with the end of the Island Grace. This was a post–Compass Point Grace, because Trevor could handle the impossible, and perhaps after that there is nowhere else to go—the perfect sound of Grace is found, and found again, and beyond that is a mystery, where Grace is always now Grace, whether you see her or not.

"Slave to the Rhythm" was intended to be a single, and because Trevor knew how to achieve the impossible but at a price, it cost a lot of money—maybe the only single ever recorded with a seven-figure budget. I decided that we should make the one song an album, or maybe ZTT's Paul Morley made that decision. Both of us would claim the idea.

AS ISLAND HAD its own momentum belonging to its staff as much as to me, I was always looking for the new and the next, not necessarily what fashion and the critics said was new, but outside of that. That was my role as much as label owner. I still wanted to be the advance guard, seeing what was out there that was interesting and not being noticed in the usual places.

I had imagined after Bob Marley's success that African music might have its time, and put some effort into signing innovative African artists like Salif Keita, Angélique Kidjo, and King Sunny Adé, when music from outside the basic English-speaking Anglo-American culture rejected the grip on what music was allowed into the mainstream. If Bob could make it out of Jamaica and fulfill global potential, I was convinced that others from less-expected places could follow.

Eventually this music from outside the usual countries, from Africa, Asia, Latin America, would be grouped together as world music in a well-intentioned but ultimately flawed attempt to create an accessible genre. The idea was that all of this music from different countries that didn't fit into the usual categories would have its own name. It worked in one way, creating a focus on usually neglected music; but it also unfortunately relegated complicated, adventurous music with a vast array of singular histories and roots into a simplistic pigeonhole.

My appetite was always for roaming off the beaten track, looking for something unexpected, a voice, a rhythm, an attitude, that would appeal to me as much as Steve Winwood had, and then Free, and Bob Marley. Even when I looked for music in New York, I preferred to hunt around the margins. My satisfaction was in uncovering music that should be heard and making it as available as the more obvious music with its more obvious commercial backing.

One thing I did decide was that I really wanted Trevor to try to use a new sound I loved and thought was the future that had come out of the Southeast district of Washington, DC: go-go. Emerging in the home city of American government in the mid-1970s as a vibrant hyper-local take on funk, go-go was connected to its place the way hip-hop was to the Bronx in its beginnings. By the mid-1980s, it seemed ready to break out into a wider world.

Go-go seemed something that should move from its local setting and travel around the world. I'd heard "We Need Some Money" by the acknowledged go-go pioneer Chuck Brown, and once I found out what it was and where it was coming from, I decided to go down to Washington to see what was going on. I went to a stadium-sized arena, and there were about six thousand people there going absolutely mad to a few bands, Rare Essence, Redds and the Boys, Trouble Funk. It was weird that outside Washington, there was hardly any knowledge this was happening. I hadn't thought of Washington having an indigenous music.

As always, it was the rhythm that got me first—the hypnotic drum pattern was astonishing, and I couldn't work out how they had done it. It was always rhythm I was looking for, rhythms that refuse to be silenced, that become blueprints for survival, and here was a spectacular rhythm.

Chuck Brown said he was chasing an everlasting beat, one that just goes and goes as time melts away, something African, and Jamaican, as well as the obvious James Brown, jazz-swing seemed to be at the root of it all, with a Latin groove tossed in. Chuck's drummer had toured with Miles, Chick Corea, and Carlos Santana. It was a nonstop rhythm I was destined to fall for, and then I got carried away.

I thought, well, it's amazing music, but by its very nature, it's live music; there's a lot of improvisation and it's not meant for radio. The rhythm is the lead; the songs aren't strong enough. James Brown had hooks and melodies, but this was continuous rhythm where the bands wanted to make sure their audience didn't leave the dance floor between songs. That's maybe where the "go-go" came from—Chuck seeing the crowd drift off during a break between songs, and him telling the drummer to "go, go." The percussion just kept coming, the rhythm kept regenerating, and it was the beat between the songs where go-go really lived, which is hard to sell outside its natural environment. It's not sound as such; it's pure experience, seeing bands play serious, sweaty funk nonstop for hours at a time.

I signed Trouble Funk, who had followed and enhanced originator Chuck Brown's sound and had released the first go-go music outside the capital, on the hip-hop label Sugar Hill. I thought they were
going to be the ones. They had a track that had started with a frenzied
attempt to play Kraftwerk's "Trans-Europe Express" as sheer funk that
people loved so much the band would have to play it for hours, and
they could.

Then we had to make them travel further without losing what they
had as go-go specialists, which was always going to be difficult. We
released a Trouble Funk live album, but that was a cheat really, because
the key was going to be how to make their recorded music equal the live
event, and how to harness their all-night energy with songs.

We got the rights to a few of the strongest go-go acts, and set up
a special go-go division to our 4th & B'way dance label. Then we
started to fly British journalists over to DC so they could experience it
as it was meant to be experienced, and go-go began to get play in the
clubs. For a moment, it seemed to be having a moment. Somehow,
though, go-go only seems to last for a brief time outside Washington,
like it can't breathe anymore and needs to race back home.

I was sure there must be another way to get more people into this
music. If it was heard, it could really break out. I started thinking of
what *The Harder They Come* did for Jamaican music, what *Saturday
Night Fever* did for New York disco, giving people a sense of where
this music came from and what it meant to the people who loved it—
and, of course, carrying the music along on an amazing soundtrack
that became an introduction to a whole new world.

The movie I ended up financing through Island's film company,
Island Alive, backfired badly. We tried to make a thriller set in the
go-go scene, and I only have to mention that Art Garfunkel was cast
as an alcoholic Baltimore news reporter investigating a rape for it to be
clear where the problems started. Perhaps the problems started with
Art's hair, and the fact that he would only allow himself to be shot
from one side. Well, the real problems started with getting people

from outside Washington to try to make a film that was totally from within Washington.

Good to Go was a mess and made the mistake of framing the film around a potential race riot in DC, with plenty of shootouts and car crashes. The Blackest music was instantly and crudely associated with street violence and Black people crazy on drugs. The relationship between inner-city tensions and the liberation of music didn't work like it did in *The Harder They Come*, which celebrated creative Black culture by seeming to be part of what it was filming, not watching from the outside.

The club in the movie was actually called the Go-Go, for God's sake. I'd help make a film that was like the worst sixties exploitation pop film. Art Garfunkel's character solves the case and announces that the Black people accused of the rape are innocent at a go-go concert, to happy-ending cheers. I remember when I saw an early version, where the film's flaws were many and brutal, I turned to the person with me and said, "I've just made a demo that cost five million dollars." I'd bet big, and I'd bet bad.

The best thing about the film was the music, the concert scenes, but the film as a whole was a terrible disservice to go-go, swamping it with thriller clichés. We tried to repackage it with the name *Short Fuse*, as there was some confusion about why this cheap and nasty thriller was called *Good to Go*. We tried to call it a "concert drama," because there was the opportunity to see great go-go groups close up in their element. It could have been the next best thing to being there, but the guns, drugs, and careering cars kept getting in the way.

Go-go didn't make it to record, or film, and perhaps its beauty was that it wasn't meant to make it outside Washington, the place where it belonged and made the most sense. It influenced swing beat, and Steve Hurley's "Jack Your Body," but that was lesser go-go. It was as though when I tried to interfere, I was cursed, which is the only excuse I can think of when I think of the film's star being Art Garfunkel.

The film did get a little more about go-go out into the world, and one accidental positive was that I originally hired Spike Lee to direct. Island Pictures was distributing his first film, 1986's *She's Gotta Have It,* but then I decided he wasn't the right person to direct the go-go musical he said he wanted to make—in hindsight, that was probably the way to go.

The go-go group E.U.—Experience Unlimited—played at the launch party Island organized in DC for *She's Gotta Have It*, and Spike used them doing "Da Butt" for the musical-comedy-with-a-message he made after I dropped him, *School Daze.* "Da Butt" didn't start as a go-go song, but E.U. added the correct relentless rhythms, and it became perhaps the best-selling go-go track ever, but unfortunately it was something of a fad, a dance craze. It did E.U.—and Spike—a lot of good, but it seemed to suggest that's as far as go-go went.

Go-go did get smuggled inside Trevor Horn's fastidious production of "Slave to the Rhythm," which is paradoxically go-go-ish and also a tremendous record. In that sense, Trevor achieved the musically impossible, and it was Grace's biggest hit—even though, for Trevor, not breaking the UK top ten and doing next to nothing in America made it a failure. It's part of the myth of Grace, though, the sound of her everlasting afterlife, and even after the Compass Point songs, you can't imagine her without it—it's almost her "My Way," or one of them; and it's ultimate Trevor Horn, an epic in spectacular isolation.

As go-go goes, it gets the swing, sass, and spirit without seeming a corruption or a watering down, and it featured the trademark snare sound of E.U.'s indefatigable drummer, William Ju Ju House, as well as members of Chuck Brown and the Searchers and E.U. fed through the expensive Synclavier sampler. The ultimate live sound was transferred onto record through an expensive machine process, its spontaneity being carefully programmed into manipulated pieces of digital sound, which was perhaps why go-go music never really crossed over—to successfully capture its essence, you needed a million dollars and a cyborg element. Or you need Beyoncé and her first solo hit, "Crazy in Love," whose famous infectious brass hook was pure joyous go-go. I knew there was something in go-go. It just wasn't Art Garfunkel.

I HAVE BEEN friends with Grace for over forty years now. We regularly talk about her work and her music, but the intensity we had in those months at Compass Point can never be repeated. Maybe now and then when we play backgammon. She is the fiercest of opponents. And the funniest. We're friends now, more than friends. Family.

She is such a survivor. She has so much power. Unbelievable determination. As soon as I saw that picture of her in an illogical position, and then got to know her, I realized she was on some sort of mission. She is destined to always be around, and always be noticed. That performance in 2012, for the Queen's Golden Jubilee, where she is outside Buckingham Palace freezing her arse off spinning a Hula-Hoop around her waist for the entire song. Everyone will remember that. Only Grace would have thought of doing that and gone and done it.

As I discovered when I first met her, she is very Jamaican, and there is something very resilient about Jamaica. Her image is Jamaican—she is ultimately from outer space, but totally Jamaican, and grounded. I think her family, her dad, her mum, they were so strong, like only Jamaicans can be. A lot of Jamaicans when they meet her ask if she is from Africa. "We are all Africans," she replies.

Grace lives in her own time. She really does have her own sense of time, and her very own timing. She is somewhere else at the same time she's in the same place as you. She moves through time in her own way. When you are going to meet her, you know that at first she'll say she will be there by 12:00. That will become 2:00. What that means is that she will make it by 4:00. Ish. So you plan for her to be with you at 5:00. And see what happens then. It's who she is.

I understand her timing. Maybe it is because, like her—and Bob, and Yusuf, and Bono—I am a sort of hybrid. A mutant. I am from

Jamaica and England and Ireland and Portugal and all the places I have visited and all the music I have made. I am many, like Jamaica. And I am at home in the recording studio, where time is exactly the same as Grace thinks it is. It is something else altogether. It is in outer space, at the edge of the ocean, at the top of the mountains, the calm at the center of the storm, deep inside the mind, from the past, in the future. I think because of studio time I was the right person at the right time to imagine what the sound of Grace was. A sound made from the rhythm of time. A sound and a time and a mysteriousness that begins and ends in Jamaica and that we captured at Compass Point like we'd put electricity into a bottle.

IN THE EARLY 1980s, in New York, Grace introduced me to Mary Vinson, a girl from Virginia who'd studied at the Parsons School of Design and was working as a stylist. I was wild about her, and she became the most important person in my life, there with me as a calm spirit throughout the eighties and nineties, which in many ways, professionally and personally, were very turbulent.

Mary tamed a restless part of me that seemed untamable—other parts remained restless—and of all people, it was Grace who brought us together. An artist in all sorts of ways, she seemed able to see something that was missing that I couldn't see and found the perfect person to be my partner. Wild, tempestuous Grace and thoughtful, dignified Mary were unlikely friends, but they had a special friendship separate from their other friends, because Grace sometimes needed some calm. When Grace suggested to Mary that she meet me because she thought we would get on, Mary was initially a little hesitant, because she always considered Grace's other friends, the ones she never got to meet, to be far too crazy for her. She thought that to be part of that side of Grace's life, there must be something wrong with their heads.

She was a little surprised to meet me, nothing like Grace's music friends; and I was surprised to meet a friend of Grace's who wasn't from her party world. As a person, Mary was as dramatic and as daring as Grace, and I could see why they were so close, but she was more discreet and careful.

Once Mary and I were together, as Grace knew would happen, the next part of Grace's plan was perhaps that stylish, meticulous Mary, with her interest in fabrics and design and her exquisite eye, might get me out of my shorts and flip-flops. She did try, but it was a losing battle. I tend to have very long relationships with people I meet, or very short ones. With Mary, I knew instantly it was going to be one of the long relationships.

CHAPTER TWELVE

MEETING U2

I was at Compass Point in the spring of 1980 when Rob Partridge, the head of Island press, first told me about U2. A former *Melody Maker* journalist, he had good instincts for what was happening, any new scene, and he called me up and said, "I think there is a band you will really like. They are Irish, and they've got something." He wasn't the excitable type, so I took him seriously. When he saw them, Nick Stewart, our new A&R man, thought they were perfect for Island, a noisy rock band like the old days, but young, enthusiastic, and with a little modern punk attitude.

Island had missed out on punk pretty much, except for the Slits, who had a very different vibe and a very particular sense of rhythm and seemed to fit into Island in a way punk bands really didn't. I never really took to punk as music even though I liked the attitude (to me, it just lacked bass), but there was a sense within the label that we had missed out on something culturally important, perhaps for the first time since we started. It was a time when Island was out of fashion, when we mostly had rock groups, even if we also had Kevin Ayers, Nico, and John Cale, whom the influential, Marley-supporting ex–*Melody Maker* writer Richard Williams had helped bring into Island when he was working in A&R; we also had the wide interests of Brian Eno after Roxy Music, whose early solo singing albums contained amongst much else some punk-like energy and post-punk disquiet.

But the punk groups weren't going to come to the Island of Cat Stevens, Jethro Tull, Free, and Nick Drake, which seemed the old days, and even Roxy Music and Sparks seemed the wrong influence.

The new punk groups would start their own labels, or go to labels with their own punkiness, like Stiff. (We did actually distribute Stiff, so we kept our hand in, not losing touch completely.) Then there were bands like the Sex Pistols, who played games with record labels, taking the money and taking the piss.

Paradoxically, even though we were seen as a big, established label at the time, we were actually having our own financial troubles. The gambler in me did like to spend money and invest incoming money in new projects, and the managing directors I put in place tended to be those who had worked for me from the very beginning. After seeing him rise through the ranks, I wasn't really going to listen to my managing director Tim Clark, much as I respected him, if he told me to stop spending money.

For a couple of years around 1976 and '77 we were forced to license our records through EMI to raise urgent money, losing our independence for a while. We got it back a couple of years later, when the Marley money started to come through, but it did mean when the bigger punk groups like the Clash were the subject of bidding wars, we actually couldn't afford them even if we wanted them.

When it came to punk as rebel music, I had Bob Marley bringing the rebel into the label, and that was rebel with rhythm, much more where I was.

I never saw U2 as punk, but they were definitely part of that next wave of groups after punk, who took the energy and attitude, and in U2's case, added something uplifting and positive, and in its own way something undeniably spiritual. They weren't exactly post-punk either, as there was something about them, perhaps the fact they were Irish, that held them back from seeming something boldly new. We didn't respond quickly to the post-punk groups, and Virgin Records, who'd begun distributed by Island, had become the more obvious destination for post-punk bands like Public Image Ltd, XTC, and Magazine—they even challenged us with their own reggae division, Front Line.

U2's name instantly hooked me even if the music didn't. I go by names, they mean a lot, and I was quite capable of not signing an act because their name wasn't right. If I thought there was nothing you could do with a name, I never had any interest. U2 you could definitely do something with—it would look great printed big on a poster, unmissable, and it was something you said every day. *You too? You too!* There was a little wobble about their name amongst the Island staff backing us to sign U2. They were being called the U2s, but I thought it was a strong name as soon as I heard it.

Rob Partridge and Nick Stewart were trying to find a way for me to go and see them while I was in England, which because of Compass Point and business in New York was happening less and less.

A gig was arranged on June 7 in South London at the Half Moon in Herne Hill; I could go there after Bob Marley's open-air show in front of fifteen thousand people at the Crystal Palace a few miles away. No one in the audience knew Marley was ill. He had less than a year to live, and some people who saw him perform said he seemed a little tired, a little slow and careful. Bob sang his new acoustic song "Redemption Song," the first time many people had heard it, just as the sun went down. For many there it was heartbreaking, but they couldn't really explain why.

After the show, everyone backstage headed into Central London on coaches, but I went off to see U2 with my girlfriend at the time, Nathalie Delon, and one or two others. I did not know it, but I was heading into another adventure, and in the same way Island had Cat Stevens, who brought the spirit of 1960s into the early 1970s, and then Bob Marley later in the 1970s, here was Island's biggest act of the 1980s. All three of them made religious music, from different places, but music with a message, songs about faith, and truth, and human dignity, which must say something about why I was so drawn to them.

Arriving at the pub, an old haunt of Dylan Thomas's, I would never have believed I was about to come across Island's next big signing, but then at the beginning of these things, it's often beyond your wildest imagination how it will turn out. You don't expect anything. You just follow your instinct and make a decision at that moment and then let it play out.

They'd played there a few times already that year. There seemed to be more people in my entourage than in the paying audience, but U2 played as though there were a thousand in front of them. They were bursting out of themselves. I was immediately blown away by their passion. I didn't really feel the music—it wasn't my kind of thing, too trebly, a bit rinky-dinky. They sounded as young as they were, and seemed overwhelmed by their influences, and their solemn-looking rhythm section barely made a dent in my memory.

The jazzer in Jamaican me needed some bass, the R&B lover wanted some swagger, and at that time I was enthralled by the cross-pollinated rhythms of the New York bands signing to ZE and excited by the rhythms of Compass Point. U2 wasn't about unusual rhythms, and if I had just heard them on a demo tape, I would have passed. Their early demo tapes would give you about 10 percent of the necessary information.

All was not lost, because I really believed in their self-confidence. It was like seeing a movie where you are not getting it all the way through. It doesn't seem to be grabbing you, and then at the end you realize you loved it. You want to see it again. There was much more to it than there initially seemed. And how that came across to me was through U2's energy, something that was really focused. In their energy was their own belief in themselves, which was irresistible.

Their twenty-year-old singer, Bono, seemed particularly driven, like he knew what his destiny was and he was charging towards it from a small stage in an unpromising pub in South London. He had some kind of rhythm, even if it was just how he engaged with an imaginary audience. Very early on in these cramped little venues in front of the smallest crowds, he was already clambering over the equipment and up the lighting rig as if he needed to reach out to the back of a vast venue, and even farther. This was either complete, delusional wishful thinking, or sheer, audacious magnetism, or a bit of both. He was already rehearsing for the big time. It stopped just about short of being too much. He didn't care if it looked a bit daft. In his head it was magnificent, and he was out to persuade everyone else it really was. They were going through where they were, without any kind of shame, to get to where they were going.

I met them after the show, in similar circumstances to when I met the Spencer Davis Group, in a very cramped dressing room, all of us on top of each other, becoming a part of music history, or perhaps just ships passing in the night. Bono was perhaps so animated because he was still in the process of proving to drummer Larry Mullen Jr., who had formed the group and was clearly the leader, that he was going to work as the lead singer, and to bassist Adam Clayton and the guitarist they were already calling the Edge, quiet but clearly smarter than the usual young rock musician. It was small talk, really, nothing much more than a bit of chitchat, but I realized pretty quickly that they were an intelligent collection of people. I believed in them as people even if the music had passed by me.

I agreed on the spot that they should come to Island. Their manager, Paul McGuinness, made a big impression on me as well. Bands at this stage of their life, playing small, dirty venues, are usually looked after by an eager pal who can't play an instrument and acts as the driver and equipment humper. But U2 had someone in place who even in this tiny venue absolutely looked the part, reminding me very much of David Enthoven and John Gaydon of E. G. He was clearly in charge of everything but their music.

Bono talks about how when I came to the gig I was dressed in shorts and flip-flops, as if it were a cold winter's day or something. It was June, but Bono likes to make a story better! He's got a way with words. Apart from whatever else he is, he is a mythmaker.

The flip-flops made a big impression on him, that the boss of the record label turned up that way. But what made an impression on me was how their manager was dressed almost exactly the opposite to me, the way I would never dress. Even though it was a scruffy venue, a basic bar with a barely there stage, he was in a suit and tie, very proper, very professional, and that really added to the sense that they all meant business.

Just a few words was all it took for McGuinness to make it clear to me that he was very smart, and he also believed in U2 and knew how to sell them. He was committing himself to this project. He was confident. *Don't worry about the size of the venue or the small crowd; this is going to happen.*

He told me, "We are not in the record business; we are in the U2 business," and I knew exactly what he meant. He was announcing, *We have stature; we have a future.* The professionalism was significant. They had things worked out. We signed them, not for a particularly dramatic amount of money. We might have offered Spandau Ballet more, but there were no other labels interested in U2, and we didn't have to enter a bidding war. Even Stiff, run by fellow Irishman Dave Robinson, wasn't keen on releasing U2 records when McGuinness asked him to help, to give them a profile. He liked the idea of them, but he thought their songs were underwhelming.

Later, when he was managing director of Island, feeling I was too soft and old-fashioned when it came to promotion, it was Dave's aggressive marketing and TV advertising of U2 that pushed them from being minor cult to the edge of the big time.

Paul McGuinness didn't blink when it came to negotiation, even though we might have been their only option. The reality was, Island was the best label for U2, because it was in an area between major and independent, and I still had the final say about what we signed, based on years of experience.

Some record companies might get nervous if they think no one else is interested, but it suited Island just fine. We had done well signing the rejects and the unwanted, because we often responded to an act not as a record company but as a potential collaborator.

Now that I was a U2 believer and we were signing them, I told everyone at Island that I wanted to give them their head; I wanted us to follow them instead of telling them what to do. I said, "These guys are in charge. This is their thing." In effect, I gave them the company to use as they wanted to make their vision come true. I gave them a platform. I gave them Island Records. I did not have any influence on them at all. I had nothing to do with their recordings, their graphics, their touring. They did everything themselves. And we left them to it. I just got out of their way, allowed them to be independent spirits. Sometimes that's what it takes. They had a producer in mind: Steve Lillywhite, who'd worked with Siouxsie and the Banshees, XTC, and Ultravox; engineered a great single for Island by Eddie and the Hot Rods called "Do Anything You Wanna Do"; and just produced Peter Gabriel. He seemed like a good choice, a little older than them but not by too much, and had also fallen for their self-belief and live performance as much as their demo tapes. We left them to it, as I promised, and let them work it out for themselves, none of them yet twenty—but then, neither were the members of Free when they made their first album.

Bono would say he took it as a compliment that I just let them be themselves. It was a good time for me to come across U2, because I was becoming more hands-off in general, certainly outside of Compass Point, and it was perfect to find a band that connected so well with Island but didn't really need much involvement from me. I just needed to be there, a living symbol of the kind of person they wanted at the head of their label.

Boy, their debut album, did not sell so well. Just like Bob Dylan was known as John Hammond's folly after his first album, U2 was thought of as Nick Stewart's folly. There was some talk in Island of dropping them—which to me didn't seem a very Island thing to do, in terms of how they clearly had a long-term plan, and we had said we were there for them. We had given them this commitment, not something we would often do to that extent, and then at the first sign of a problem we pulled out? There were discussions, my point of view was obvious, Rob Partridge reported on their great press, minds were changed, and we picked up the option. To me it made perfect sense—even if it was a gamble, when had we ever not gambled on what turned out to be the right thing to do?

I had made a new deal with Atlantic to distribute our records, turning the deal on its head—instead of the usual way, where they offered us an advance, I offered them an advance for a much better profit share. An accountant is never going to turn down free money. This was just before Island, in particular U2, took off. That led to Atlantic's cofounder Ahmet Ertegun, one of my heroes, calling me "the baby-faced killer."

Now and then I would give the group some advice, offer an opinion. I still had a point of view. I remember after they had used Steve Lillywhite to produce the first three albums—*Boy*, *October*, and *War*—they decided a change would be good. Lillywhite had been like their teacher, and now they needed another one.

I suggested that they might try using Jimmy Iovine for their fourth studio album. He'd worked on Springsteen's *Born to Run* and Meatloaf's *Bat Out of Hell*, as well as producing Patti Smith's *Easter* and her first hit, "Because the Night." He'd produced their 1983 live album *Under a Blood Red Sky* from their American War tour and I thought he would be a good match for U2, at an especially important time for them—to make them a bit more wide-screen and international. They seemed on the verge of becoming massive, but, being overthinkers, this worried them as much as it excited them. They feared that they might break through with a basic rock sound they could never escape from, and they wanted to demonstrate they had an artistic fluidity.

I heard that they were going to use Brian Eno as their new producer. This was a real surprise at the time, one I wasn't sure about at all, thinking of those abrasive and cold no-wave recordings Eno had done in New York a few years before, more than of early Roxy Music. I thought it was commercial suicide, even when Neil Storey and Rob in the press department, with their ears close to the ground, tried to persuade me it was a brilliant idea, however unexpected.

This motivated me to fly out to Dublin to meet the group and talk it through. They listened politely as I explained why I didn't think it was a good idea. They had clearly made their minds up that they were going to use Eno, who up to that point had been involved with plenty of innovative new music but never with anything close to direct rock success. Where we did meet on Eno was the work he had done with Talking Heads, but that hadn't sold the kind of copies I thought U2 could. Eno doing with U2 what he had done with Talking Heads wasn't as bad an idea as him doing to U2 what he had done with Teenage Jesus and the Jerks, but I was still not convinced.

Full of themselves—because that was part of their attraction—they said, "Well, if you are here as the record company concerned about your investment, you should go now. If you are here as a fan of the group, well, we have thought hard about this, and we think this is what we need to do to sound more modern, more serious."

They politely told me they would use Iovine when the time was right (and they did on *Rattle and Hum* in 1988, which gave them their first UK number one, "Desire"), but they were very wedded to the idea of using Brian Eno along with Daniel Lanois on what became *The Unforgettable Fire*.

I was concerned that Eno would take them in an experimental direction, which would have been absurd; but of course they knew what they were doing, searching for their own sound, this ambient abstraction of rock stardom, conceptualizing the idea of a massive rock band without losing any authenticity. It was a dramatic—and at the same time subtle—change for the group, and absolutely the right one. I didn't see it coming. They did. It was why I trusted them, even if now and then I pointed out what I thought was an error. Once they explained why they were doing it, I left as a fan, understanding what they were doing and looking forward to it.

It turned out they had also needed to persuade Eno, as he wasn't sure what he could do for them when they first asked him. He needed persuading from the other side. Bono, of course, eventually talked him into it. Bono is a very good talker. Eno had initially recommended that they use Lanois on his own; but when he decided to do it, it was hearing about my fears that he would turn them into art rock, or worse, that made him bring Lanois with him. Then, he reasoned, the album would at least sound great. So I made some sort of contribution to this clever change in direction.

With U2, Eno experimented in a different way, not sacrificing their rock dynamics, but working out how to enhance them through a combination of spontaneity, emotion, and strategy. He was like a kind of intellectual Guy Stevens, a cerebral Jimmy Miller, creating a mood, someone who understood how a recording studio worked and how to get the best out of the group he was working with. He created a landscape for U2 to occupy, and that alone meant they didn't end up as their worst nightmare, just another high-powered rock band.

Unforgettable Fire went to number one in the UK charts, and in the US it reached number twelve, the highest position for a U2 album so far, and in 1985, *Rolling Stone* named them Band of the Eighties, the only band that mattered. It opened up America in the way I had hoped, but with the added bonus of a new, adaptable sound for the group, because Eno—with his lapsed-Catholic background, with Lanois's vast sound—had reimagined them as a spiritual rock band.

And of course the partnership with Eno, with his firm, theoretical approach to the idea of U2 as a kind of commercial art object, became one of their most important relationships. Often Eno played a similar role to me—he was a symbol of their ultimate producer, a talisman, even if his influence was sometimes just a matter of him being there, part of their mental picture, and someone they needed to live up to.

Before they worked with Jimmy Iovine on *Rattle and Hum* (which led to some of the criticism about a tendency to melodrama and bombast they had originally feared), they were still using Brian Eno (with Daniel Lanois) and his different, slyer thinking about rock dynamics for 1987's *The Joshua Tree*—which was again the correct course of action. It won a Grammy for Album of the Year and put them on the cover of *Time* magazine, certifying superstar status, and was the first of eight straight number-one albums. They were now a group who could change from record to record without changing their central purpose or losing their commercial impact. Four years later, for 1991's *Achtung Baby,* they returned to Lanois and Eno, their favored studio partnership, which allowed the group to experiment with pop culture and their place in it, to introduce electronics and other non-rock elements but still sound like they were artists who meant business. Eno was with them for the next album, *Zooropa,* extending the *Achtung Baby* experiments, and in 1995 even merged with U2 to become the Passengers (the name they recorded under when Eno was even more involved than usual), making the kind of eclectic, conceptually playful album I had imagined their first collaboration would have been.

For quite a time they always seemed to know what they were doing, and how to do it, and they turned into the kind of group they were acting out when I first saw them in front of a handful of people in an obscure part of London. They just kept on being serious, and smart, and hardworking, often overanalyzing what they were doing but for good reason, finding the best people to work with, and Bono kept on talking, never afraid to fail, and Paul McGuinness kept on dressing the same way, and Island kept following them, at least while I was around.

The only time it went wrong was much later, when they released *Pop*, in 1997—without Brian Eno—which was an odd, self-conscious title, although slightly better than one they'd had in mind, *Pop for Men*, and they launched it in a supermarket, which was so out of place. It was the only time that a direction they went in was a failure, with a combination of bad reviews and bad sales. Because everything up to then had worked—all their choices about management, artwork, producers, photographers, designers, tours, titles, songs—when it didn't work, no one quite knew how to respond. There was no precedent for a really bad set of U2 decisions. There was no model for anybody to say to them, "Hold on. This is a mess. . . ." Because nothing like that had ever happened with them before. They hadn't put a foot wrong, so it was very disorienting when they did. I guess they recovered. They got it right about what to do when you get it wrong. Maybe it was all part of their plan, even if at the beginning there didn't seem to be a clear plan other than: let's go with this plan until we come up with a better one.

Forty years after I first met them, as a fan and a friend, as someone who likes to go with the flow, I still look forward to seeing what they do next and how they're going to start over again one more time.

CHAPTER THIRTEEN

THE NINETIES:
SHIFTING GROUND

Looking for a different kind of rhythm, I had started producing films, which requires a very different level of investment. Dave Robinson always used to say when Trevor Horn spent blockbuster amounts of money on making an album or a Grace Jones single, "Well, it's the price of a small independent movie." Which meant that hundreds of thousands of pounds, even a million, only got you a small independent movie. I wanted to make an impact, so even though I was interested in making interesting independent movies, it took a lot of money, and a lot of gambling. The game you were in increased in intensity. You could make more, but of course you could lose more.

Island Alive as a production and distribution company formed in 1983, two years after I'd produced *Countryman*, which made me want to do more. We chose our films very carefully, all of them intended to be unusual, challenging, low- to medium-budget, and as much as possible from all over the world.

Our first release was Godfrey Reggio's plotless, wordless *Koyaanisqatsi*, an experimental environmental documentary as an incredible hypnotic experience, with a spectacular soundtrack by Philip Glass, who initially said he didn't write music for films. Once Glass had written the music, Godfrey cut the film to the music, and the soundtrack album was released on Island, one of the label's best secrets.

It was a very personal film, and Godfrey chose Island even though we were a new company precisely because we were small and agile. He wanted to be involved with the release, and at first he didn't want it to have a title, just a symbol.

We were involved with the grand and moving *El Norte*, about the realities of immigrating to the US, which *Variety* described as an independent epic; writers Gregory Nava and Anna Thomas received an Oscar nomination for the screenplay.

In 1984, we became Island Pictures, and there was Stephen Frears's crime thriller *The Hit*, and Jonathan Demme's music-film masterpiece representing Talking Heads in concert, *Stop Making Sense*. In 1985 we were really getting into our stride—we distributed Héctor Babenco's *Kiss of the Spider Woman*, which garnered five Oscar nominations and a Best Actor Oscar for William Hurt; *Mona Lisa*, with an Oscar nomination for Bob Hoskins; and *The Trip to Bountiful*.

We were hitting that sweet spot that reflected where we were as a record label, which in film terms put us in between large-scale mainstream studio releases and small-scale specialty films. We wanted to make the kind of intelligent, commercially difficult films the major studios didn't want to risk producing. I thought of it as the creation of an identity niche, where people came to Island for a certain kind of record or film. If the act is brilliant, the niche expands, as was happening with U2.

I was still doing the same thing—looking for talent and then developing it. This meant my schedule involved even more travel, because there were not only the music artists to follow around the world where they were playing and recording but also the film festivals I wanted to attend. In 1987, I would top 250,000 frequent-flier miles, always traveling without baggage, because it's a nightmare otherwise, and I always liked to walk onto a plane as the doors were closing before the flight. Usually, as soon as I sat down, we would be ready for takeoff.

THE FILMS WERE a sign that I was looking for ways of finding new stimulation as the record label continued to grow but facing new sorts of problems as the music business became more corporate.

We were feeling the squeeze between the major labels and the smaller, nimbler independents, neither one thing nor the other. We had U2, who by the time of *The Joshua Tree* were selling millions of albums, the kind of act you'd usually need the resources and organization of a major to support; but we also pursued the oddball and outsider acts, which was part of our independent spirit. We were getting too big to be small, yet still too small to be big. As a small label, you can have a guerrilla-force type spirit. As we became a small corporation, it was difficult to compete. As a guerrilla force, you can compete with an army; but as a small army, which we had become, it is difficult to compete with a big army.

Whenever there was a suggestion we should become a kind of major, maybe sign more acts like U2, as if that sort of thing were our specialty, I didn't like it; it didn't feel right, but it was also tricky when we signed acts that made the trademark unusual Island records, but were not exactly setting the world on fire.

The business side wanted me to build pressing plants and open offices all over the world. Once you have a U2 and the money starts to pour in, there is a tendency as a company to feel that the more esoteric music, the African, reggae, and odd, unique records by wanderers and misfits that were always the soul of the label, is a waste of time. When you are used to selling in seven figures, why bother with an iconic African act that might be loved and well-reviewed but only sells 30,000 copies? They are never going to sell a million records, so what's the aim?

The discussions about what the point of the label was were becoming more complicated and were not the kinds of conversations I was having in the late 1960s and early 1970s, as the label moved from John Martyn, Nick Drake, Free, Traffic, Jethro Tull, and Cat Stevens to Roxy Music and Brian Eno, and then to Bob Marley and the Wailers. Slowly, the numbers started to take over. It wasn't anyone's fault; that's how it was, but it didn't suit me. I started to feel, as the eighties progressed and the business changed around me, that I was in no-man's-land.

For me, it was signing Tom Waits that represented pure Island, whether it made conventional commercial success or not. If you look at the artists we had worked with, the likes of Fairport Convention, Toots, Kevin Ayers, Marianne Faithfull, John Cale, the B-52's, and Kid Creole, it all led to Tom Waits.

He wasn't a signing you'd make because you read what was selling in *Billboard*, what the latest trends were, but it was where I found myself one day, another of those days when it seemed I'd turned the right corner and found myself in the right room with a character who seemed more alive than most people, and who in his work made a stand to ensure eccentricity and strangeness never disappeared from the world.

That was the kind of artist I wanted to sign, and it was both a surprise and no surprise to me that Island signed Tom Waits. It's great to have U2 over here, their hearts set on taking over the world, but it's even better when, somewhere else on the label, you have Tom Waits making the world something else altogether.

He had made some fine, jazzy, softly skewed singer-songwriter records for David Geffen's Asylum in the 1970s, one nicely following the last, but he was becoming a little trapped. He fancied a change, a few changes, in pretty much everything he was as a musician, singer, and performer. He'd presented Elektra/Asylum with his seventh album: to them, it sounded like he was just sticking together some musical styles from across the board and bashing them out of shape and breaking some glass just for the sake of it. They passed on the album. They thought he was going to lose all his old fans and not pick up any new ones.

I couldn't understand, to be honest, how you could turn down a record by Tom Waits. It shocked me. One song he'd done that made me such a fan was his poignant, powerful version of "Waltzing Matilda," which you hear and know he's on a level with Louis Armstrong or Lead Belly. I loved how he had made himself a character in his own story.

When I heard that he had been dropped, I asked Lionel Conway—who had worked for me at our publishing company, Island Music, and who lived in Los Angeles—to set up a meeting for me. I hadn't heard the record, but I was very interested in the whole idea of Tom Waits, and the fact he'd made a record that Asylum had rejected. That had to mean it was something of interest.

So there I was having a coffee with Tom and his very striking Irish-American wife of three years, Kathleen Brennan, in Los Angeles, which of course is the perfect place to meet him, where many of his songs are set. The story goes, of course, that as a performer Tom took a turn for the wilder and weirder after he met Kathleen, marrying, as he said, a beautiful woman and a great record collection, filled with bizarre new delights that he couldn't get enough of. The influences piled up and fell all over the album that Asylum wouldn't put out.

We met in a little café-bar place in Los Feliz on the edge of Hollywood. Tom didn't have much to say, which never puts me off, and left most of the talking to Kathleen, who had become his manager. Actually, I can't remember him saying anything at all. Oddly, it reminded me of the last time I saw Nick Drake. Looking down, no eye contact, very tight shoulders, not a word coming out of his mouth.

Tom was a bit lost at the time, incredibly introverted, and if Kathleen hadn't been there, I don't know what kind of meeting it would have been. Quiet, I suppose. She was in the process of getting his messy, meandering life in order. We worked out a deal with Kathleen because it was meant to be.

And then what do you do with Tom Waits? You make him feel comfortable and let him get on with what he's got in mind to do. If artists like that have got a problem or need any help, you make sure you're there for them.

Later, I learned he had just listened at that first meeting in order to get the measure of me. He seemed to like what he heard—that I was going to let him have as much freedom as you can have as an artist making records for a record label, that it was okay by me if he wanted to produce his own records. He appreciated, he said, that in our dealings, he never felt that he was at Texaco or Heineken or Budweiser. He wasn't keen on record companies, certainly the major ones. He thought they were more like countries than companies. Or they were like jellyfish: they had no anatomy. I like to think the relationship we had with Tom shows that Island had anatomy. It had heart.

You don't direct Tom Waits. You don't tell anyone with talent like that what kind of records to make. When I did get to hear the rejected album, *Swordfishtrombones* (after we'd done the deal—so for all I knew, Asylum could have been right), I couldn't believe it. I would have been happy with the old Tom Waits, but this was a new Tom Waits, all sorts of sounds and styles connecting with each other from all over the world and the twentieth century and musical history, elements that you would never think belonged with each other, but for Tom absolutely did.

It didn't sell many copies, it didn't get much airplay, it had a peculiar glimpse of the bottom of the Billboard Top 200 for a moment, but it was in a lot of music paper end-of-year lists of best albums of the year. He wasn't everybody's cup of tea, and he didn't aspire to be. But if you found him, he took you places, and people tended to find him almost by word of mouth, back when someone like him did most of his appearing through magazine interviews.

At the end of the 1980s, *Spin* magazine named *Swordfishtrombones* the second-best album of all time, in between James Brown's *Sex Machine* and Bob Dylan's *Blonde on Blonde*. Which made a lot of sense. It's the kind of record that's never going to run out of steam, because it's as much a great novel or a classic film as a record, set to always make sense of time and place and whatever state of mind you're in when you listen to it.

Tom and Kathleen moved to New York, and they made albums for Island for as long as Island was independent, and as long as I was in sole control—before the big fish ate the little fish—and they are a perfect example of how if you give an artist freedom and let them take ownership of their own songs, they will flourish: *Rain Dogs, Franks Wild Years, Big Time, Night on Earth, Bone Machine, The Black Rider.* You just get out of the way and let them do their thing.

Tom Waits sneaked into Island, and he was a kind of secret compared to a lot of our other acts, but some of the best Island acts were secrets, from Dr. Strangely Strange, White Noise, and Ijahman Levy to Stomu Yamashta and the early Ultravox, doing their thing under cover. U2 was a secret for a while.

WHILE TOM WAS in the shadows digging deeper into his music and life, U2 was conquering more and more territory, staking a claim to be the biggest band on earth. It was while U2 was working on *The Joshua Tree* that I got a dose of reality about why it can be dangerous to have a massive hit group on an independent label. It was exactly why I had licensed Millie and the Spencer Davis Group to Fontana in the sixties. You can end up being crushed by too big a success.

In the same way that, in the mid-seventies, building Compass Point took a considerable amount of money away from Island and then put the label in trouble, the investment in film meant that in 1986 I owed U2 many millions of dollars in royalties, and Island didn't have the money to pay them. The label was close to collapse.

I had overreached. I was doing too many things at the same time, possibly because after Bob died, I was always looking for something that could equal what I had with him, that excitement, that discovery of something that was bigger than music. There was Grace, there was U2, there was Tom, there was ZTT, there was Compass Point, and there were the films, and one of those things perhaps should have been satisfying enough, but I just kept trying to fill the space that Bob had left behind. Which was impossible.

Bob's death didn't come as a shock, because we were prepared for it, but I was not prepared for what happened afterwards, which made me realize how much I had lost, and how much the world had lost. It hit me during his funeral in Jamaica where, the day before he was buried, tens of thousands of people filed past his coffin. His funeral procession traveled from Kingston, passing by 56 Hope Road, out of the city towards his Nine Mile burial site in the hills, where he had been born. The streets were lined all the way along, with different Bob Marley songs being sung or played at different stages. It was incredible. It was difficult to get as excited about the record business after that—but that didn't mean I stopped doing things. The opposite, really.

I took on too much. I did too much. Island was more relevant than it had ever been, and more people wanted to sign with us. I came across Melissa Etheridge in much the same way I had Steve Winwood, catching her performance in a small bar in Long Beach, Los Angeles, not expecting much before I arrived. I got as carried away as I always did when I found something exciting. I could never stop being excited when I heard something I hadn't heard before.

I told her almost immediately that I thought the future of rock and roll had a female voice, thinking of that line in the seventies about Bruce Springsteen being the future of rock and roll. She'd quickly become tagged as the female Bruce Springsteen, and she was, if he had been the male Janis Joplin.

I used a trick I'd used not long before when Melissa was finishing her first album, when she'd done that thing I purposefully didn't do with the B-52's—made it glossy and slick, getting dazzled by the studio. The production knocked off all the rowdy, rough edges and the pain and hunger that made her so compelling.

The reason I'd signed her was that I wanted a record that cut *against* the glossiness and synthesizers of the mid-1980s. We'd done a photo session for the album using George DuBose, who had taken the photo for the B-52's' debut, where DuBose had gotten Melissa to move while he played one of the most passionate songs on her album, "Like the Way I Do." The photo with her head thrown back and her fists clenched reminded me more of how she was onstage, energetic, carefree, and committed to her feelings. The photo was better than the album.

I got a large print of it sent into the studio with the message: "Make the album sound like this." She remade the record with just drums, bass, and guitar; it was much more powerful, and who she was, which didn't stop it selling over a million and getting high in the Billboard 200. Some of her albums would become multimillion-sellers, and I think it was good that she started with an uncompromising sound. If she'd started glossy, she would have been trapped. Starting raw gave her places to go.

Mostly, though, it was getting hard for me to keep up with new artists like I used to. There wasn't enough of me to stay in touch with it all, even though I wouldn't admit it to myself.

I wanted to keep up-to-date with everything, because Island was at its best when it was ahead of the game. We didn't sign many rap artists, but when we did, they were the very best—through 4th & Broadway we signed Eric B. and Rakim, releasing their debut album in 1987. One view was that Island's golden age was between Traffic's "Paper Sun" single in 1967 and U2's *The Joshua Tree* in 1987; but another version is that it went from John Martyn's "Fairy Tale Lullaby" in 1967 to Eric B. and Rakim's *Paid in Full* in 1987.

There were a lot of Island stories and histories, lots of labels, lots of current acts and acts from the past, and slowly and inevitably the label had become more corporate even as we were releasing King Sunny Adé or Tom Waits. There was a staff of 120 in the US alone; it's difficult to keep the label identity when you have lots of different people all doing their thing. It drifts further and further away from where it began, which was essentially me making it up as I went along.

In the eighties, the jazz went out of it for me. I couldn't impro-
vise like I used to. In the sixties, it was a new business, and you were
always breaking new ground. You could still do that in the eighties,
but it was a very different music business, and a very different world.
We still put out great records, but I couldn't help but wonder, well,
what's so special about us now; we're not as unique as we once were.
Many records we put out could have been on any label. If we got
too big, we lost what we were; if we stayed small, we weren't making
progress.

I owned up to U2 about the finances and we managed to work
something out. If they hadn't trusted me or Island as much as they did,
it would have been very messy. U2 didn't want to bankrupt Island,
and there was no other label they wanted to go to, so we worked it out
between us very civilly. In the middle of everything, the biggest band
in the world was treating their label as though it were still a family
affair, and they were part of the family.

We both benefited from the deal—U2 got to own their masters
and 10 percent of the company, while I got to make sure Island continued without having an undignified end, and without its history
being broken up and scattered to the winds. In March 1987, *The
Joshua Tree* was released on Island, U2's first number-one album, and
to the outside world, all was normal.

WHAT IT ALL meant internally was that, emotionally and financially,
it was time to sell the label, ending its existence as an independent.
It was a sign of the times. It was also the best time for me to get
the most value for the company. The industry was changing. Danger
was looming. The managing director of Philips told me in 1987 how
fantastic the compact disc was, that it was going to revolutionize the
music world. He would say that—Philips had the patent on it, and
effectively that's what they were selling, the discs themselves. It didn't
much matter to the company what was on them.

Once I'd made the decision to let go, I never wavered. In 1989 I sold Island to the Netherlands-based conglomerate PolyGram for close to $300 million, which certainly gave me and the label a chance to regroup. There were other shareholders involved in this, including U2. (It was estimated that the buyout earned them five times more than the missing back royalties—we were a long way from the Half Moon in Herne Hill.)

I'd had relationships with PolyGram over the years—they distributed Island in France and Germany—and even though there were offers from other major labels, PolyGram's was the best, both financially and in terms of the structure of the deal. I sold my shares, but I was still closely involved with the running of the label as chief executive. I didn't want any withdrawal symptoms, so it suited me, even though I knew what they expected from me was to help identify and sign acts, not really run it in the way I had. There wasn't going to be the same sense that when I signed an act, there would be time for it to develop. Corporate time scale took over. If an act wasn't having hits, the attitude would be, why keep them? Put it this way: once the change happened, it didn't suit Tom Waits, suddenly exposed to exactly the atmosphere that freezes him as an artist. He was soon on his way, although I did try to put Tom together with trip-hop traveler Tricky, which was either as mad an idea as putting John Martyn with Scratch Perry, or as inspired an idea.

I was a figurehead as much as anything, but still with a responsibility to maintain continuity. It wasn't as bad as I thought it would be, at least for a while. I was sad having to end Island's relationship with the first European company I ever did a deal with, the Swedish label Sonet. I'd connected with them when I was still in Jamaica, when they were known for importing jazz records.

I'd worked with them consistently since 1959; then thirty years later, PolyGram ended the Sonet deal, and they were themselves forced to become absorbed into PolyGram. It was the beginning of a period when labels were eating each other up, on the way to the world we're in now, which is like it was at the beginning when a couple of labels owned 96 percent of record distribution.

Seagram's Edgar Bronfman would buy PolyGram in 1998 and merge it with the MCA family of labels to form the Universal Music Group, owning most record labels along with Sony and Warner Music, the Big Three. They have monopoly power, and Island exists somewhere in the middle of it all as an imprint, made distinctive and relatively culturally valuable by its early history.

Island ended up where it was always destined to end up, but with a few extra years of activity it might not have had if U2 didn't have the trust they had in the label. Other labels that were being absorbed as the industry tried to prepare itself for dangerous times ahead, such as A&M and Virgin, would become more or less shells of what they'd been. Island, to this day, long after I had an official connection, long after it lost any link with how it functioned as an independent, continues with about as much profile as a label can have in this day and age, responsible for signing Amy Winehouse, and twenty-first-century superstars like Drake, The Weeknd, Post Malone, and Ariana Grande. Maybe that's because its story goes back to my selling records from the boot of my car, beginning a momentum that the label's own ups and downs, being absorbed into Universal, and the transformation of the business itself by streaming, never completely extinguished.

FOR A FEW years, there was a post-independent Island history that I was directly involved with. Working inside PolyGram was the first real job I'd had since leaving Jamaica, speaking as someone who ended up doing what I did because I was fundamentally unemployable. There was still a surviving Island spirit represented in acts we signed under PolyGram like PJ Harvey, the Cranberries, Angélique Kidjo, Tricky, the Disposable Heroes of Hiphoprisy, Stereo MC's, and Pulp, not least because Island UK's managing director during this period, Marc Marot, was a self-confessed fan of the label who admitted he had been collecting Island records for years.

I did feel it was a chance to keep trying new things while a little more protected by the PolyGram structure, which, as much as it could be brutal, was also a realistic shield against the worst excesses of the decisions and gambles I had made. I still couldn't resist a gamble.

The day after I sold Island, I had a meeting with bass player, producer, bandleader, arranger, and Miles Davis fanatic Bill Laswell at my Central Park apartment. This wasn't necessarily going to lead to the new U2 or Bob Marley that PolyGram would have been expecting, but that was okay by me. He'd worked as the main member of Material, ZE's free-floating rhythm section for hire, after a period in New York's improvisational downtown scene with John Zorn and Fred Frith. Along the way, he'd studied studio technique with Brian Eno and contributed to the groundbreaking album Eno made with David Byrne, *My Life in the Bush of Ghosts*. He once put free-jazz saxophonist Archie Shepp with an unsigned Whitney Houston on an old Soft Machine track.

Laswell had a huge hit while not really straying from his weird, experimental urges producing, via Material, Herbie Hancock's "Rockit," jazz tipping over into hip-hop; but, allergic to the obvious, after producing Mick Jagger at Compass Point, as well as Sly and Robbie and Public Image Ltd, his instincts were to form a loud free-jazz noise band called Last Exit. He talked about collaborating with Miles and had some ideas of making a record with him that mixed the endless rhythms of Trouble Funk with African beats and classical sounds. Of course, it never got made, although it sounded like something you'd want to play after Tricky produced by Tom Waits.

Bill had a very restless, eclectic mind and I was always interested in what he was thinking of doing next, so the timing of our meeting was fortuitous. I was about to start a whole new era, and I was in the mood to make sure that, having taken the money, I didn't immediately look like I had succumbed to the predictable and compromised my standards.

The night before, Bill had been out with German free-jazz saxophonist Peter Brötzmann, the great improvisational pianist Cecil Taylor, and character actor Nick Nolte, famous for wearing surgical scrubs everywhere because they were comfortable, and I think he had come to see me straight from being with them, on no sleep. Bill was definitely seeing things, and somehow still dreaming.

He had an idea for a label he wanted to do, international, avant-garde, experimental, industrial, ambient, but also dub, hip-hop, spoken word, and jazz. He didn't really have much of a prepared plan, but to give me an idea of his intentions, he quoted a twelfth-century mystic, "Nothing is true, everything is permitted," and that seemed a good place to start.

He was very enthusiastic about having a label that included all music, which seemed both very vague and absolutely specific, an idea that had come to him after drinking all night with Taylor, Brötzmann, and Nolte. Essentially, he was thinking of extending Material's roaming brief as a musical production company into a record label, and I liked the idea of a rhythm section, which they essentially were, forming a label. Maybe, he admitted, he just wanted a label that gave him the chance to work with musicians he liked.

Based on his track record and the musicians he had collaborated with, and his interest in what he called "collision music"—putting together cross-cultural, cross-generational musicians from different backgrounds and countries to see what happened—it seemed like a good way to consolidate a lot of ideas that were in the air at the time. He was like a Lee "Scratch" Perry for new times, and a little easier to work with.

Island had always helped other labels, from Chrysalis, Bronze, and Virgin to ZE, ZTT, and Beggars Banquet, and it seemed the perfect way to refresh that side of the label in our new setting. We were also always very keen on working with innovative producers, and at the end of the eighties, Bill was one of the more interesting producers, and one who was more from the playing side than the engineering or conceptual.

I thought it was also a good way to challenge the new relationship with PolyGram to see how much they understood what they had bought and appreciated how wide-ranging it had been away from the obvious and more visible artists.

Nobody seemed to get in my way, and I wasn't going to get in Bill's way, and so for a few years what Bill called Axiom, based at Greenpoint Studios in Brooklyn, released an extraordinary number of records from around the world, including recording the Master Musicians of Jajouka in their village in the Rif Mountains of Morocco, and combining master Indian musicians such as Zakir Hussain and Sultan Khan with electronics.

He conceived extravagant immersive studies in ambient, world fusion, metal, devotional, Hendrix, and funk, with collaborators including Ginger Baker, Sly Stone, Sly and Robbie, Jah Wobble, and various members of the Parliament-Funkadelic axis including Bootsy Collins.

Billboard magazine handily described Axiom as specializing in three things: traditional world music, experimental jazz, and "what seems to be the heart of the label, anarchistic music that combines and mutates traditional world music, jazz, hip hop, funk, industrial no wave noise and more into a sonic mélange of noise."

Billboard also reported that because Axiom was so different from other labels at PolyGram, PolyGram staff needed a little education about what the music was. Bill was quoted as saying he chose the label name because it began with the first letter of the alphabet and had an X in it. He expressed gratitude that I didn't feel the need to police every detail of each record, "which is generally the problem with record companies." And still no one from PolyGram knocked on my door and asked me what the hell was going on. I guess the fact that elsewhere U2 had renegotiated their PolyGram/Island deal in 1993, for six albums, satisfied various quotas and projections, and Bill could carry on trying to put all music from everywhere in the world onto one label.

Bill thought Axiom was releasing the greatest progressive fusion music of all time, music that would last for centuries, and who was I to disagree with him? It was being done, possibly the only way it could be done, using PolyGram-sized budgets, often to fly Laswell around the planet, whether to Ginger Baker's olive farm in Italy to lure him out of retirement or to Nigeria to find musicians for Ornette Coleman to work with.

There was no stopping Bill, and I think he was quite capable of keeping Axiom going permanently, a constantly reconfigured soundtrack to infinity, an ongoing development of the conversation we'd had after his all-night drinking session. I also asked him to produce some ambient dub versions of Bob Marley, part of a series I envisaged where various Island classics were remixed with dub tradition in mind.

In 1997, it was me who inadvertently brought Axiom, and this remix series, to an end. I was starting to feel I was working for a boss, and that boss wasn't allowing me to work the way I liked. I wish I'd had as much freedom as Bill. It turned out I couldn't keep working at Island forever.

I had suggested to PolyGram CEO Alain Levy that he should think about acquiring the video channel The Box and buy a half stake in Ted Field and Jimmy Iovine's Interscope, which at the time was the most successful record company in America, with acts like Nine Inch Nails, Tupac Shakur, and those of Dr. Dre and Marion "Suge" Knight's Death Row. It would have made PolyGram the number-one music company in the world. MCA (which was owned by Seagram) bought in, and by the end of the decade, Interscope sales were one-third of Seagram's 27 percent share of the US music market. I hadn't done any market research, but I could see it coming.

Levy shut the ideas down. He just wanted me to keep running Island, keep me in my place, but I had done that for thirty-five years, and I wanted to broaden out and make decisions as a member of the PolyGram management board. I didn't want to keep doing the same thing, and I was seeing how much the music business was changing and wanted to keep moving with it.

I ultimately fell out with PolyGram because of how they were dealing with a film Island Pictures was making directed by Robert Altman, *Gingerbread Man*. It hadn't tested well, and PolyGram moved to edit it without speaking to Altman. It was exactly how I didn't like to work, changing things behind an artist's back without telling them. When you work with someone like Altman, you are placing your confidence and trust in him as an artist and what he wants to do. It was sorted out, but Levy was furious that I had made a stand.

There were other petty and not so petty things going on as well, and I'd had enough trying to make it work. I rang Levy and told him he had repeatedly disregarded my judgment and I wanted to resign. He was restricting me, and I didn't understand why. Maybe he was wondering where the next U2 was, the next Bob Marley.

I might have looked a little like a spoiled brat, but I was angry and I'd realized that it was impossible for me to carry on as the kind of entrepreneur I wanted to be within the PolyGram corporate structure. The deal between us was voided with a few curt faxes, and I think Axiom lasted at PolyGram for about a second after I was no longer formally connected with Island.

AXIOM MOVED WITH me into my next, deliberately and defiantly independent venture, Palm Pictures. It was an attempt to begin another Island Records, scouting the world for enterprising talent, combined with another Island Pictures, committed to intelligent independent films. Being foolish, or stubborn, I founded another company, more in tune with my way of working and with where I saw music and entertainment going culturally and financially.

For old times' sake, but also because he was still playing lively, inventive guitar forty years after he was one of the first Island artists, we began with an album by Ernest Ranglin, and Sly and Robbie were still part of the mission. We signed artists like Cousteau, Supreme Beings of Leisure, and Nortec Collective, and we continued the relationship we had with Baaba Maal, convinced he had the voice and presence to be the international African superstar I still can't believe he hadn't become.

I made a lot of mistakes setting up Palm. I think I acted rashly because I wanted to react to the parting of the ways with PolyGram as soon as possible. I was driven by my frustration at not getting my own way, by effectively being expelled from Island and, for the first time in nearly forty years, no longer having the name.

I began much bigger than I normally would have. I was in fact encouraged to do so, because the feeling was that I would be able to raise a good amount of financing to speed up the whole process. But we were not able to raise that financing, and we never started with the right amount of money for the size of the venture. It was always a struggle. We couldn't sign expensive new acts, we couldn't spend money on marketing, we were always on the back foot.

Palm started in 1998, almost forty years after Island, and it was a completely new venture. When you start new you have no catalogue, you have nothing, so you have nothing already generating revenue while you're working and developing the new things you're establishing. We had the kinds of acts where selling 30,000 of their first album would have been a very respectable jumping-off point in the sixties and seventies but in the nineties was just a blip. No serious player was interested in such a number. Even selling a million could lead to questions about whether it was worth it. The music was once the reason for it all. Eventually it was hardly part of the equation.

I never did much talking in public before I left Island for good in 1997, and made it policy that, as much as possible, I was never photographed with the artists. You will be hard-pressed to find any photos of me with Bob Marley, for instance. It was one of the first things I ever said to him—that we would never have our picture taken together. There might be one or two, if that. He was Che Guevara with a guitar, and he couldn't be seen to be friends with me—I was the industry, the enemy.

I came from an era when even producers were not credited on a record, and no one outside of a few aficionados had any idea who was behind the record labels. No one cared. I started to talk more after I left Island, protecting my place in history just in case PolyGram—and then Universal when they absorbed PolyGram—decided to remove me from that, and remove Jamaica, where it all began, what gave the label its flavor. I could yet be the last man standing at Island Records, even though I have been out of the official picture for a quarter of a century.

I also formed a music site, Sputnik7, with Les Garland as president, who'd worked at MTV in the "I want my MTV" era and had made a success rolling out The Box music channel in America. I was anticipating a big next-generation switch to audiovisual, a world where everything came to you, on demand, on the web. I'd fallen heavily for the web, all the connections it made and the speed at which it moved. I had received my first email in the early nineties, when there was hardly anyone using it, and so I had to wait for everyone to catch up. I was an early supporter of Napster, believing it was going to be a new way to break new artists, that Napster fans would be the type interested in different and unusual artists.

The industry was panicking, thinking that music online was going to mean music would be free, but I was thinking of Napster as a new service that wouldn't mean people stopped buying music. I might have been right, I might have been wrong, but it was a time when, really, who knew what was going on? My instinct was to support something new and disruptive, even as it took me further and further away from what I knew.

We spent a lot of time, and money, talking about delivering fulfilling audiovisual content, about building niche communities that connected with each other to build a bigger community. We spent a lot of time talking at cross-purposes. We didn't have the language, or the sense of the changes about to happen, to think of a model like Spotify or Netflix. We were on the way, but there was a lot of fear of the future.

And when we did get some investment from the usual less-forgiving places, the attitude within a few months was, of course, where is the new Bob Marley, the new U2? Trying to explain that in fact the originals took a few years to even begin to become what they became, I would be treated as some kind of dreamer, a shaman. Bankers and investors would look at me as if I were no different from Scratch Perry, and in some ways they were right. I was interested more in creating things than in business, even if I'd developed my own form of business aptitude to make sure I could keep creating things.

Palm and Sputnik7 merged, which somehow made them smaller. The truth was, I was trying to build something on foundations that were moving all the time, so much so that in a few years, there would be no foundations at all.

I'd carefully planned for an entertainment future I knew was coming, but I based my plans on the technology that existed at the time and wasn't ready for how much the future of music as an industry, as a technology, kept changing. I knew a good song when I heard one, I could spot a star as soon as they walked through the door, but the ground was shifting under my feet.

CHAPTER FOURTEEN

MOVING ON: FOR THE LOVE
OF JAMAICA

After Palm wound down and Sputnik crashed, I was already wandering in a different direction, and ultimately that was in the direction of a place I had never really left, because it filled my heart and increasingly my mind. I was heading back to Jamaica, perhaps the one thing amazing enough to replace the blank space that Bob had left behind.

Jamaica not just as a place where I lived, but the country as a kind of artist, something to develop and distribute to a wider audience. In a way, I became interested in marketing the country more explicitly. It was part of the motive for setting up Island in the early sixties and the hunt I went on to find what turned out to be Bob Marley, but after 2005 I was interested in representing almost as a kind of informal ambassador the country itself. I never wanted to go into politics or work officially for the tourism board, like my cousin John Pringle did in the 1960s after opening Round Hill. That requires the sort of thinking I was no good at doing within PolyGram. I like to walk my own path and answer to no one.

I was the kind of ambassador who launched his own rum and put his name on the label. Blackwell Rum is the only thing that I have ever put my name on, and it seemed right that I did so, because it was a connection with when as a teenager I was set up to run the family's drinks company, J. Wray & Nephew. I was supposed to be in the rum business, and now I could be.

It was champion New York advertising man and friend Richard Kirshenbaum who first suggested the idea to me, claiming dark rum was going to be the next big thing. One of the campaigns that made his name was marketing Hennessy cognac to the rap crowd, so he wasn't coming in without experience. At first, as usual when I came to using my own name so directly, I wasn't so sure; but the more I thought about it, and the more I considered how apt it would be to collaborate with J. Wray & Nephew, the more the idea grew on me. It would be like my life going full circle, not in a sentimental way, but as a tying up of loose ends.

Joy Spence was a wonderful, pioneering master blender who worked on some fine rums for Wray & Nephew, and we did a deal where she would develop a new rum to my brief. I was treating the rum like an artist, and Kirshenbaum devised a mysterious rough-and-ready black-and-gold bottle that gave it the look of something you might find in a pirate's treasure chest.

Joy came up with three samples to try. I liked the first and third very much, not so much the second. Eventually I decided on the one I liked the most. I was sampling them in the bar at GoldenEye, and as I was making my mind up, Grace Jones turned up with some girl-friends, starting a night out, or ending one from the day before. I asked them what they thought. They were all delighted to try, drinking it the way I prefer, neat or on the rocks, like a fine cognac, even though it works great in a cocktail.

All four chose the one I didn't like. Grace was especially fond of it. Her face lit up, always a good sign, except when it's a bad sign. I had learned over time that you never argue with Grace, so I went with her choice. She was right, of course. I probably had the best person on the planet help me choose my rum. In a way, she had produced me. Is Blackwell Rum selling like early U2 or biggest-band-in-the-world

U2? Put it this way: as a rum, earthy and ethereal, it will be interesting forever.

AS I MADE money in the music business, I had always invested in property in Jamaica. My mother, Blanche, told me in 1976 that Ian Fleming's GoldenEye estate was on the market, twelve years after he had died, and that I should buy it. I hadn't seen it since 1962. She had been keeping an eye on it for Fleming's tormented twenty-two-year-old son Caspar, but he committed suicide and it went up for sale.

She had great memories of the place, but I didn't have the liquid capital to buy it when she suggested it. I had just paid Bob Marley about £70,000 in royalties, so I knew that he could afford it. I told him what a fabulous place it was, and he decided to buy it unseen. I asked him if my mother could keep swimming there, which she had done when Fleming was alive and while she guarded it when Caspar Fleming was in London. He agreed.

He went to see it just before the sale went through and decided he didn't like it. It was too posh for him, not anywhere he thought he could be comfortable. It wasn't exactly a mansion—it was as basic as Fleming had wanted it to be—but it didn't appeal to Bob. He asked me if there was a way out of the deal. Luckily, by then I had the cash. We scratched out his name on the contract and replaced it with mine. I thought of living there, but I never did. I would visit it sometimes, swim there, let friends and family stay there sometimes. It was a house I used as an entertaining place.

Whenever I had the cash after that, I would buy a property, a little bit of land in different places. In 1972, I had purchased another place I'd visited when I was younger, Strawberry Hill, a 26-acre eighteenth-century estate once owned by the son of the first British prime minister, 3,000 feet above Kingston in the Blue Mountains surrounded by tropical forest. In the nineteenth century it had been a navy hospital before it was transformed into a grand house, and my mum would take me there for tea, driving for an hour along the winding road that led there. I had never forgotten the place, never thinking I would one day be in a position to buy it. It had a dazzling view across the island, and even after I traveled the world, I never saw one as magnificent.

For twenty years, it was somewhere private, where I would invite friends and family. It's where I immediately took Bob Marley when he had been shot in Hope Road down in Kingston, the city you can see from Strawberry Hill, especially lit up at night, as if it is in another world altogether. At the back of my mind, I thought of it as becoming a hotel, and we opened a restaurant there in the mid-eighties.

I had always loved hotels. I'd worked at the Half Moon, which led to my first record with Lance Hayward, and I had been inspired by what John Pringle had done with Round Hill in the 1950s. John was a cousin, his family had known mine for two hundred years, and because he was somewhere between my age and my father's, I always looked upon him as a big brother.

He had an innovative approach to the idea of hotels, and it made me think about them in a different way when I started traveling with bands. I would also notice when a room worked or didn't work. I hated it if I stayed in a hotel by the sea and there was a class division between those with sea views and those without. When I started hotels, I always made sure everyone had a sea view, so there was no sense of feeling let down if you were on the wrong side of the building.

In Los Angeles, I was always taken by the Sunset Marquis in West Hollywood when I stayed there in the 1970s. It was built with the idea that the people staying there would be in the entertainment business. They were after something different from standard hotel amenities. Each room had a little kitchenette, so you didn't have to rely on room service and could be in control of your own room, organize your own self-catering, get on with your life.

It was a boutique hotel long before there was such an idea, and it worked not only as a hideaway but also as somewhere you could meet people and feel part of a community. It would be filled with stars and creatives just passing through or hanging out at the bar.

I filed ideas at the back of my mind, because I tended to spend a lot of time in hotels, and I vaguely compiled an idea of the perfect, most practical room in my mind. It was at Compass Point that I really started thinking of opening hotels, because there were always people staying, mixing with each other, exchanging ideas and stories. Part of the reason I had built Compass Point as a residential studio was so that artists and other interesting people would visit.

At the end of the 1980s, with Island now with PolyGram, the idea of hotels became as interesting to me as the music, the idea of making something happen, of finding new ways to meet people and put people together. It was creating little scenes really, small, mobile centers of discussion.

I'd slowly added cottages to GoldenEye; it wasn't officially a resort, but it was a place where friends and colleagues could come and visit. Sting wrote "Every Breath You Take" and other songs while he was visiting, Apple CEO Steve Jobs celebrated his twenty-ninth birthday at GoldenEye. Slowly, discreetly planning for the future, I was working towards opening some hotels in Jamaica, as an extension of my work in the music business as much as anything.

I GOT DISTRACTED by Miami. I stumbled onto a tempting investment project, which involved rebuilding an entire district. I was walking along South Beach at the end of the 1980s, and it seemed most of the buildings were for sale. Filled with retirement homes, flophouses, crack dens, and a lot of obvious drug activity on the street—the kind of stuff that became the weekly plot on the *Miami Vice* television series—it wasn't very appealing.

It had a bad reputation and, considering what the nostalgic view would be of the area, with its dramatic art deco buildings and beautiful architecture, the pastel colors and geometric shapes set against the sun and sea, this was a shame. It had been a playground for the rich and famous in the fifties and sixties, but had become something of a depressed no-go area. If you looked beyond the ruins and edginess, there was a whole lost world to rediscover. Something in me stirred, perhaps because the empty beach was still beautiful, and I thought it was a place that could do with an input of energy, just to see what happened. Sometimes the derelict can seem more promising than the so-called orderly.

I decided Miami had the potential to be a serious music center and took it from there. I formed a company called Island Outpost, so I still had an Island name, planning to build hotels tapping into the experience I'd had staying at some of the best, and occasionally some of the worst. I liked the idea of it being an outpost because you don't have high expectations for an outpost, and I wasn't sure at the beginning how it would turn out. I established the Island Outpost dress code: no jackets, no ties, flip-flops allowed.

I started to buy up some of the decrepit deco buildings, a job lot, including the old Marlin Hotel, which was the first building I renovated. I'd learned a few things at Compass Point. We put in a recording studio steps from the ocean, and it had twelve suites, a model agency, a great bar, and a restaurant. A potent mix of models and musicians crossed paths there—U2, Madonna, Beyoncé, Mick Jagger, Aerosmith, and Prince recorded at the studio, and celebrities started to turn up to see what was going on. Celebrities make the gossip columns and always draw a crowd—the effect on the area was almost instantaneous. It became the center of the transformation.

Barbara Hulanicki was a vital part of the change we made to the area and the exuberant, imaginative enhancement of the art deco district. A fashion legend, she'd founded Biba with her husband, Stephen Fitz-Simon, in the sixties when London was the capital of pop culture. She had become a great interior designer and was in Miami working on a club on the beach for Ronnie Wood, Woody's.

She was recommended to me, and when we met, I asked her

to design a corridor, just to see what she came up with. She passed what she called the Corridor Test, and I gave her my apartment to design. She did such a great job, I asked her to do more spaces and rooms.

As I kept buying hotels and buildings along Ocean Drive and Collins Avenue—the Leslie, Cardozo, Carlyle, Kent, Casa Grande, Netherland, and Cavalier—she kept coming up with stunning décor. We were both mad for color, we both had our memories of the Swinging Sixties that we didn't want to be sentimental about but to relocate and rewire, and I loved how she would use the lobby areas to go wild with ideas.

I treated her as I would an act that I thought knew exactly what they were doing, giving her a brief or an idea of what I wanted and leaving her to it. I would say, "This hotel I want to be Jamaica in Miami," and she would do it, better than I could even imagine. I also commissioned her to work on two hotels in the Bahamas: Pink Sands on Harbour Island, a fusion of Morocco, India, and Bali; and Compass Point, within walking distance of the studio, a riot of color. I could begin to travel the world by spending time at my hotels. The world would come to me, wherever I was. I could be close to artists, entrepreneurs, actors, and musicians in spaces I had created myself based on my own likes and desires.

Barbara stayed in the Miami area while she worked on my buildings, and is still living there, and she would work for me when I started to concentrate more on Jamaica, which had been my original intention. Miami was magical for a few years, and it was like having a series of hit records. When I opened a refurbished Tides in 1997, the grandest of the art deco hotels along Ocean Drive, which I'd remade into a forty-five-suite luxury boutique, I persuaded my cousin and mentor, John Pringle, then seventy-two, to come out of retirement to introduce his exacting taste and standards to the relaunch. He treated the task with immense style, connecting the hotel spiritually to the era of Noël Coward, Errol Flynn, and the Kennedys. Tides was as good as it got, the last hit, the ultimate sign that South Beach had gone up and up in the world, and a certain social history had been refreshed.

It was fun while it lasted, but soon it was time to move on. When I started, South Beach seemed to be a blank canvas where we could be spectacular; but once the main work was completed, I seemed to end up sitting in meetings whenever I visited.

Around 2003, Palm Pictures was in trouble, I'd lost a lot of money with Sputnik7, and I was having to sell my Miami real estate to make sure that I could still protect the properties I was developing in Jamaica. It was a loss, some of it very emotional, but it ended up being a choice between Miami and Jamaica, and there could be only one winner. I wanted to make a difference in Jamaica the way I had along South Beach.

Miami had been a blast of rock and roll, especially as I dealt elsewhere with the increasingly depressing reality of Island now being part of PolyGram, and it was a demonstration of my need to be independent and create vibrant music scenes from scratch.

I think that's why I was so upset when I started to be ignored by PolyGram—in another part of my life, I had helped revamp an entire Miami neighborhood and revive dead parts of the city. I wasn't running out of steam, which they seemed to be implying. I was still chasing ideas I was excited about, still causing things to happen. I can never stop doing that because I am useless at doing nothing.

COMPARED TO MIAMI, GoldenEye, Strawberry Hill, and a piece of undeveloped land on the western tip of the island in Negril that became the Caves in 1997—twelve cabins on top of a cliff—were more personal projects. I was the artist with these projects. They reflected my vision of Jamaica, and my experiences as a traveler and entrepreneur. I didn't want them to be hotels with lobbies or corridors. I wanted them to be unobtrusive, embedded in the nature around them, so they didn't loom above the landscape and scream "tourist." My hotels worked undercover.

I wanted to employ only local people from nearby the premises. I wanted them to be places that pointed you into the island to explore the real Jamaica, because the best thing about Jamaica is its people, their positivity and charisma. I wanted what we did to rub off on other parts of Jamaica, not exist in sterile isolation. I even fought against them having air-conditioning. Sweating is good for you.

I've been working on GoldenEye since I bought it, constantly remixing it, adding cabins, villas, huts, bungalows, unfussy individual units spread around the property without making it seem cluttered, keeping intact the original Fleming elements, including the room where he worked. I'm still making plans for its future, even though I'm reaching the age where it might be that I never get to see the results of those plans.

I can't stop making plans. To this day I wake up every morning looking forward to seeing where current projects are, and what new ideas I will think of, sending ripples into the future in a way you can never imagine. I always want to re-create that moment when I first sat in Ken Khouri's small Kingston studio in 1959 and we were about to record a track by Lance Hayward. That moment when Cat Stevens was about to sing me "Father and Son," when Bob, Peter, and Bunny walked into my office, when Grace Jones was ready to perform with the Compass Point All Stars for the first time. I don't want to repeat myself, to be a prisoner of my past. Yesterday's gone, but I want to come across more moments that lead to change, even if, sometimes, change takes time.

INITIALLY, WE IMAGINED opening GoldenEye as a James Bond–themed hotel. The bar was going to be the Shaken Not Stirred, the waitresses would be Bond girls, the villas would be numbered 001, 002, 003. We planned to open after the main renovation on July 7,

2007—070707. We missed that 2007 deadline, and by the time we were ready to open a few years later, I'd realized that this GoldenEye was my GoldenEye. It wasn't Ian Fleming's. He had passed through, and now I was passing through. He'd established the name and certain traditions, and I had added to them, using the same instincts I had when running Island Records and promoting my artists. I wanted it to become the most relaxed place in the world, in the same way that Bob Marley's music became known as the most relaxed political music in the world. And the James Bond image just didn't work in the barefoot sanctuary I imagined. (When Prince Charles and the Duchess of Cornwall visited GoldenEye in 2008, I greeted them barefoot. I hadn't even thought about it until someone mentioned it later.)

When it's full, GoldenEye still seems empty, and you can spend a lot of time there without seeing anyone, as if the place is all for you. It's on another planet from Kingston, but it is also one part of what makes Jamaica so special—because, after all, it exists, and there is a world where you can wander over the footbridge that leads to the beachfront Bizot Bar, and there's Elon Musk on his own having a drink; Ryan Gosling is on the phone to his agent at the other end of the bar, Sly and Robbie are coming out of the speakers, Jay-Z and Beyoncé are hidden in their villa on a romantic weekend, and in the ocean, Grace Jones is having a swim. I want that to be as much what Jamaica is as anything else, a glamorous Jamaica I experienced in the 1950s, a Jamaica I have contributed to, bringing in different forms of energy to mingle with what is already there.

I have a circular wooden hut there as well, nothing fancy, at the end of a dirt road, one room and a covered porch, just enough for my immediate needs. Very much in the Jamaican tradition of there being a little inside but a lot outside, where you are going to spend most of your time.

You could say that part of the time, when I am not in New York, or London, or Theale, I live in a hotel, one that can seem like a club, a place for friends, a resort hotel, a remote paradise, a luxury village, and a hip boutique hotel. It's whatever you want it to be, like the island itself.

Jamaica is not the easiest environment in which to run such a venue; but on the other hand, it's the only place in the world where it could exist. It's a complicated island, and it still has a reputation for violence and crime that sometimes seems hard to shake off. Like other places, Jamaica does have crime, and, yes, murders are committed, but there is no history of violence against tourism. When you read reports in the papers, it's easy to think you can't go there. These incidents are generally confined to specific places. If you want to find trouble and danger and you're stupid, it's like anywhere else in the world—you'll find it. But if you know where to look, it can be heaven.

MARY VINSON, THROUGH her home furnishing company Royal Hut, an offshoot of Island Trading, contributed to the décor of GoldenEye's villas and huts, sourcing materials, furniture, linen, towels, and crockery from around the world, from tiny factories in small villages in exotic places, which helped make the rooms and suites both very Jamaican but also from everywhere. We used to travel together looking for fabric throughout Africa, where we seemed to be hunting for treasure.

She used local craftspeople to decorate the interior walls, make the sinks, and build the outdoor showers, thinking of details I never would. She became an expert in the relaxed mood and timing of Jamaica, the sense of timing intended to avoid useless stress and fuss.

We worked and lived together well—how clever was Grace seeing we belonged together!—and her designs for the hotels, especially GoldenEye, came out of what she decided we needed for our life together. It all reflected her own aliveness, her own relish for color, as though it had soul. She had a hut adjacent to mine, his-and-hers huts where we could be apart and come together. We had worked out the best way we could be as independent as we were as people while living together.

She fell ill during the 1990s. She struggled for years with myeloma, a nasty, painful bone cancer that's treatable but incurable. It's not the kind of illness where you recover. It comes and recedes. It goes away and then it reappears. She was in very bad shape around 1997, and then she came out of it. It was a miracle really. To celebrate, we got married in 1998. She wore something spectacular, me something less so. The rest of our life together was our honeymoon. Of course, the cancer was in hiding.

She came to pick me up at JFK one time in 2004 after I had been away for a short while. She was suffering, and the prognosis did not look good. When she picked me up, she seemed more vivacious than she had been for a while—she was normally a very vivacious woman— and very excited about something. As we drove into Manhattan, she told me about someone she had met at her specialist's office. He had the same type of cancer and had had it for longer than she had, but he was following a cure that he said was making him better.

He had offered to show her what he was taking that was helping him, and invited us both to his house outside New York. Mary had nothing to lose, so we went to visit him. He showed us what he said was some form of cure the Chinese used, a traditional diet based on a certain animal.

He opened a container, and inside there was the weirdest-looking creature I had ever seen, not a worm, not a snake, maybe some kind of gnarled, mashed caterpillar. It was truly horrible-looking. Mary and I didn't know what to make of it and went quiet. After a short while, Mary admitted she didn't think she could eat what she was seeing. "No way can I put that in my mouth," she said. "It can save you," her friend said.

She asked me what I thought. I had to agree with her. It looked vile, and to be honest, it seemed like the person showing it to us was following some crackpot alternative cure that wasn't really going to work.

Mary politely declined and we left, somewhat crestfallen. The drive back to Manhattan was particularly quiet. Mary died a few months later. Her funeral was extraordinary, as it needed to be, the proper Jamaican send-off to send her soul in the right way to the right place, rising off the earthly plane so that she could watch over us. Dancing, singing, chanting, eating, gambling, drinking, playing games, a spectacular party with plenty of Afro-Jamaican music—Maroon drummers continuing the traditions of the escaped slaves and their rolling heartbeat rhythms invoking the spirits of ancestors, and great, loud Jamaican pop music blasting from the twentieth-century Jamaican tradition, the glorious sound systems.

Weirdly, in the months after Mary died, I started to see those strange things that man had been eating at the edge of the sea around GoldenEye. I don't know what they were, but there they were. And the man who showed us how they were part of his diet is still alive today. If I had been more forceful with Mary, insisting that she try the diet, as peculiar as it seemed, she might be around now. She would still only be in her mid-sixties. It wasn't meant to be, as some things aren't. She disappeared from the path we were on together it seemed forever, and it forced me even harder into Jamaica, where you find light even when all goes dark.

WHATEVER NEXT . . .

I've been working on this book during the Covid-19 pandemic—finding a way to travel at least in my mind—which has been the most extraordinary time I have experienced in my life. I've been watching things with a mixture of shock and deep interest. We are obviously moving into very different times, and living through lockdowns has intensified a general self-consciousness about how different our lives are going to be. As a hotelier, professionally I have found it a real challenge keeping the Island Outpost properties open when for months at a time there have been no bookings. We have set ourselves up to be places that people come to from around the world, and because international travel has been almost impossible, we have been forced to be quiet and empty. I'll let you know how we get on when hotels are needed again, and easier to get to.

It would have been impossible to keep GoldenEye running without my new partner in life and work, Marika Kessler, who has been an enormous help for many years now. After Mary, I never imagined anyone new coming into my life, but I was fortunate enough to fall in love with Marika and begin a relationship that keeps growing. She possesses extraordinary people skills and has energized both me and Island Outpost and opened my life in all sorts of exciting and unpredictable ways. Alongside Marika, I have fallen even more in love with Jamaica and its future possibilities.

People I know and have had enjoyable dealings with seem to have spent the pandemic striving to literally leap off the planet, to get the hell out of here. They want to go to Mars or travel into space. The billionaires, needing to scratch nonstop itches, to stretch their empires. Elon Musk, Jeff Bezos, and an old colleague of mine, Richard Branson, desperate to see space and open new territory off earth. I wonder what is on their minds. It's not something I think about.

Maybe I'm a little envious of Elon's latest mind-blowing exploits, and Richard has always been very brave, circling the world in a balloon, crossing the Atlantic in a one-man boat. We started more or less in the same place, with records and eccentric rock artists, and I helped him in the early days; but I'm happier with my rum and resorts than I would be with planes and rockets.

I respect it, but it's not for me. The only person I have ever met whom I felt ill at ease with was an American astronaut who had walked on the moon. I find all the space I need, all the adventure, in Jamaica, and my mission is to make people aware of the island and its beauty, which can be as lusciously alien as anything.

The center of my Jamaican outer space is a former cattle farm I bought when I sold Island—as a kind of celebration—Pantrepant, located in Jamaica's cockpit country thirty miles inland from Montego Bay. It's embedded in Jamaica, and it is also lost in time, otherworldly, hidden inside itself. Sometimes on the noisiest island on the planet all you can hear is an owl, the breathing of a horse, or some whistling frogs. It takes some getting to, as the last mile or so is a jarring drive along a winding dirt road that means I can see when people are approaching a long time before they arrive.

I wanted a house by the turquoise Martha Brae River, and first of all I was shown a majestic seventeenth-century property, which was far too big for my needs. Then they showed me a farm nearby, with a more modest but beautiful house underneath the most enormous tree I had ever seen.

I bought the tree first and foremost, and got everything that came along with it: the river, the house, a natural watering hole, roaming wildlife, hummingbirds, lizards, cattle, a cave that was home to the Taínos hundreds of years before any Europeans arrived, and acres of almost ancient isolation. There was also Lion, a hardy, enigmatic Rasta living somewhere in the woods, locks spilling languidly past his waist and reaching towards the floor, living like a king in his paradise found, making himself useful as he saw fit, materializing out of the soft morning mist and disappearing just as suddenly, as if into another dimension.

It was a very private retreat for Mary and me, but a few years after she passed I opened it up publically to guests at GoldenEye, the Caves, and Strawberry Hill for farm-to-table lunches and overnight stays, and developed it as a working organic farm to supply Island Outpost hotels with produce and meat.

The stately three-hundred-year-old guango tree sits there like a great solitary person. There is something about it that seems holy, preaching the ancient law of life. You imagine the roots heading into the earth forever. It represents nothing but itself. When I look at it, I don't need any rockets. I've somehow traveled somewhere even farther and more awe-inspiring.

ONE WAY OR another, I have lost many fellow travelers, friends, and colleagues over the last months. I have to keep a distance as I hear that people who meant a lot to me have died. An ex-girlfriend I always remained close to, the actress Nathalie Delon, passed away in Paris after battling pancreatic cancer. I heard she didn't stop fighting to the end, which would have been typical of her. She was so smart, energetic, and passionate; you have to wonder where that goes.

I met her in 1978, and I quickly fell for her, and we never really fell out. She was there when I first saw U2, and she took the photograph on the cover of this book, where I was sitting on the set of the *Countryman* film with director Dickie Jobson and Countryman himself. Because of Covid, I couldn't fly out to see her at the end of her life, which was devastating, but Suzette Newman managed to get to Paris from London on the Eurostar. They spent a couple of days remembering old times and, because it was Suzette, laughing a lot. Nathalie's ashes were scattered in Jamaica on the reef outside the Fleming villa where my Mom's ashes were also scattered.

One of the great, joyous reggae pioneers, Toots Hibbert, died in September 2020, just after he had released his first album in a decade—after performing for fifty-eight years—which featured a cover of Bob Marley's "Three Little Birds" recorded with Bob's son Ziggy. It was said that the Maytals were the Beatles to the Wailers' Rolling Stones, and I always thought that Toots, for his fantastic soul voice alone, should have been as widely known as Bob.

Millie Small died in May 2020 at seventy-two, which totally shook me. In many ways it all started for me with Millie, and working with her set me on my way. Suddenly she was gone, a death made more horrible and untidier because it was during the pandemic. It made me think about how she had come from nothing and how for a few fantastic months we traveled the world together, travels I have never stopped since, until the pandemic. Millie was so important to me—sure, I changed her life, but she changed my life in such a positive way, and those changes are still reverberating today. Sean Connery, my favorite James Bond, who had become a friend, died in October 2020. I loved how he put some Jamaica into the character. And then Neville "Bunny Wailer" Livingston died in March 2021, the last surviving Wailer, one of three distinctive songwriters who in the end had to be apart to develop their own identities. He stayed with Island even after he felt pushed away, recording the powerful and spiritual *Blackheart Man* in 1976, three years after he'd left the Wailers, another hidden Island classic. Whatever he thought of me, I always knew he mattered.

The self-styled, free-spirited "miracle man" Lee "Scratch" Perry died at the end of August 2021. He produced the Wailers before me and contributed more than most to the innovative and inventive modern reggae sound—it all started at his table, said Bunny. Scratch said some pretty outlandish things about me—that I was a vampire who wanted to steal Africa was one of the milder comments—but because of what he gave to Jamaican music, I wouldn't have wanted him and his imagination any other way. Scratch died just five days after another of my favorite masters of rhythm, Charlie Watts of the Rolling Stones, whom I had seen in the early 1960s classily introduce the kind of jazz drumming I loved into British rock music.

Bob Marley's longtime friend and Wailers percussionist Seeco Patterson passed in November 2021, just a month short of his ninetieth birthday. He had been with Bob during the attempted assassination at Hope Road, and he was close to him during his illness. He took a lot of Bob with him. And then in December 2021, Robbie Shakespeare of Sly and Robbie died, and the world got a whole lot less bass. On those great Grace Jones Compass Point albums, his playing was so fierce, and so musical and melodic. No other bassist could understand how to get his sound, and that's because of who he was and the way it just flowed out of him. He was the originator. I was lucky to have him as a friend.

Good friends we have, as Bob sang in "No Woman, No Cry," and good friends we've lost. Nathalie, Millie, Sean, Toots, Bunny, Scratch, Charlie, Robbie, and Seeco made me think of others who have died along the way. Nick Drake, John Martyn, Robert Palmer, Bob Marley, Peter Tosh, Rob Partridge, Alex Sadkin. Mary . . . a day can't pass without me being reminded in some way of someone I worked with, or spent some time with, or shared a life with. It starts to crowd the mind.

Every day you hear a song; are asked a question; get sent a link to some way that Bob Marley has had an impact on the world, how he brought people of different faiths together; see a photo or a design that reminds you of a space that someone has left; and you can't help but tear up. It's as if life, as wonderful and surprising as it has been, has also been a battlefield, and you find that you have survived a series of battles, and others didn't make it. It shows how songs and memories can give back life to those who no longer exist. Memories and songs can become stronger and stranger. Songs themselves have a life of their own you could never see coming.

I was never directly involved, but Suzette Newman and I talked about the idea of a Bob Marley musical. At first, we weren't sure whether it could work, the idea of reducing his vitality and vision to simply a series of songs taken out of context, elevating his melodies above his militancy. We quickly realized that of course there should be a Bob Marley musical, a new kind of hybrid, an unexpected collaboration between one energy and another, in the way he had continually and with an open mind collaborated with musicians, producers, writers, singers, friends, and also places, strangers, and cities, always developing as a writer and musician.

Get Up Stand Up! premiered at the Lyric Theatre in London in October 2021. When I saw it after it had been developed, I was really blown away. I don't think it would have happened the way it did without Suzette driving it forward as one of the producers. It was definitely a stimulating musical, but there were special extra qualities. I realized how much this was exactly the kind of collaboration Bob loved. The energies of different people working on a common mission carried on his work perfectly, making sure his songs, and spirit, endure. It was like seeing Bob in a small club, still fighting to win people over, tapping into something deep and mysterious, sure of himself and his message. It was like watching a gig as much as it was theater.

It was like Bob used to say—it was a fact, he announced: His music was going to last forever. Seeing the musical, you can see it coming true. You realize Marley's songs are something more than songs, and their strength keeps growing. It's been amazing to see that growth continue in my lifetime. His global reach keeps extending, and I am looking forward over the next few years to seeing his songs becoming something else again.

WHEN I WAS in my sixties at the turn of the century, I always said I would live to ninety-four, and that would give me plenty of time to get done all the things I wanted to do. Now at eighty-four, ninety-four seems to be getting a little close. I am reasonably fit, I can walk faster than most people half my age, and my memory, all things considered, is fine—although occasionally I need a prompt, but then I think I always did. I need to revise that number, push it on a little. I don't want to be greedy, but my mother lived to be 104.

I remember once when *Countryman* was being filmed, we had finished shooting for the day and were sitting on the beach at the end of a lovely evening. We were near where Countryman himself lived in his simple hut that gave him everything he wanted in the world.

There was director Dickie Jobson and *The Harder They Come*'s Perry Henzell and his wife, Sally, and we started to smoke a well-earned end-of-day spliff. We got involved in a very intense, intellectual conversation about life and death. The smoking was helping us along, and perhaps we didn't make much sense, and then we drifted over to wondering what the point of life is. We were asking, in all seriousness, why are we here?

Countryman, who had been very quiet sitting on some rocks in the shadows, suddenly started chuckling. "What's so funny?" I asked him.

"I tell you what the purpose of life is," he said. "The purpose of life is to live as long as possible."

We fell quiet and watched the sun set over the sea, a magical event in Jamaica that seems to calm the mind, body, and soul. After the sun dipped below the horizon, you could see millions of stars twinkling against a jet-black sky. I swear mixed in with Countryman's soft laughter we could hear drums beating relentlessly in the distance, being played somewhere high up in the mountains, the mesmeric Jamaican rhythms that have no beginning and no ending.

ACKNOWLEDGMENTS

CHRIS BLACKWELL

Thank you:

Paul Morley, whose magic touch and friendship helped me tell this story.

Marika Kessler; Meg Friedman; Cathy Snipper; the Marley family; Mark Painter, keeper of the photos; Adrian Boot, taker of many of those photos; and Tony Wright, designer of most of the album covers.

Tim Clark and Tom Hayes for their invaluable contributions over the years.

David Betteridge, my first Managing Director. Lionel Conway, who ran Island Music.

Rob Partridge, who was Press Officer; Denny Cordell and Jerry Moss.

Elsa Hoken, my right hand back in the day, and Denise Mills, who sadly passed. Dicky Jobson, my close friend.

Michael Seltzer and Eric Greenspan for their friendship and support.

All the Islanders over time; in the UK, the US, and Jamaica.

All the artists, musicians, producers, engineers, designers, film-makers, and the many talented people I've been lucky enough to work with.

The Andrew Wylie Agency.

Everyone at Gallery Books, especially my editor, Aimée Bell.

And of course . . . Jamaica.

One Love

PAUL MORLEY

Thank you:

Chris and Suzette, Elizabeth Levy (e.s.p.), Madeleine Morley, Carol Morley, and Michael Zilkha.

The dedicated Gallery Team, including Aimée Bell, Max Meltzer, publisher Jennifer Bergstrom, publicists Jill Siegel and Sally Marvin, copyeditor Joal Hetherington, and editorial advisor David Kamp.

David Godwin and Philippa Sitters, my agents at DGA.

Mark P and Ramus for reading early drafts.

INDEX